THE ONE YEAR®

LOVE
LANGUAGE
— MINUTE —
Devotional

GARY CHAPMAN

TYNDALE HOUSE PUBLISHERS, INC.
CAROL STREAM, ILLINOIS

Visit Tyndale's exciting Web site at www.tyndale.com.

TYNDALE and Tyndale's quill logo are registered trademarks of Tyndale House Publishers, Inc.

The One Year is a registered trademark of Tyndale House Publishers, Inc.

The One Year Love Language Minute Devotional

Copyright © 2009 by Gary D. Chapman. All rights reserved.

Cover photo copyright © by Tetra Images/jupiterimages. All rights reserved.

Author photo copyright © by Boyce Shore & Associates. All rights reserved.

Edited by Kathryn S. Olson

Unless otherwise indicated, all Scripture quotations are taken from the *Holy Bible*, New Living Translation, copyright © 1996, 2004, 2007 by Tyndale House Foundation. Used by permission of Tyndale House Publishers, Inc., Carol Stream, Illinois 60188. All rights reserved.

Scripture quotations marked NIV are taken from the HOLY BIBLE, NEW INTERNATIONAL VERSION®. NIV®. Copyright © 1973, 1978, 1984 by International Bible Society. Used by permission of Zondervan. All rights reserved.

Scripture quotations marked KJV are taken from *The Holy Bible*, King James Version.

Scripture quotations marked NASB are taken from the *New American Standard Bible*®, copyright © 1960, 1962, 1963, 1968, 1971, 1972, 1973, 1975, 1977, 1995 by The Lockman Foundation. Used by permission.

Scripture quotations marked NKJV are taken from the New King James Version®. Copyright © 1982 by Thomas Nelson, Inc. Used by permission. All rights reserved. *NKJV* is a trademark of Thomas Nelson, Inc.

Scripture quotations marked ESV are from *The Holy Bible*, English Standard Version®, copyright © 2001 by Crossway Bibles, a publishing ministry of Good News Publishers. Used by permission. All rights reserved.

ISBN 978-1-4143-2973-4

Printed in the United States of America

20	19	18	17	16	15	14
13	12	11	10	9	8	7

INTRODUCTION

I'VE BEEN PRIVILEGED to counsel couples for more than thirty years, and in that time I've seen my share of marital struggles. But what I've also seen, time and time again, is the power of God to transform relationships. When two people commit to each other—and especially when they commit to communicating love to each other through the five love languages—positive change occurs.

Because my background is in marriage counseling, I tend to use the language of marriage when I write. Some of the issues I address are marriage specific. However, if you're a dating or engaged couple, I hope you will read this book too. There is plenty of helpful information for you as well. The building blocks of marriage—such as good communication, respect, unconditional love, and forgiveness—are foundational to any romantic relationship. And learning to identify and speak your loved one's love language will benefit a couple at any stage.

You can use this devotional individually, or sit down together as a couple to read it each day. Use the prayer at the end of each devotion as a starting point for your own prayer—whether you pray silently together or aloud, one at a time. In just a minute or two every day, you can discover encouraging biblical insights.

Whether your relationship is strong or struggling, stable or challenging, my prayer is that this devotional will encourage you and give you renewed joy in each other. May your relationship be strengthened this year as you focus on loving and growing together.

Gary Chapman

COMMUNICATING LOVE

Three things will last forever—faith, hope, and love—and the greatest of these is love. Let love be your highest goal! 1 CORINTHIANS 13:13–14:1

AFTER THIRTY YEARS of counseling couples, I'm convinced there are five different ways we speak and understand emotional love—five love languages. Each of us has a primary love language; one of the five speaks to us more profoundly than the other four.

Seldom do a husband and wife have the same love language. We tend to speak our own language, and as a result, we completely miss each other. Oh, we're sincere. We're even expressing love, but we're not connecting emotionally.

Sound familiar? Love doesn't need to diminish over time. The end of the famous "love chapter" of the Bible, 1 Corinthians 13, says that love is of great value and will last forever. In fact, the apostle Paul says that love should be our highest goal. But if you're going to keep love alive, you need to learn a new language. That takes discipline and practice—but the reward is a lasting, deeply committed relationship.

Lord, thank you for creating each of us so differently. Keep me from assuming that my partner thinks and feels the way I do. Please give me the patience to find out how I can most effectively communicate love to my spouse.

LEARNING THE LOVE LANGUAGES

Dear friends, since God loved us that much, we surely ought to love each other. No one has ever seen God. But if we love each other, God lives in us, and his love is brought to full expression in us. 1 JOHN 4:11-12

MY RESEARCH INDICATES that there are five basic languages of love:

- ∾ Words of affirmation—using positive words to affirm the one you love

- ∾ Gifts—giving thoughtful gifts to show you were thinking about someone

- ∾ Acts of service—doing something that you know the other person would like

- ∾ Quality time—giving your undivided attention

- ∾ Physical touch—holding hands, kissing, embracing, putting a hand on the shoulder, or any other affirming touch

Out of these five, each of us has a primary love language. One of these languages speaks more deeply to us than the others. Do you know your love language? Do you know your spouse's?

Many couples earnestly love each other but do not communicate their love in an effective way. If you don't speak your spouse's primary love language, he or she may not feel loved, even when you are showing love in other ways.

The Bible makes it clear that we need to love each other as God loves us. The apostle John wrote that God's love can find "full expression" in us. If that's true for the church in general, how much more true is it for a couple? Finding out how your loved one feels love is an important step to expressing love effectively.

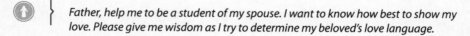

Father, help me to be a student of my spouse. I want to know how best to show my love. Please give me wisdom as I try to determine my beloved's love language.

FOLLOWING THE CLUES

I am giving you a new commandment: Love each other. Just as I have loved you, you should love each other. Your love for one another will prove to the world that you are my disciples. JOHN 13:34-35

WHAT DOES YOUR SPOUSE most often request of you? This is usually a clue to a person's love language. You may have interpreted these requests as nagging, but in fact, your spouse has been telling you what makes him or her feel loved.

For example, if your mate frequently requests that you take a walk after dinner, go on a picnic, turn off the TV and talk, or go away for a weekend together, these are requests for *quality time*. One wife told me, "I feel neglected and unloved because my husband seldom spends time with me. He gives me nice gifts on my birthday and wonders why I'm not excited about them. Gifts mean little when you don't feel loved." Her husband was sincere and was trying to demonstrate his love, but he was not speaking her love language.

As we see from the verse above, Jesus instructed his disciples to love each other as he had loved them. How does God love us? Perfectly and with complete understanding. He knows us, and he knows how we can experience his love. We can never love perfectly this side of heaven, of course. But discovering the love language of your spouse is an important step in the right direction.

Lord, thank you for knowing me perfectly and loving me perfectly. Help me to think carefully about what my spouse most often asks of me. Give me the wisdom to interpret that correctly so I can communicate love better to him or her.

REVEALING YOURSELF IN MARRIAGE

The LORD gives righteousness and justice to all who are treated unfairly. He revealed his character to Moses and his deeds to the people of Israel.

PSALM 103:6-7

WHAT DO YOU KNOW about the art of self-revelation? It all began with God. God revealed himself to us through the prophets, the Scriptures, and supremely through Christ. As the verse above mentions, he revealed himself to the ancient Israelites through his actions. They saw him guiding them out of Egypt and into the Promised Land, and as they did, they learned about him. If God had not chosen self-revelation, we would not know him.

The same principle is true in marriage. Self-revelation enables us to get to know each other's ideas, desires, frustrations, and joys. In a word, it is the road to intimacy. No self-revelation, no intimacy. So how do we learn the art of self-revelation?

You can begin by learning to speak for yourself. Communication experts often explain it as using "I" statements rather than "you" statements. For example, "*I* feel disappointed that you are not going with me to my mother's birthday dinner" is very different from "*You* have disappointed me again by not going to my mother's birthday dinner." When you focus on your reaction, you reveal your own emotions. Focusing on the other person's actions places blame. "You" statements encourage arguments. "I" statements encourage communication.

Father, help me to remember that revealing more of myself is the first step toward greater intimacy with the one I love. Thank you for revealing yourself to us, and please give me the courage to share myself with my spouse.

EXPRESSING FEELINGS

For everything there is a season, a time for every activity under heaven. . . .
A time to cry and a time to laugh. A time to grieve and a time to dance.

ECCLESIASTES 3:1, 4

SOME PEOPLE WONDER WHY they would ever want to share their feelings with their mate. The truth is, if you don't openly share your feelings, they will likely show up anyway in your behavior. However, your loved one will have no idea why you are behaving as you are. That's when you get the proverbial question, "Is something wrong?" Your spouse knows something is wrong but doesn't know what.

Emotions are a natural part of life. King Solomon wrote in Ecclesiastes that there is a time for everything, including joy and sorrow, grieving and celebration. All feelings have their place in our lives, and many of them communicate a lot about us. Most of our feelings are tied to some experience we have had in the past or something we're going through now. The next time you feel disappointed, ask yourself, *What stimulated my disappointment?* Then try to share whatever it is with your spouse.

Revealing your feelings lets your spouse know what is going on inside you—what you are feeling and why. For example, you might say, "I'm feeling angry with myself because I came home late last night and we missed our ride in the country." Such a statement may encourage your mate to say, "I'm disappointed too. Maybe we can do it on Thursday night." Revealing your feelings creates an atmosphere of intimacy and trust.

Lord, expressing emotions does not always come easily to me. Help me to remember that holding back my feelings only makes my spouse guess why I'm acting the way I am. Please give me the courage to share what I am feeling. May it bring us closer together.

SHARING DESIRES

Hope deferred makes the heart sick, but a dream fulfilled is a tree of life.

PROVERBS 13:12

AS I'VE WRITTEN in the last few days about self-revelation, we've looked at sharing experiences and feelings. Today I want to talk about sharing desires. The failure to share desires is a source of much misunderstanding and frustration in any romantic relationship. Expecting your mate to fulfill your unexpressed desires is asking the impossible, and that makes disappointment inevitable. If you want your spouse to do something special on your birthday, for example, then say so. Don't expect your partner to read your mind.

In Proverbs 13:12, King Solomon presented a striking word picture of fulfilled and unfulfilled desires. Of course, not all our daily wishes rise to the level of making us heartsick if they're not fulfilled, but the basic idea is that when good, healthy desires are filled, joy can result. Why wouldn't you want to do that for your spouse? And why wouldn't your spouse want that for you?

Letting your spouse know what you want is a vital part of self-revelation. Several statements reveal desires: "I want . . . ," "I wish . . . ," "Do you know what would really make me happy?" or "I'd like to . . ." If you express your desires, your spouse has a chance to accommodate them. You are not demanding; you are requesting. You cannot control your spouse's decisions. You can clearly state what you would like. It's a step toward intimacy.

Father, help me to communicate my desires more openly. I don't want to be demanding, but I want to reveal more of myself—and the things I hold close to my heart—to the one I love. Please bless our relationship as we strive to fulfill each other's desires.

EXPLAINING OUR BEHAVIOR

O LORD, you have examined my heart and know everything about me.
You know when I sit down or stand up. You know my thoughts even when
I'm far away. . . . Such knowledge is too wonderful for me, too great for me
to understand! PSALM 139:1-2, 6

THE ABOVE VERSES from Psalm 139 are some of the best loved in Scripture because they reveal that God knows us inside and out. He knows our thoughts, our feelings, and why we do the things we do. We can't even comprehend that level of understanding, much less reproduce it. That's why self-revelation is so important for a couple.

We've talked about sharing desires and emotions, but it's important to share about our behavior as well. Your spouse can observe your behavior, but he or she may not interpret it correctly unless you explain it. For example, my wife may observe that I dozed off while she was talking to me. It would be helpful for me to say, "I nodded off on you. I'm sorry. I took a pill for my head-ache, and it is making me sleepy. It's not that I don't want to hear what you have to say." That explanation helps her understand my behavior correctly.

Explaining your behavior ahead of time can also be helpful. "I plan to mow the lawn as soon as I get home from the ball game. Okay? I love you." Now, she doesn't have to fret all afternoon about the long grass while you are off to the ball game. She knows what you intend to do.

Revealing past behavior can also give your spouse valuable information. "Today I went by the furniture store and looked at a bedroom set. I really like it, and I think it is a good deal. I'd like for you to look at it." Explaining what you've done regarding a decision or request helps your spouse process it appropriately. All of these things promote understanding and intimacy for you as a couple.

Lord Jesus, thank you that you know us completely and love us anyway. Help us as a couple to aspire to a deeper knowledge of each other. Please encourage us as we learn to share about our behavior.

WHERE CHANGE BEGINS

[Jesus said,] "Why worry about a speck in your friend's eye when you have a log in your own? . . . First get rid of the log in your own eye; then you will see well enough to deal with the speck in your friend's eye." MATTHEW 7:3, 5

AS A MARRIAGE COUNSELOR, I've drawn one conclusion: Everyone wishes his or her spouse would change. "We could have a good marriage if he would just help me more around the house." Or, "Our marriage would be great if she was willing to have sex more than once a month." He wants her to change, and she wants him to change. The result? Both feel condemned and resentful.

Jesus' words in Matthew 7 vividly illustrate the problem. We think we see others' faults clearly, and we put forth a lot of effort to try to correct them. But in reality, our own sin blinds us. If we haven't dealt with our own failings, we have no business criticizing our spouse's.

There is a better way: Start with yourself. Admit that you're not perfect. Confess some of your most obvious failures to your spouse and acknowledge that you want to change. Ask for one suggestion each week on how you could be a better husband or wife. To the best of your ability, make changes. Chances are, your spouse will reciprocate.

> *Father, it's so much easier to concentrate on my spouse's flaws than to deal with my own. Please give me the courage to look at myself honestly. Help me today to try to change one thing that will make me a better marriage partner.*

TURNING AROUND

[John the Baptist's] message was, "Repent of your sins and turn to God, for the Kingdom of Heaven is near. . . . Prove by the way you live that you have repented of your sins and turned to God." MATTHEW 3:1-2, 8

A WOMAN SAID to me recently, "We have the same old arguments about the same old things. We've been married for thirty years, and I'm sick of his apologies. I want him to change." This woman wanted her husband to repent. The word *repentance* means "to turn around." In the context of an apology, it means that I deeply regret the pain my behavior has caused, and I choose to change my behavior.

John the Baptist preached that people needed to repent—to turn away from their sins and turn toward God. When Jesus began his ministry, he had the same message. As we see in verse 8 above, the proof of our heart change is in our actions. When Christ rules in our hearts, we are not happy to keep repeating the same old sins. Instead, we reach out for divine help to change our ways.

When we hurt our spouse, we must acknowledge that what we have done is wrong and that just apologizing is not enough to make it right. We also need to make a plan to change our actions so we don't hurt our loved one in the same way again. Why would we not want to do that in our closest relationship? Repentance is a vital part of a genuine apology.

Lord, I know I need to do more than say I'm sorry. I need to turn away from my wrong patterns of relating to the one I love. I want to change, but I need your help. Please give me the strength to repent.

DECIDING TO CHANGE

Repent, and turn from your sins. Don't let them destroy you! Put all your rebellion behind you, and find yourselves a new heart and a new spirit.

EZEKIEL 18:30-31

ALL OF US NEED to learn to apologize, for one simple reason: We are all sinners. From time to time we all hurt the people we love the most. When we apologize, we hope the person we have offended will forgive us. We can make that easier if we include in our apology a statement of repentance or change. As one woman said, "I don't want to just hear words; I want to see changes. When he indicates that he intends to change, I'm always willing to forgive him."

All true repentance begins in the heart. The decision to change shows that we are no longer making excuses or minimizing our behavior. Instead, we are accepting full responsibility for our actions. As the above Scripture says, we are putting our sinful behavior behind us and seeking "a new heart and a new spirit." Only God can give those. He can renew in us a desire to change the way we act. He can help us do better. When we share our desire to change, the offended party gets a glimpse of our heart. That often leads to forgiveness.

Father, what a wonderful promise that you can give me a new heart and a new spirit. Change my heart, O God, and help me to change my behavior. I want to communicate that to my loved one so he or she can fully trust me.

EFFECTIVE APOLOGIES

People who conceal their sins will not prosper, but if they confess and turn from them, they will receive mercy. PROVERBS 28:13

EFFECTIVE APOLOGIES REQUIRE a willingness to change our behavior. Proverbs 28:13 makes it clear that when we don't admit our wrongs—whether toward God or toward our spouse—we can't expect a good result. But when we do admit ("confess") the hurtful things we do and make a plan to stop doing them ("turn from them"), forgiveness is possible.

I remember Joel, whose wife, Joyce, was extremely negative. No matter what Joel said, Joyce disagreed with him. In our counseling sessions, I discovered that Joyce saw everything as either good or bad, right or wrong. Thus, if she disagreed with Joel, it couldn't just be a difference of opinion—his idea must be *wrong*.

It took a while, but eventually Joyce apologized for her negative attitude and came up with a plan to change it. She learned to say, "That's an interesting way to look at it." Or, "I can appreciate that." She learned to share her ideas as opinions rather than as dogma. She learned to say, "My perception of that is . . . " Joel freely forgave Joyce when he saw her genuinely trying to change. Effective apologies can save marriages.

God, it's hard to admit my own wrong patterns, but I know I hurt my spouse in the same way over and over again. Please give me the courage to confess those wrongs and turn away from them. And when my loved one does the same, help me to be gracious and to forgive.

DIVISION OF LABOR

Two people are better off than one, for they can help each other succeed. If one person falls, the other can reach out and help. But someone who falls alone is in real trouble. ECCLESIASTES 4:9-10

I VACUUM THE CARPET and wash the dishes at my house. What do you do in your home? Who will do what? is a question that every couple must answer. In my opinion, the gifts and abilities of each person should be considered. One may be more qualified than the other for certain tasks. Why not use the player best qualified in that area?

This does not mean that once one person accepts a responsibility, the other will never offer to help with the task. Love seeks to help and often will. In Ecclesiastes, King Solomon wrote clearly about the value of teamwork. As a couple, we can accomplish more together than we could as two individuals because we are there to help each other. The Scriptures do not tell us exactly who should do what, but they do encourage us to agree on the answer.

The prophet Amos once asked, "Can two people walk together without agreeing on the direction?" (3:3). The answer is, "Not very far and not very well." I encourage you to keep negotiating until both of you feel good about who is doing what in your home.

> *Lord, thank you that my spouse and I can work as a team. Help us to find the best tasks for each of us, and help us to support each other as we work for the same goal.*

SHARING THE GOAL

At last the wall was completed to half its height around the entire city, for the people had worked with enthusiasm. NEHEMIAH 4:6

AS A COUPLE, what is your shared goal? Perhaps it's a smoothly running home, a harmonious relationship, and a sense of fairness. Recently, a woman was in my office complaining that her husband didn't help her with household responsibilities. "We both work full-time," she said. "But he expects me to do everything around the house while he watches TV and unwinds. Well, maybe I need to unwind too." Clearly this couple had not defined their shared goal.

The players on an athletic team do not all perform the same tasks, but they do have the same goal. That was also true when Nehemiah led the Israelites to rebuild the wall around Jerusalem. Some of them rebuilt gates, some carried materials, and others stood guard, watching for those who wanted to sabotage the work. The individuals had separate tasks, but they were united in their ultimate goal: making the city of Jerusalem safe again.

If we want harmony and intimacy in our relationship, then we must each do our part of the work. A spouse who feels put upon is not likely to be interested in intimacy. Why not ask your spouse, "Do you feel that we make a good team around the house?" Let the answer guide your actions.

Father God, thank you for the great example of teamwork from the book of Nehemiah. I want to keep our end goal in mind as my spouse and I negotiate the tasks in our home. Help me to do my part willingly and lovingly.

MUTUAL SEXUAL FULFILLMENT

A newly married man must not be drafted into the army or be given any other official responsibilities. He must be free to spend one year at home, bringing happiness to the wife he has married. DEUTERONOMY 24:5

TWO QUESTIONS I HEAR fairly often in my counseling practice are "How can I get my wife to have sex more often?" and "How can I make sure we both enjoy it?" How often a wife desires sex will be influenced by how her husband treats her. And finding mutual sexual fulfillment is a process; it does not happen automatically. In Deuteronomy 24:5, we read that God instructed the Israelites not to give a newly married man any official responsibilities, particularly those, such as military service, that would take him away from home. During the first year of marriage couples were to bring happiness to each other. We can conclude that helping couples develop marital intimacy was important to God.

One of the best ways to learn about sexual intimacy is to expose yourself to good information. I suggest that you and your spouse read one chapter each week in the book *The Gift of Sex* by Clifford and Joyce Penner. At the end of the week, discuss the ideas presented in the chapter. This is one way to better understand male and female sexuality and to discover how to give each other sexual pleasure.

Your attitude should always be one of love, looking out for each other's enjoyment. Share your desires with each other, but never force any particular sexual expression on your spouse. Open communication in an atmosphere of love will lead to mutual sexual fulfillment.

Father, thank you for the gift of sex. As we seek to become closer sexually, help us to value each other's enjoyment as much as our own. Guide us in showing love to each other through sex.

POSITIVE VIEW OF SEX

Your love delights me, my treasure, my bride. Your love is better than wine, your perfume more fragrant than spices. SONG OF SOLOMON 4:10

I'D LIKE TO TALK about making sex a mutual joy. Please note the word *mutual.* When it comes to sex, anything less than a deep sense of fulfillment on the part of both the husband and the wife is less than God intended. What, then, are the guidelines that lead us to such mutual satisfaction?

Number one is a healthy attitude toward sex. For any number of reasons, some people have very negative attitudes toward sexual intimacy, even within marriage. The answer to negative attitudes begins with a Bible study on sex. In 1 Corinthians 7, Paul affirms sex as an important part of marriage. If you read through the Song of Solomon, you will see that married sex is celebrated in detail as a gift from God. Let this knowledge free you. After all, Jesus said, "If you remain faithful to my teachings . . . you will know the truth, and the truth will set you free" (John 8:31-32).

The second step toward changing your attitude is prayer. Ask God to transform your view of sex into a positive one. Positive attitudes lead to positive behavior.

Father, you know that sometimes I struggle with a negative attitude toward sex. But I read in your Word that sex is wholesome and good. Help me to believe that wholeheartedly. Guide me as I talk with my spouse and try to grow in this part of our marriage.

DEALING WITH SEXUAL SIN

Now there is no condemnation for those who belong to Christ Jesus. And because you belong to him, the power of the life-giving Spirit has freed you from the power of sin that leads to death. ROMANS 8:1-2

ONE OF THE REALITIES of contemporary society is that many couples come to marriage with previous sexual experience, either with each other or with other partners. Our culture would have us believe that sexual experience before marriage better prepares people for marriage. However, all the research indicates otherwise. In fact, the divorce rate among those who have had previous sexual experience is twice as high as those who haven't.

The reality is that previous sexual experience often becomes a barrier to achieving mutual sexual intimacy in marriage. The Christian answer to such barriers is to confess wrongdoing and genuinely forgive each other for past failures. The wonderful verses above from Romans 8 remind us that nothing is beyond God's grace and forgiveness. If you are in Christ and have confessed your sin, you are forgiven and free from the past. The scars of the past may remain forever, but healed scars can serve as reminders of the grace and love of God. Accepting the scars and forgiving each other is a step on the road to mutual sexual fulfillment.

Lord, you know the role that sexual sin has played in our relationship. Please forgive my sins and help me to start anew, forgiven and ready to develop a healthier sexual relationship with my spouse.

EMBRACING EMOTIONS

[Jesus] looked around at them angrily and was deeply saddened by their hard hearts. Then he said to the man, "Hold out your hand." So the man held out his hand, and it was restored! MARK 3:5

SOME CHRISTIANS ARE CRITICAL of emotions. Have you ever heard a statement like this? "Don't trust your emotions. Faith, not feelings, is the road to spiritual growth." Why do we so disapprove of our emotions? In Mark 3 we read that Jesus felt anger and sorrow—and for good reason. It was the Sabbath, and when Jesus was in the synagogue, he noticed a man with a shriveled hand. He was compassionate and healed the man, but all the watching Pharisees could think about was that Jesus had broken their Sabbath laws. Jesus' anger and sorrow over their reaction was entirely appropriate and reflected the Father's own heart. Few of us would condemn Jesus for having those emotions. So why do we condemn ourselves?

God gave us emotions for growth, maturity, fulfillment, and enjoyment. Feelings were made to be our friends, and they can serve as important signals. When we experience a negative emotion, it tells us that something needs attention. Think of it like the dashboard light that appears when your car needs oil. We don't curse the light; we address the problem it's alerting us to. Why not do the same with your emotions? When you experience a negative emotion, especially regarding your spouse, stop for a moment and figure out the real problem. If you take constructive action, the emotion will have served its purpose.

Lord, thank you for emotions. You have made us in your image as emotional beings. Help me to look at my feelings as a gift. Please give me the wisdom to see the problem behind the emotion and deal with it before my strong feelings hurt my spouse.

DEALING WITH FEAR

When I am afraid, I will put my trust in you. I praise God for what he has promised. I trust in God, so why should I be afraid? PSALM 56:3-4

WOULD IT SURPRISE YOU if I told you that Jesus experienced fear? Fear is an emotion that pushes us away from a person, place, or thing. In Matthew 26:39 we read that Jesus prayed in the Garden of Gethsemane, "My Father! If it is possible, let this cup of suffering be taken away from me." As he approached the time of his death, he saw the physical and emotional suffering ahead, and he was afraid. His emotions pleaded for a different way. But he didn't let his fear cause him to lash out at others or turn away from what he knew was right. Rather, Jesus showed us what we should do with our fear—express it to God.

The psalmist reminds us that God has promised his presence and protection. When we trust in God, we know he's in control, so there is no reason to be afraid. In fact, the Bible records 365 times when God says, "Fear not, for I am with you." Our fear leads us to God, and we rest in his strength to protect us.

When you feel fear, don't put yourself down and don't blame it on your spouse. Instead, run as quickly as you can to the loving arms of God.

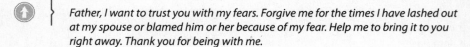

Father, I want to trust you with my fears. Forgive me for the times I have lashed out at my spouse or blamed him or her because of my fear. Help me to bring it to you right away. Thank you for being with me.

RELEASING ANGER

"Don't sin by letting anger control you." Don't let the sun go down while you are still angry, for anger gives a foothold to the devil. EPHESIANS 4:26-27

DO YOU FIND YOURSELF overreacting to little irritations? Your spouse forgot the milk, and you grimace or make a sarcastic comment. Your child tracked mud on the new carpet, and you explode. If so, there is a good chance that you are suffering from stored anger—anger that has been living inside of you for years.

Perhaps your parents hurt you with harsh words or severe punishment. Maybe your peers made fun of you as a teenager or your boss treated you unfairly. If you've held all of these hurts inside, now your stored anger may be showing up in your behavior. The Bible wisely tells us not to let the day end when we're still angry. In other words, we need to deal with our anger right away rather than letting it build up. In my book *Anger*, I talk about getting rid of stored anger. It all begins by releasing your anger to God. Tell him about your emotions, and ask him to help you handle the situations that caused them. He can help you release the hurts from long ago and forgive those who wounded you.

Experiencing anger isn't wrong. But as Ephesians 4 tells us, letting anger control us *is* wrong—and can be very damaging to a marriage.

Lord, sometimes I experience so much anger over such little things. I know I'm hurting my spouse, and I don't want to do that anymore. Please forgive me. I release this anger to you. Help me to figure out why I have it and then let it go.

EXPRESSING LOVE

*Jesus replied, "The most important commandment is this: 'Listen, O Israel!
The LORD our God is the one and only LORD. And you must love the LORD
your God with all your heart, all your soul, all your mind, and all your
strength.' The second is equally important: 'Love your neighbor as yourself.'"*

MARK 12:29-31

THE WORD *CHRISTIAN* MEANS "Christlike." In the first century, *Christian*
was not a name chosen by the followers of Jesus. Rather, it was a name given
to them by others. Believers based their lifestyle on the teachings of Christ, so
the best way to describe them was to call them Christians.

What if Christians really were Christlike? Central in Jesus' teachings is
the command to love. In fact, in the verses above, Jesus said that the greatest commandment is to love God and the second is to love our neighbors.
These commands supersede all others, because everything else flows out from
them.

Love begins with an attitude, which in turn leads to acts of service. "How
may I help you?" is a good question with which to begin. Today is a good day
to express love to our neighbor. In my opinion, that starts with those closest to
us—first our spouse, then our family—and then spreads outward.

*Father, you made it clear that loving you and loving others is the most important
thing I can do. Help me to make that a priority. Let me show Christlike love to my
spouse today.*

KINDNESS

Be kind to each other, tenderhearted, forgiving one another, just as God through Christ has forgiven you. EPHESIANS 4:32

"BE YE KIND ONE TO ANOTHER" (Ephesians 4:32, KJV). We may have memorized it as children, but have we forgotten it as adults? Kindness is one of the traits of love, as defined in the Bible's famous "love chapter," 1 Corinthians 13: "Love is patient and kind" (v. 4). Do you consciously think of being kind to your spouse throughout the day? Kindness is expressed in the way we talk as well as in what we do. Yelling and screaming are not kind. Speaking softly and respectfully is. So is taking the time to have a meaningful conversation with a spouse who is lonely, upset, or uncertain.

Then there are acts of kindness—things we do to help others. When we focus our energy on doing kind things for each other, our relationship can be rejuvenated. What could you do today to be kind to your spouse? Maybe it's taking on a chore that's not typically your responsibility, or bringing him or her a cup of coffee in bed. Or perhaps it's giving an encouraging note or bringing home a favorite treat. These are small things, but they can have a big impact. Imagine what your relationship would be like if you both emphasized kindness.

Lord Jesus, I want to show my love through kindness. Please help me to think of great ways today to be kind to the one I love.

SHOWING PATIENCE

Always be humble and gentle. Be patient with each other, making allowance for each other's faults because of your love. EPHESIANS 4:2

PATIENCE MEANS ACCEPTING the imperfections of others. By nature, we want others to be as good as we are (or as good as we think we are), as on time as we are, or as organized as we are. The reality is, humans are not machines. The rest of the world does not live by our priority list; our agenda is not their agenda. It's especially important for couples to remember this. In a loving relationship, patience means bearing with our spouse's mistakes and giving him or her the freedom to be different from us.

When is the last time you were impatient with your significant other? Did your impatience come because he or she failed to live up to your expectations? I don't think it's coincidence that Ephesians 4:2 links humility with patience. When we're humble, we realize that the world doesn't revolve around us and that we don't set the standard for behavior. And when that's our mindset, we're far less likely to become impatient.

The Bible says, "Love is patient and kind" (1 Corinthians 13:4). If in impatience you lash out at your loved one, love requires that you apologize and make it right. Work for more patience in your marriage.

Lord, I need more patience. Please teach me to let go of my expectations—for what others should be like, for what I should be able to accomplish, and for what I think I'm owed. Help me to treat my husband or wife with loving patience.

LEARNING TO LISTEN

Fools think their own way is right, but the wise listen to others.

PROVERBS 12:15

WE WILL NEVER RESOLVE conflicts if we don't learn to listen. Many people think they are listening when in fact they are simply taking a break from talking—pausing to reload their verbal guns. The above verse from Proverbs doesn't pull any punches when it calls those who don't listen *fools*. We may not like that word, but the truth is, refusing to listen reveals a lack of humility. Wise people listen to others—especially those they love. Genuine listening means seeking to understand what the other person is thinking and feeling. It involves putting ourselves in the other person's shoes and trying to look at the world through his or her eyes.

Here's a good sentence with which to begin: "I want to understand what you are saying because I know it is important." One man told me that he made a sign which read, "I am a listener." When his wife started talking, he would hang it around his neck to remind himself of what he was doing. His wife would smile and say, "I hope it's true." He learned to be a good listener.

Lord Jesus, thank you for listening to me when I pray. Help me to listen to my spouse—really listen—so I can understand him or her better.

HONORING THROUGH LISTENING

Love each other with genuine affection, and take delight in honoring each other. ROMANS 12:10

WE ARE ALL BUSY. Often, too busy to listen. And yet, listening is the only way we will ever come to understand our spouse's thoughts and feelings. Listening takes time and requires focus. Many people pride themselves in being able to listen while reading e-mails or watching television, but I question if that's really listening. One husband said, "My wife insists that I sit down and listen to her. I feel like I'm in a straitjacket, like I'm wasting time."

In Romans 12, Paul tells us to "take delight in honoring each other." One way to honor someone is to listen intently and to give him or her our full attention. It's a question of respect. When we drop everything, look at our spouse, and listen, we communicate, "You are the most important person in my life." On the other hand, when we try to listen while doing other things, we communicate, "You are just one of my many interests." Listening is a powerful expression of love.

Father, I want to honor my spouse by being a good listener. Help me to be willing to focus my full attention on him or her so I can really understand the words being said.

WHEN FAMILY GETS IN THE WAY

"A man leaves his father and mother and is joined to his wife, and the two are united into one." Since they are no longer two but one, let no one split apart what God has joined together. MATTHEW 19:5-6

A WOMAN ONCE ASKED ME, "We are supposed to leave our families and cleave to each other, but my husband is so attached to his family that I feel left out. What can I do?" Of course, this situation can happen with either women or men.

The concept of "leaving and cleaving" is central to the Bible's teaching on marriage. It first appears in Genesis, right after the very first woman and man were united. Both Jesus and Paul quoted this verse as well, and for good reason. When the principle isn't followed, marriages suffer.

If you find yourself in the circumstances of the woman I mentioned above, you will feel left out because your spouse is not meeting your emotional need for love. You might even feel that his family is more important to him than you are. However, the answer is not to blast your spouse with angry lectures about being overly attached to his parents. When you do that, you drive him away. His parents are giving him love while you are angry and demanding. You will argue endlessly about the time he spends with his parents—which is the symptom rather than the root problem. Your relationship will suffer.

A better approach is to focus on meeting each other's need for love. Leave the in-laws out of the discussion. Find out what makes your spouse feel loved, and share what makes you feel loved. Then concentrate on speaking the right love language. You and your spouse will be drawn together as you begin to feel loved by each other. Spending time with each other will become even more appealing than spending time with your parents, and your relationship will be strengthened.

Lord, sometimes I get frustrated when I feel my spouse's family is more important to him or her than I am. Help me to avoid pointless arguing and instead focus on showing love. May we truly cleave to each other and be united in love.

DEALING WITH PARENTAL ADVICE

Timely advice is lovely, like golden apples in a silver basket. PROVERBS 25:11

A COMMON QUESTION I hear in counseling is this: "I want to honor my parents, but they are constantly trying to give us advice. How do I let them know that we need to make these decisions on our own?"

Three things are important when you are dealing with parents who give advice too freely. First, you must understand that their intentions are good. They are not trying to make your life miserable; they are trying to help you avoid making poor decisions. Second, there is a good chance that your parents have more wisdom than you, since they have been around longer and have had more experience. Third, it is true that your parents should not control your life after you are married.

How do you put these three together and get the best of both worlds? I suggest that sometimes you ask for your parents' advice before they have a chance to give it. Don't immediately discount it; often their advice will be beneficial. After all, the book of Proverbs speaks highly of timely, appropriate advice. Then pray for God's wisdom, discuss the matter as a couple, and make the decision you think is best. If your parents object, tell them that you appreciate their input and found it very helpful, but you are doing what you and your spouse think is best. In time, they will come to see you as adults and respect your wisdom.

Father, thank you for parents who care for us and want us to make good decisions as a couple. Please give us the wisdom to weigh advice carefully and to seek the direction you have for us.

THE TRANSFORMING POWER OF ATTITUDE

A glad heart makes a happy face; a broken heart crushes the spirit.... For the despondent, every day brings trouble; for the happy heart, life is a continual feast. PROVERBS 15:13, 15

HOW DO YOU ENHANCE the seasons of your relationship? Or, how do you get from what I call a winter marriage—one that's negative and full of frustration—to a spring marriage—one that's full of hope and renewal? One strategy is to choose a winning attitude.

Most athletes would agree that winning is 90 percent attitude and 10 percent hard work. If that is true in the world of sports, it is certainly true in the world of relationships. Spring marriages are created and sustained by positive attitudes. Winter marriages are characterized by negative attitudes. What we think largely influences what we do. In turn, our actions greatly influence our emotions. King Solomon acknowledged some of these truths in the verses from Proverbs above. Optimism breeds more joy, but negativity feeds on itself to make us feel even more downcast. When faced with the choice between constant trouble and life being a "continual feast," who wouldn't choose the latter?

This connection between attitude and actions opens a door of hope for all couples. If we can change our thinking, we can change the atmosphere of our marriage. The most common mistake couples make is allowing negative emotions to dictate their behavior. By failing to recognize the power of a positive attitude, they don't achieve their marriage's highest potential. The good news is that you can choose your attitude.

Heavenly Father, I know my attitude can make all the difference in how I view my marriage and even how I interact with my spouse. Please renew my attitude with hope and optimism.

CHANGING YOUR ATTITUDE

And now, dear brothers and sisters, one final thing. Fix your thoughts on what is true, and honorable, and right, and pure, and lovely, and admirable. Think about things that are excellent and worthy of praise. PHILIPPIANS 4:8

CHANGING YOUR ATTITUDE can be a catalyst that sets in motion a seasonal change in your marriage. I must confess that I learned this truth the hard way. Earlier in my marriage, I spent a great deal of time in the winter season because of my negative attitudes. And when I was in the midst of winter, I found it hard to admit that my attitude was part of the problem. It was much easier to blame my wife, Karolyn's, behavior. Today I readily admit that my negative thinking was the culprit.

If your relationship is filled with frustration and strain, my guess is that you, too, have the tendency to blame your spouse and are failing to recognize your own negative attitudes. If you want to break free from the coldness and bitterness of a winter relationship, I challenge you to change your attitude. As long as you curse the darkness, it will get darker. But if you look for something good in your marriage, you'll find it.

This famous verse from Philippians 4 reminds us to fix our thoughts on good things—things that are true, right, honorable, pure, lovely, and admirable. This kind of focus can change the way we see everything around us. Focusing on the positive creates a warmer climate. Express appreciation to your spouse for one positive action, and you'll likely see another.

Father, I have so much to be thankful for. There are reasons to hope all around me, if I will only look for them. Forgive me for my negativity and the effect it's had on my outlook and my marriage. Help me to see the positive.

LOOKING AT THE POSITIVE

Some people make cutting remarks, but the words of the wise bring healing.

PROVERBS 12:18

ONE OF THE MOST POWERFUL things we can do to enhance the seasons of our marriage is to choose a winning attitude. How do we do this?

First, we must admit our negative thinking. As long as you think negatively, you'll never be able to choose a winning attitude. The second step is to identify your spouse's positive characteristics, even if that's difficult for you. You might even get help from your children by asking, "What are some of the good things about Daddy or Mommy?" Third, once you've identified those positive characteristics, thank God for them. Then, fourth, begin to express verbal appreciation to your spouse for the positive things you observe. Set a goal, such as giving one compliment a week for a month. Then move toward two per week, then three, and so on until you're giving a compliment each day.

The book of Proverbs has a lot to say about the importance of words. Proverbs 18:21 says, "The tongue has the power of life and death" (NIV). Proverbs 12:18 talks about words bringing healing. Proverbs 15:4 calls gentle words "a tree of life." You can give your marriage new life when you replace condemnation and criticism with compliments and words of affirmation.

Lord God, thank you for all the wonderful things about my spouse. Please keep those fresh in my mind. Help me to use my words to acknowledge those things. May what I say heal and bring life.

UNRESOLVED CONFLICTS

Starting a quarrel is like opening a floodgate, so stop before a dispute breaks out. PROVERBS 17:14

WHY IS IT SO IMPORTANT to resolve conflicts? Because unresolved conflicts stand as barriers to a couple's unity. Conflicts arise over those issues about which we have differences and where we both feel that our side is right. If we don't find a way to meet in the middle, we become enemies instead of teammates, and life becomes a battlefield. The proverb above reminds us that starting a quarrel or an argument can often lead to places we didn't mean to go. It's always better to try to resolve things before they get heated. Few people like to fight. So if conflicts continue, sooner or later someone gives up and walks away.

How sad that thousands of relationships end because couples never learn to resolve conflicts. The first step is to get out of the "arguing mode" and get into the "understanding mode." Stop trying to win an argument and start trying to understand each other.

Lord, you know the areas of conflict between me and the one I love. We need your grace to resolve these things without continual arguing and battling. Help me to seek first and foremost to understand my spouse.

BE A CONFLICT RESOLVER

Love is not jealous or boastful or proud or rude. It does not demand its own way. It is not irritable, and it keeps no record of being wronged.

1 CORINTHIANS 13:4-5

WHY DO PEOPLE ARGUE? In one word, rigidity. When we argue, in essence we are saying, "My way is the right way. If you don't do it my way, I'll make your life miserable." The arguer insists on getting his or her own way.

Conflict resolvers have a different attitude. They say, "I'm sure we can work this out in a way that will be positive for both of us. Let's think about it together." They look for a win-win resolution. They begin by respecting each other's ideas and looking for a solution instead of trying to win an argument.

The Scriptures say that love "does not demand its own way." Love is not proud, either, so it doesn't consider its way best. Actually, love means looking out for the other person's interest. Philippians 2:4 says, "Don't look out only for your own interests, but take an interest in others, too." "What would be best for you?" is the question of love.

Father, I want to stop being an arguer and start being a conflict resolver. Help me to think first of my spouse and second of myself. Help me not to demand what I want but to look for a solution that will work for both of us. I need your help to combat my innate selfishness.

SERVING THE LORD THROUGH OTHERS

Work willingly at whatever you do, as though you were working for the Lord rather than for people. Remember that the Lord will give you an inheritance as your reward, and that the Master you are serving is Christ.

COLOSSIANS 3:23-24

THE CHRISTIAN MESSAGE is that we serve Christ by serving others. As Colossians 3:23 says, we should do everything as if we are doing it for the Lord—in other words, willingly, cheerfully, and enthusiastically.

We all have idealistic visions of our spouse asking, "What could I do to help you tonight?" or "How could I make your life easier this week?" But the fact is, many of us grew up in homes where we had to fight to survive. We did not learn to appreciate the value of serving others. How do you develop an attitude of service if you grew up in a home where it was dog-eat-dog?

Let's start with your family of origin—the family you grew up in. On a scale of zero to ten, how would you rate your father on having an attitude of service toward your mother? Zero means he never lifted a finger to help her; ten means that he was almost Christlike in his servanthood. Next, rate your mother. How well did she demonstrate an attitude of service? Now let's make it personal. How would you rate yourself? Are you more like your father or your mother? Do you have a lot of room for growth? Or are you already serving Christ by serving your spouse?

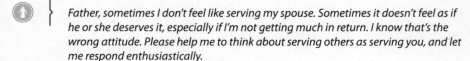

Father, sometimes I don't feel like serving my spouse. Sometimes it doesn't feel as if he or she deserves it, especially if I'm not getting much in return. I know that's the wrong attitude. Please help me to think about serving others as serving you, and let me respond enthusiastically.

"I REALLY APPRECIATE THAT"

Whoever wants to be first among you must be the slave of everyone else. For even the Son of Man came not to be served but to serve others and to give his life as a ransom for many. MARK 10:44-45

THE THEME OF THE CHRISTIAN LIFE is serving Christ by serving others. Jesus came to earth to serve others—first by his love, his teaching, and his healings, and ultimately by his death. When we serve others, we are not only serving Christ, but we are being Christlike. So why not begin developing an attitude of service in our closest relationship? The fact is, we do acts of service for each other every day. However, we don't often talk about them, and consequently, we begin to take them for granted.

I want to suggest a little communication exercise that will bring service to the front burner. It's a game called I Really Appreciate That. Here's how you play it: The husband might say to the wife, "One way I served you today was by putting away a load of laundry." The wife might respond, "I really appreciate that." Then she says, "One way I served you today was by cooking dinner." The husband responds, "I really appreciate that." Play the game once a day for a week, and you will become more aware of the acts of service that you are already doing for each other. You will elevate them to a place of importance by talking about them. If you have children, let them hear you playing the game, and they'll want to get in on the fun.

Lord Jesus, thank you for your example of service. Please transform me more each day into your image. Help us as a couple to serve each other with love and to show our appreciation for each other.

SERVING WITH GLADNESS

Make a joyful noise to the Lord, all the earth! Serve the Lord with gladness!
Come into his presence with singing! PSALM 100:1-2 (ESV)

A HEALTHY MARRIAGE will include a positive attitude of service between a husband and wife. She will want to do things for him, and he will want to do things for her. But how do you know what things to do? Simple: You ask questions.

How about asking your spouse, "What is one thing I could do for you this week that would make your life easier?" When he or she tells you, you respond, "I'll try to remember that." All true service must be given freely, so the choice to do what your spouse suggests still rests with you. But now you have a concrete idea of how to invest your time and energy in a way that he or she will appreciate.

When you choose to do what your spouse has requested, you are serving Christ by serving your loved one. The first verses of Psalm 100 remind us that we're called to serve with gladness. Serving God—whether directly or through serving others—can be joyful and energizing, and it can certainly bring blessing. It is the road to greatness, and it will also give you a growing marriage.

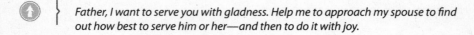

Father, I want to serve you with gladness. Help me to approach my spouse to find out how best to serve him or her—and then to do it with joy.

LEAVING A LEGACY

Come, my children, and listen to me, and I will teach you to fear the LORD.

PSALM 34:11

IF WE HAVE CHILDREN, how can we leave them a positive legacy? A legacy is an inheritance handed down from one generation to the next. In a legal sense, a legacy is a deposition of personal property that is made by terms of a will. But a real legacy goes beyond material things, and its impact is usually much deeper. Our legacy will have a powerful influence on the lives of those who follow us.

The most important legacies are not monetary but emotional, spiritual, and moral. They center around the character of the person leaving them. Legacies from the past affect a family's future. We all know families with long-standing reputations of good character—kindness, honesty, and decency. On the other hand, we all know families who received a negative legacy of character and behavior—perhaps dishonesty, lack of a strong work ethic, or poor relationship choices. While we like to believe that an individual can overcome any disadvantage, the legacy we receive can be either a blessing or a curse on our lives.

Psalm 34 talks about the ultimate blessing we can give our children: teaching them to love and serve the Lord. We do that through reading and talking, but most of all through modeling. What changes do you need to make in your life or in your relationship as a couple in order to leave a positive legacy for your children?

Father, it's good to stop and think about what I'm teaching my children—and how that lines up with the lessons I want to leave them. Please show me where I need to change. Guide me as I seek to leave my children a positive legacy.

GIVING UP OUR LIVES

We know what real love is because Jesus gave up his life for us. So we also ought to give up our lives for our brothers and sisters. 1 JOHN 3:16

BEFORE MY WIFE and I got married, I thought that every morning when the sun rises, everybody gets up. But after we were married, I found out that my wife didn't do mornings. It didn't take me long not to like her, and it didn't take her long not to like me. For several years we struggled, greatly disappointed in our marriage.

What finally turned our marriage around? The profound discovery that it was not my job to demand that she meet my expectations. My job was to give away my life to make her life easier and more meaningful. My model? Christ himself, who gave away his life for our benefit. The apostle John reminds us that Christ's sacrifice exemplifies genuine love. Because of his sacrifice, we should also give up our lives for others—starting with our spouse.

In a thousand years, I would never have come up with that idea. But then, God's ways are not our ways. (See Isaiah 55:8-9 for a beautiful description of this.) In God's way of doing things, the road to greatness lies in serving others. What better place to start than in your own marriage? My wife is my first responsibility. When I choose to serve God, he says, "Let's start with your wife. Do something good for her today." When I got the picture, my wife was quick to respond. She was a fast learner.

Love begets love. That's God's way.

Lord Jesus, words can't express how grateful I am for your sacrifice. You gave up your life for us when we had done nothing to deserve it. Please transform my heart so I may have that same attitude toward my spouse. May I be willing to lay down my own desires and expectations to serve him or her. I know that will reap wonderful rewards in our relationship.

DEALING WITH DEPRESSION

The LORD is close to the brokenhearted; he rescues those whose spirits are crushed. PSALM 34:18

JOHN WAS A SUCCESSFUL BUSINESSMAN whose wife was suffering from depression. "She spends most mornings in bed, and in the afternoons she just sits around the house," he told me. "She seems to have no ambition. She doesn't have the energy to cook, and many nights she doesn't eat with us. She has lost forty pounds over the last year. To be truthful, life is pretty miserable at our house. I feel sorry for the kids, although they get more attention than I do. But I know they must wonder what is wrong with their mother."

John had just described some of the classic characteristics of depression. Unfortunately, depression is quite common and does not go away simply with the passing of time. John's wife needed medical and psychological help, and without it, things would get even worse.

Many Christians don't understand depression and think it is only a spiritual problem. While it may have a spiritual dimension, it is often rooted in physical and emotional imbalance. In the next few days, we'll talk about the causes and cures of depression. If this is an issue for you or your loved one, remember Psalm 34:18. The Bible promises that the Lord has compassion for you and deals tenderly with you in your time of depression.

Father, you know how depression affects us as a couple. Thank you for your tenderness toward us even when we feel weak and vulnerable. Help me not to criticize my spouse but to be supportive and get the help we need.

TYPES OF DEPRESSION

He heals the brokenhearted and bandages their wounds. PSALM 147:3

WHAT DO YOU DO when you or your loved one is depressed? First, you must get information so you understand the basic facts about depression. It is helpful to think of three categories. First, depression may be the by-product of a physical illness. When we are physically sick, our minds and emotions often move into a depressed state. We temporarily check out. It's nature's way of protecting us from constant anxiety about our physical condition.

The second kind of depression is called situational or reactive depression and grows out of a particularly painful situation in life. Many of these experiences involve a sense of loss: the loss of a job, the loss of a child, a significant transition such as a child going to college, or the loss of a friendship.

The third category is depression rooted in some biochemical disorder. This is a physical disease and must be treated with medication.

Visit the library or talk to your doctor to learn about depression. It's the first step in getting help.

Lord, thank you for your promise to bandage our wounds when we're hurt and brokenhearted—whether the cause is physical, emotional, or spiritual. When we're affected by depression, please help us to deal with the situation as a couple.

TREATING DEPRESSION

Why am I discouraged? Why is my heart so sad? I will put my hope in God!
I will praise him again—my Savior and my God! PSALM 42:5-6

LONG-TERM DEPRESSION can be extremely detrimental to a relationship.
Therefore, if you or your loved one is depressed, you need to do all you can
to get help.

The first step is generally to see a medical doctor or a counselor. The
physician will often prescribe an antidepressant medication. If the depression happens to have a biochemical root, then the medication can be helpful.
Typically, it takes three or four weeks to determine if a given medication is
producing positive results. If it does not, the physician will usually try another
type of medication.

However, only about one-third of all depressions have a biochemical root.
Whether or not medication helps alleviate the symptoms, it is also valuable
to see a trained professional counselor who has experience in dealing with
depression. The counselor can help you discover the emotional root of the
depression and begin therapy. If the depression has lasted for several weeks
or months, I urge you to take action. Depression is not an incurable disease.
There is hope, but you need to get help. Psalm 42 gives us a vivid picture of
hope being renewed. Keep this image in mind as you go through your time of
depression. Both of you will one day again be filled with joy and praise.

Father, when I can't see the end of this difficult situation, please renew my hope.
Renew my faith that you can heal and restore. You care, and you are with us. Thank
you, Lord.

PAST FAILURES

No one is righteous—not even one. No one is truly wise; no one is seeking God. All have turned away; all have become useless. No one does good, not a single one. ROMANS 3:10-12

DO YOU EVER WONDER why we can't just forget the past and move on? It's usually because we haven't dealt with the past appropriately. Harsh words and selfish attitudes may have left their mark on the soul of our relationship. But healing is available, and it begins with identifying past failures so we can confess them and ask forgiveness. The wall that has been built between you and your spouse must be torn down one block at a time. The first step is to identify the blocks.

Why not ask God to bring to your mind the times you have failed your spouse? Get your pencil ready and write them down. Then ask your spouse to make a list of the ways he or she thinks you have failed in the past. Consider asking your children or your parents to share times they have observed you speaking harshly or being unkind to your spouse. As you make your list, you may discover that the wall of past failures is high and thick. That's okay. The Bible is clear that everyone has sinned—against God and against others. Admitting and identifying past failure is the first step in "wall demolition."

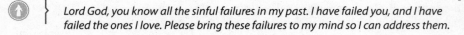

Lord God, you know all the sinful failures in my past. I have failed you, and I have failed the ones I love. Please bring these failures to my mind so I can address them.

TEARING DOWN THE
WALL OF FAILURE

Have mercy on me, O God, according to your unfailing love; according to your great compassion blot out my transgressions. Wash away all my iniquity and cleanse me from my sin. PSALM 51:1-2 (NIV)

YESTERDAY WE TALKED about identifying the past failures in your relationship. Today I want to talk about confessing the failures. Both of you know that there is a wall between you. So why not tear down the wall?

Once you've made a list of the ways in which you have failed your spouse, confess these things to God. Psalm 51, written after King David's greatest moral failure—committing adultery with Bathsheba and conspiring to murder her husband—offers a heartfelt model for confession. Thank God that Christ has paid the penalty for your sins, and ask him to forgive you.

Next, go to your spouse and confess your failures. Confession says, "I was wrong. I'm sorry. I know that I hurt you, and I don't want to do that again. Will you forgive me?" True confession opens the door to the possibility of forgiveness. When you have been offered forgiveness, your side of the wall is torn down. If your spouse is also willing to confess and receive forgiveness, the entire wall can be demolished, and your marriage can move forward.

Father, I confess my sins to you—sins of selfishness, impatience, and lack of love, among others. Thank you for your promise of forgiveness. Please give me the strength to confess also to my spouse, whom I have hurt greatly.

FORGIVING EACH OTHER

Make allowance for each other's faults, and forgive anyone who offends you. Remember, the Lord forgave you, so you must forgive others.

COLOSSIANS 3:13

IN THE PAST TWO DAYS, we have talked about how to identify our failures and how to confess those failures to God and to our spouse. Now I want to talk about forgiveness.

When your spouse confesses past failures and requests your forgiveness, it is time to forgive. In fact, refusing to forgive is to violate the clear teachings of Jesus. He taught his disciples to pray: "[Father,] forgive us our sins, as we have forgiven those who sin against us" (Matthew 6:12). If we refuse to forgive when others confess to us and repent, we jeopardize our own forgiveness from God. The apostle Paul underscored this point in Colossians 3:13, when he wrote that we must forgive others because the Lord has forgiven us. And one of Jesus' parables made clear that our "forgiveness debt" to the Lord is far greater than the debt anyone can "owe" us.

Nothing is to be gained by holding on to past failures. By contrast, a willingness to forgive opens the door to the possibility of future growth. Trust can be rebuilt and love restored. When a couple is willing to confess and forgive past failures, a marriage can move from a place of bitterness and hardship to a place of renewal and joy.

> *Father, I am so grateful for your forgiveness. Help me to extend that same gracious forgiveness to my spouse when he or she requests it, even when that's hard. I know the benefits will be great.*

EXPRESSING LOVE

Let love be your highest goal! 1 CORINTHIANS 14:1

WOULD YOU LIKE TO KNOW your spouse's love language? Then observe how he or she most often expresses love to you. Is it through words of affirmation? gifts? acts of service? quality time? or physical touch? The way a person expresses love to you is likely the way he or she wishes you would express your love.

If he often hugs and kisses you, his love language is probably *physical touch*. He wishes you would take initiative to hug and kiss him. If she is always weeding the flower beds, keeping the finances in order, or cleaning up the bathroom after you leave, then her love language is probably *acts of service*. She wishes that you would help her with the work around the house. If you don't, then she feels unloved. One husband said, "If I had known that my taking out the garbage would make her feel loved and more responsive sexually, I would have started taking out the garbage years ago." Too bad it took him so many years to learn his wife's primary love language. As the Bible says, love should be our highest goal. To reach that goal, we need to put forth an effort to know how our spouse can best receive love.

Lord Jesus, help me to make love my highest goal—both in life and in my marriage. Please give me wisdom as I observe my spouse and try to figure out his or her love language. I want to love him or her well.

FINDING THE GOOD IN COMPLAINTS

Love never gives up, never loses faith, is always hopeful, and endures through every circumstance. 1 CORINTHIANS 13:7

WHAT DOES YOUR SPOUSE complain about most often? We usually interpret complaints as negative criticism, but they are actually giving us valuable information. Complaints reveal the heart. A person's recurring complaint often reveals his or her love language.

If a husband frequently says, "We don't ever spend time together. We're like two ships passing in the night," he is telling his wife that *quality time* is his primary love language and his love tank is sitting on empty.

If a wife says, "I don't think you would ever touch me if I didn't initiate it," she is revealing that *physical touch* is her love language.

If a husband returns from a business trip and his wife says, "You mean you didn't bring me anything?" she is telling him that *gifts* is her love language. She can't believe that he came home empty-handed.

If a wife complains, "I don't ever do anything right," she is saying that *words of affirmation* is her love language, and she is not hearing those words.

If a husband says, "If you loved me, you would help me," he is shouting that his love language is *acts of service*.

Do you feel frustrated because you don't seem to be communicating love to your spouse? First Corinthians 13 reminds us never to give up. Things can improve when we maintain hope. Discovering and speaking your spouse's love language is one way to help your relationship grow.

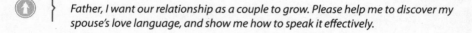

Father, I want our relationship as a couple to grow. Please help me to discover my spouse's love language, and show me how to speak it effectively.

TAKING THE INITIATIVE TO LOVE

God showed how much he loved us by sending his one and only Son into the world so that we might have eternal life through him. This is real love—not that we loved God, but that he loved us and sent his Son as a sacrifice to take away our sins. Dear friends, since God loved us that much, we surely ought to love each other. 1 JOHN 4:9-11

I BELIEVE OUR DEEPEST emotional need is the need to feel loved. If we are married, the person we most want to love us is our spouse. If we feel loved by our spouse, the whole world looks bright. If we do not feel loved, the whole world looks dark. However, we don't get love by complaining or making demands.

One man told me, "If my wife would just be a little more affectionate, then I could be responsive to her. But when she gives me no affection, I want to stay away from her." He is waiting to receive love before he gives love. Someone must take the initiative. Why must it be the other person?

Why are we so slow to understand that the initiative to love is always with us? God is our example. We love God because he first loved us (see 1 John 4:19). He loved us even when we were sinful, even when we weren't responsive, even when we had done nothing to deserve it. That's the ultimate example of love that takes the initiative. If you choose to give your spouse unconditional love and learn how to express love in a language your spouse can feel, there is every possibility that your spouse will reciprocate. Love begets love.

Father, you have shown us the way to love—unconditionally, by taking the initiative and not waiting for the other person to reciprocate. Please help me to express that kind of love to my spouse.

INTELLECTUAL INTIMACY

My heart has heard you say, "Come and talk with me." And my heart responds, "Lord, I am coming." PSALM 27:8

MOST OF US GOT MARRIED not because we wanted someone to help us cook meals, wash dishes, maintain the car, and rear children. Rather, we married out of a deep desire to know and to be known, to love and to be loved, and to have a genuinely intimate relationship. How does this lofty goal become reality? It helps to look at the five essential components of an intimate relationship, which we'll do in the next few days.

First is intellectual intimacy. So much of life is lived in the world of the mind. Throughout the day, we have hundreds of thoughts about life as we encounter it. We also have desires, things we would like to experience or obtain. Intellectual intimacy comes from sharing some of these thoughts and desires with our spouse. These may focus on finances, food, health, current events, music, or church. Whether or not they're important in and of themselves, these thoughts and desires reveal something about what has gone on in our mind throughout the day.

Psalm 27:8 describes a way to increase our intimacy with God—by responding when he invites us to talk with him. The same principle applies to human relationships. In marriage, we have the pleasure of learning some of the inner movements of our spouse's mind. That is the essence of intellectual intimacy.

Father, thank you for wanting to talk to me and hear from me! I know that conversation builds relationships. Help me to share my thoughts freely with my loved one and listen carefully to his or her thoughts as well.

EMOTIONAL INTIMACY

I am bent over and racked with pain. All day long I walk around filled with grief. PSALM 38:6

EMOTIONAL INTIMACY is one of the five components of an intimate relationship. Feelings are our spontaneous, emotional responses to what we encounter through the five senses. I hear that the neighbor's dog died, and I feel sad. I see the fire truck racing down the road, and I feel troubled. My wife touches my hand, and I feel loved. I see her smile, and I feel encouraged.

Your inner life is filled with emotions, but no one sees them. Sharing your feelings builds emotional intimacy. Allowing your mate into your inner world means being willing to say, "I'm feeling a lot of fear right now" or, "I am really happy tonight." These are statements of self-revelation. Psalm 38:6 gives just one of many examples of the psalmist pouring out his heart to God. King David and the other writers of the psalms were honest about their feelings of sadness, depression, anger, and grief, as well as their feelings of joy, adoration, and celebration. And that kind of straightforward self-revelation only increased their intimacy with God.

Learning to talk about emotions can be one of the most rewarding experiences in life. Such sharing requires an atmosphere of acceptance. If I am assured that my spouse will not condemn my feelings or try to change my feelings, then I am far more likely to talk about them.

Lord, thank you for wanting to hear our feelings. I know sharing emotions as a couple will help us grow closer. I pray that you will help us cultivate a loving, accepting atmosphere where we can share freely.

SOCIAL INTIMACY

All night long I search for you; in the morning I earnestly seek for God.

ISAIAH 26:9

MUCH OF LIFE CENTERS on encounters that happen throughout the day—things people say or do or situations that develop. When my wife and I share these with each other, we feel that we are a part of what the other is doing. We develop social intimacy and sense that we are a social unit. In other words, what happens in my wife's life is important to me.

Another aspect of social intimacy involves the two of us doing things together. Attending a movie or athletic event, shopping or washing the car together, or having a picnic in the park are all ways of building social intimacy. Much of life involves doing. When we do things together, we are not only developing a sense of teamwork, but we are also enhancing our relationship. In the verse above, we see that the prophet Isaiah wrote about strongly desiring to spend time with God. That same sense of urgency to be in another's company—which often is prompted by our good memories of previous encounters—is beneficial in marriage.

The things we do together often form our most vivid memories. Will we ever forget climbing Mount Mitchell together? Or giving the dog a haircut? Social intimacy is an important part of a growing marriage.

Lord Jesus, I am grateful for the memories we have developed as a couple. Thank you for fun and laughter and times we can just enjoy being together and doing things together. Help us to cultivate social intimacy as we grow in our relationship.

SPIRITUAL INTIMACY

We also pray that you will be strengthened with all his glorious power so you will have all the endurance and patience you need. May you be filled with joy, always thanking the Father. COLOSSIANS 1:11-12

MARITAL INTIMACY has five essential components. We've talked about intellectual, emotional, and social intimacy, and today we'll look at spiritual intimacy. We are spiritual creatures. Anthropologists have discovered that people from cultures around the world are religious. We all have a spiritual dimension. The question is, are we willing to share this part of our lives with those we love? When we do, we experience spiritual intimacy.

It may be as simple as sharing something you read in the Bible this morning and what it meant to you. Spiritual intimacy is also fostered by shared experience. After attending a worship service with her husband, one wife said, "There is something about hearing him sing that gives me a sense of closeness to him." Praying together is another way of building spiritual intimacy. If you feel too awkward praying aloud, then pray silently while holding hands. No words are uttered, but your hearts move closer to each other.

You might also consider praying for each other as a way to strengthen your relationship. Many of Paul's epistles contain beautiful prayers for those to whom he was writing, including the one above from Colossians 1, which asks the Lord to strengthen the believers and give them patience, endurance, and joy. Praying passionately for your spouse's relationship with God can be a supremely intimate experience.

Father, I know there is nothing more important in our lives than our relationship with you. Help me to be an encouragement to my spouse in this area. Let us be willing to share our thoughts and prayers with each other. Draw us closer to each other, Lord, as we draw closer to you.

SEXUAL INTIMACY

The husband should fulfill his wife's sexual needs, and the wife should fulfill her husband's needs. The wife gives authority over her body to her husband, and the husband gives authority over his body to his wife.

1 CORINTHIANS 7:3-4

BECAUSE MEN AND WOMEN are sexually different, we often come at sexual intimacy in different ways. The husband's emphasis is most often on the physical aspects. Seeing, touching, feeling, and the experience of foreplay and climax are the focus of his attention. The wife, on the other hand, comes to sexual intimacy with an emphasis on the emotional aspect. To feel loved, cared for, appreciated, and treated tenderly brings her great pleasure. In short, if she truly feels loved, then the sexual experience is but an extension of this emotional pleasure.

Sexual intimacy requires an understanding response to these differences. In 1 Corinthians 7, the apostle Paul writes directly that each spouse should fulfill the other's sexual needs. In other words, sexual intimacy requires self-lessness. For the sexual relationship to be a source of relational closeness, each spouse must think first of the other and how best to make sex a source of joy for him or her.

It should be obvious that we cannot separate sexual intimacy from emotional, intellectual, social, and spiritual intimacy. We cannot attain sexual intimacy without intimacy in the other areas of life. The goal is not just to have sex, but to experience closeness and to find a sense of mutual satisfaction.

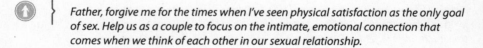

Father, forgive me for the times when I've seen physical satisfaction as the only goal of sex. Help us as a couple to focus on the intimate, emotional connection that comes when we think of each other in our sexual relationship.

WHAT'S OUR ATTITUDE TOWARD MONEY?

Those who love money will never have enough. How meaningless to think that wealth brings true happiness! The more you have, the more people come to help you spend it. So what good is wealth—except perhaps to watch it slip through your fingers! ECCLESIASTES 5:10-11

SOMETIMES IT SEEMS as if the more we have, the more we argue about what we have. The poorest couple in America has abundance compared to masses of the world's population. I am convinced that the problem does not lie in the *amount* of money that a couple possesses, but in their *attitude* toward money and the way they handle it.

I think a lot of us have a mental "magic sum" that seems to be the benchmark of what would make us happy. We get there and then realize, *No, that's not quite enough.* In Ecclesiastes 5, King Solomon—who was himself one of the wealthiest kings on record—writes bluntly about the never-ending search for "enough" money. If we think a certain amount of money will bring happiness, we're doomed to disappointment.

Author Jeannette Clift George has said, "The great tragedy in life is not in failing to get what you go after. The great tragedy in life is in getting it and finding out it wasn't worth the trouble!"

When our life focuses on "getting more money," we have the wrong focus. Our marital relationship and our relationship with God are far more important than how much money we have. Getting our priorities straight is the first step in making money an asset to marriage rather than a liability.

Lord, you know how easy it is for me to think everything would be better if I had just a little more money. Thanks for the reminder that if that's the way I think, I'll never be satisfied. I pray for better priorities and a stronger sense of contentment.

SHARING MONEY

I appeal to you, dear brothers and sisters, by the authority of our Lord Jesus Christ, to live in harmony with each other. Let there be no divisions in the church. Rather, be of one mind, united in thought and purpose.

1 CORINTHIANS 1:10

WHEN YOU GET MARRIED, it is no longer "your money" and "my money" but rather "our money." Likewise, it is no longer "my debts" and "your debts" but rather "our debts." When you accept each other as partners, you accept each other's liabilities as well as each other's assets.

Before marriage, both partners should make a full disclosure of their financial assets and liabilities. It is not wrong to enter marriage with debts, but you ought to know what those debts are, and you should agree on a plan of repayment.

The motif of marriage is two becoming one. When this is applied to finances, it implies that all of your resources belong to both of you. One of you may be responsible for paying the bills and balancing the checkbook, but this should never be used as an excuse for hiding financial matters from the other. One of you may have a higher salary, but that doesn't mean you get more say in how finances should be allocated.

Since the money belongs to both of you, both of you ought to agree on how it will be used. Full and open discussions should precede any financial decision, and agreement should be the goal. Follow the apostle Paul's advice and be "of one mind, united in thought and purpose." This is fitting for followers of Christ, whose priorities should be the same. Remember, you are partners, not competitors. Marriage is enhanced by agreement in financial matters.

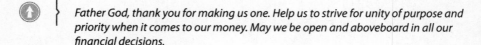

Father God, thank you for making us one. Help us to strive for unity of purpose and priority when it comes to our money. May we be open and aboveboard in all our financial decisions.

GOOD STEWARDSHIP

After a long time their master returned from his trip and called them to give an account of how they had used his money. The servant . . . said, "Master, you gave me five bags of silver to invest, and I have earned five more." The master was full of praise. "Well done, my good and faithful servant. You have been faithful in handling this small amount, so now I will give you many more responsibilities. Let's celebrate together!" MATTHEW 25:19-21

ARE YOU HONORING GOD by the way you use your money? God cares about how we use what he gives us. In Matthew 25, we read the famous parable of the talents. Jesus told the story of the master who entrusted certain amounts of money to various servants while he was away. When he returned, some of the servants had been wise stewards and had increased the money. As we see from the verses above, the master responded with praise—and by giving those servants greater responsibility with more money.

Financial resources, whether abundant or modest, have tremendous potential for good. Sound planning, buying, saving, and investing are all part of our stewardship. Another aspect of faithful stewardship is giving to God through the church and other Christian organizations.

More important than the amount we give is our attitude. Christian giving is an act of the will prompted by love for God, not a legalistic duty to be performed for merit. Have you and your spouse discussed recently what you are giving to God? Does what you are giving reflect your love for God? When the two of you decide to honor God in your giving, you have taken a big step toward creating a growing marriage.

Father, as a couple we want to be good stewards of all that you have given us. Help us to use our money wisely and to give generously to your Kingdom work.

WISDOM FOR THE FUTURE

A prudent person foresees danger and takes precautions. The simpleton goes blindly on and suffers the consequences. PROVERBS 22:3

SAVING MONEY is a sign of wisdom. Hoarding money is not. King Solomon wrote in Proverbs that wise people plan for potential difficulties in the future; foolish people assume that everything will be fine and then find themselves in trouble. The wise husband and wife plan for difficult times. Financially, this involves saving and investing. Of the two, saving is the most fundamental. Many Christian financial advisers suggest that 10 percent of a couple's income be allotted to savings and investments. You may choose more or less, but you should make the choice deliberately. If you plan to save what is "leftover," you will likely not save.

If you give 10 percent to the Lord's work and save 10 percent, that leaves 80 percent to be divided among mortgage payments (or rent), heat, electricity, telephone, groceries, and so forth. The couple who regularly saves a percentage of their income will have not only the reserve funds they need for emergencies, but also the satisfaction that comes from being good stewards. Regular savings ought to be a part of your financial plan.

> *Lord, as a couple we want to be wise in the way we use our money. Please give us the discipline to be deliberate about saving, investing, and giving. We know all we have is yours, and we want to use it well.*

HOW DO YOU MEASURE YOUR LIFE?

A generous man will himself be blessed, for he shares his food with the poor.

PROVERBS 22:9 (NIV)

USING CREDIT to buy things is a huge issue in today's culture. The media screams, "Buy now, pay later." What is not stated is that if you "buy now," you will pay *much more* later. Interest rates on credit-card debt can be more than 21 percent.

Credit cards encourage impulse buying, and most of us have more impulses than we can afford to follow. This can lead to some extreme marital stress every month when the credit-card bill arrives. Rather than "buy now, pay later," why not agree as a couple that what you cannot afford, you will not purchase? Most of us can live with less, and perhaps live more happily. Jesus taught, "Life is not measured by how much you own" (Luke 12:15). Life finds its greatest meaning in relationships—first with God, then with our spouse, children, extended family, and friends. After a point, using our money for ourselves has little meaning or significance. But as Proverbs 22:9 points out, using our money generously for others—whether those we know or others who are in need—can bless us. It can strengthen our relationships, give us a sense of purpose, and encourage others.

Things have meaning only as they enhance relationships. Why must you have the biggest and best now, if doing so puts stress on your marriage? *Things* bring only momentary pleasure, while relationships last for a lifetime.

Father, it's easy to get caught up in things I think we need now. Please give me the right perspective. Help me to realize what is really meaningful—our relationship with you and others. May we invest heavily in those things.

WHEN PERSONALITIES CLASH

In his grace, God has given us different gifts for doing certain things well.

ROMANS 12:6

IN MY COUNSELING OFFICE, I often hear of personality clashes within marriage that result in disharmony. By personality, I mean our patterned way of responding to life. We speak of people being extroverted or introverted, neat or sloppy, pessimistic or optimistic, decisive or indecisive, excitable or calm. These are all personality traits. They are predictable ways in which one tends to respond to life's situations.

One wife said of her husband, "He is so slow and deliberate that by the time he makes a decision, it's too late." She was describing how one of his personality traits annoyed her. We all have a mixture of personality characteristics, and someone who knows us well can usually predict how we will respond in a given situation. Most personality traits have both strengths and weaknesses. The key in marriage is to make the most of our strengths and learn how to minimize the weaknesses.

It's important to remember, as Romans 12 tells us, that God has created us as unique individuals. We have different personalities and different things we do well. That's something we should celebrate rather than allow to frustrate us. When as a couple we understand each other better, our distinct personalities can become an asset rather than a liability.

Father, thank you for making us distinct individuals. It's so easy to get annoyed with some of my spouse's personality traits that are different from mine. Please help me to view those as a gift instead of a problem. Help me to learn from my spouse.

THE PEACEMAKER

God blesses those who work for peace, for they will be called the children of God. MATTHEW 5:9

IF WE ARE GOING to understand each other, we must identify our personality differences. There are many personality types, all of which have positives and negatives, and in the next few days we'll look at a few. Today we'll look at the peacemaker. This is the calm, slow, easygoing, well-balanced personality. This person is typically pleasant, doesn't like conflicts, seldom seems ruffled, and rarely expresses anger.

The peacemaker has emotions but does not easily reveal them. In a marriage, the peacemaker wants calm, tends to ignore disagreement, and avoids arguments at all costs. This person is very pleasant to be around; however, the downside of this personality is that conflicts are often left unresolved. If the couple does get into an argument, the peacemaker will try to calm the other person by acquiescing, even if he does not agree. He is kindhearted and sympathetic and wants everybody just to enjoy life. However, if a peacemaker is married to a controller, she may be steamrolled and eventually suffer in silent anger.

In the Sermon on the Mount, Jesus expressed blessing for the peacemakers and said that they will be called children of God. What a wonderful statement! James 3:18 gives a further accolade for this personality type: "Those who are peacemakers will plant seeds of peace and reap a harvest of righteousness." If you are married to a peacemaker, thank God for it. Also, be careful not to take advantage of your spouse's easygoing nature.

Father, I am thankful for my spouse's desire to be a peacemaker. I know that you bless this attitude. Please help me to appreciate it fully, and not to use it for my own gain.

THE CONTROLLER

Diotrephes, who loves to be the leader, refuses to have anything to do with us. . . . Not only does he refuse to welcome the traveling teachers, he also tells others not to help them. And when they do help, he puts them out of the church. 3 JOHN 1:9-10

WHAT IS IT LIKE to live with someone who has a controlling personality? Controllers are quick, active, practical, strong-willed people. They tend to be self-sufficient, independent, decisive, and opinionated. Finding it easy to make decisions, they often make decisions for other people as well as for themselves.

Controllers will take definite stands on issues and can often be found crusading for special causes. They do not give in to pressure from others but will argue to the end. Controllers see problems as challenges. They have dogged determination and do not sympathize easily with others. Also, the controller does not easily express compassion or warm emotions. While controllers typically accomplish much in life, they often run over others who stand in their way. In a marriage, this leaves the spouse feeling like his or her ideas and feelings are not respected. The spouse may also complain of feeling unloved.

It's possible that some of the biblical prophets had this personality, and in their case, it was often a positive. They needed strong, decisive personalities to fulfill their God-ordained purpose while facing pressure and persecution. Another biblical example is not so positive. In the verses above, the apostle John refers to a controlling person named Diotrephes. He not only chose not to help the traveling Christian teachers who were common in that era, but he also wanted to keep others from helping them. When we move from making our own decisions to wanting to be in charge of others' choices, that's negative controlling.

If you have a strong controlling personality, you will likely need help in understanding how your actions affect others. If this describes your spouse, you may need to confront him or her gently when you feel ignored or disrespected.

Father, help us to deal with issues of control in our marriage. I thank you for the ability to be decisive and efficient, but help me not to exercise those personality traits on my spouse. Rather, help us both to be respectful and loving.

LIFE OF THE PARTY

David went there and brought the Ark of God from the house of Obed-edom to the City of David with a great celebration. . . . And David danced before the LORD *with all his might.* 2 SAMUEL 6:12, 14

WE'VE BEEN TALKING about personality types, and today we'll look at the party maker. This is the warm, lively, excited personality. For this person, all of life is a party. Party makers enjoy people, do not like solitude, and are at their best when surrounded by friends and the life of the party. Party makers are never at a loss for words. They can turn a simple meal into a celebration. These people make life exciting not only for themselves, but for others. Filled with stories, dramatic expressions, and songs, the party maker's objective is for everyone to be happy.

The Bible certainly doesn't look down on celebration. The verses above highlight King David leading a national celebration when the Ark of the Lord was brought back to Jerusalem. He "danced before the LORD with all his might"! He knew that some things deserve celebration.

The downside of this personality is that others may see party makers as undependable and undisciplined. Why? They can be so into the moment that they forget previous commitments. It's not that they intend to be delinquent; it's just that they forget. If you are married to a party maker, enjoy the ride—and ask your spouse how you might help him or her keep life on track.

Father, thank you for celebrations—and thank you for my spouse's joyful spirit that makes so many things enjoyable. Help me to appreciate it and be gentle when I try to help.

PERSONALITY DIFFERENCES ON THE SAME TEAM

The one who plants and the one who waters work together with the same purpose. And both will be rewarded for their own hard work. For we are both God's workers. 1 CORINTHIANS 3:8-9

IN THE PAST FEW DAYS, we have talked about marriage and personality differences. It's important to understand personality types because we generally seek to meet our psychological and spiritual needs in a way that fits our personality.

For example, a caretaker will find her significance in caring for a needy friend. She may spend hours trying to help this friend solve problems and find meaning in life. However, her efforts will often be incomprehensible to the controller. "Why would anyone spend so much time and energy trying to help such a loser?" is the attitude of the controller. He fails to recognize that the caretaker is finding her own significance as she cares for the needy person. The controller, on the other hand, will likely find his significance in accomplishing projects and making things happen.

If we understand the role that personality plays in motivating our behavior, we will understand each other better. Understanding leads to greater harmony in marriage. We need to remember that as a couple, we're working together as a team. Paul wrote in 1 Corinthians 3 that he and Apollos, another preacher, were not competitors but teammates with different strengths and responsibilities. The important thing was that they were working for the same goal. Similarly, in marriage, we have different strengths and weaknesses, and we often accomplish different tasks. However, we can still work together in unity and understanding for the good of our relationship.

Father, thank you for the ways I am different from my spouse. Please help us to understand each other, to have patience with each other, and to celebrate the fact that we can work as a team.

CONFRONTING DEFENSIVENESS

[Samuel asked,] "Why haven't you obeyed the LORD? Why did you rush for the plunder and do what was evil in the LORD's sight?" "But I did obey the LORD," Saul insisted. "I carried out the mission he gave me." 1 SAMUEL 15:19-20

WHY DO WE GET so defensive? Defensiveness is part of human nature. We see defensiveness even in the Bible. Job, fed up with advice from his so-called friends, angrily stated at one point that he knew just as much as they did. (See Job 13:2.) In the verses above, we see that King Saul, Israel's first king, responded defensively and untruthfully to the prophet Samuel when Samuel confronted him about going against the Lord's instructions.

Consider this example: Eric was chopping onions, and Jennifer was pouring oil in the pan. When Eric left to adjust the radio, Jennifer plopped the onions in the oil. He returned and said, "You know, there's a better way to do that." Jennifer responded, "Why do you always have to be in charge of everything?" "I just thought you would want my advice. You know this meal is my specialty," Eric said. "Then cook your special meal," Jennifer snorted as she walked out of the kitchen.

What happened in this kitchen adventure? Eric's statements touched one of Jennifer's emotional hot spots. She already felt that Eric was exerting too much control over her life. Now he was telling her how to cook, and she became defensive.

All of us have emotional hot spots. We don't know where they are until we hit them. When we do, the key is taking time to ask some questions: What can we learn from our defensiveness? What was there about my statement that caused you to get defensive? Once we take this approach, we will come to understand our defensiveness and find ways to deal positively with the problem.

Father, it's easy for me to become defensive when I feel put on the spot or accused. Please help me to understand why I'm reacting that way. Help me to choose a better response.

DEALING WITH EMOTIONAL HOT SPOTS

Always be humble and gentle. Be patient with each other, making allowance for each other's faults because of your love. EPHESIANS 4:2

ALL OF US have emotional hot spots. When our spouse says or does certain things, we get defensive. Usually our response is rooted in our history. You may find that often your spouse is echoing statements made by your parents that hurt or embarrassed you. The fact that you get defensive indicates that the hurt has never healed. The next time you get defensive, ask yourself why. Chances are, you will have a flood of memories. Share these past experiences with your spouse, and he or she will develop greater understanding.

What if you are the spouse? Once you learn why your husband or wife gets defensive in a certain area, then you can decide how to move on. You might ask, "How would you like me to talk about this issue in the future? I don't want to hurt you. How could I say it in a way that would not be hurtful to you?" Now you are on the road to defusing the defensive behavior of your spouse. You're also following Scripture by being patient and making allowances for your spouse's struggles, as Paul encourages in Ephesians 4:2. Learning to negotiate the "hot spots" of life is a big part of developing a growing marriage.

Lord Jesus, please help me to uncover why I get so defensive about certain things, and give me the wisdom to change my reaction. I know I also need to extend special patience and grace to my spouse when he or she becomes defensive. Help us to avoid each other's hot spots rather than triggering them.

PHYSICAL TOUCH

Kiss me and kiss me again, for your love is sweeter than wine.

SONG OF SOLOMON 1:2

KEEPING EMOTIONAL LOVE alive in a relationship makes life much more enjoyable. The husband or wife who feels loved is less likely to stray. How do we keep love alive after the "in love" emotions have evaporated? I believe it is by learning to speak each other's love language. In the next few days, I want to focus on the love language of physical touch.

When some husbands hear the words *physical touch*, they immediately think of sex. But sexual intercourse is only one of the dialects of the love language physical touch. Holding hands, kissing, embracing, giving back rubs, putting an arm around the shoulder, or gently putting your hand on your loved one's leg are all ways of expressing love by physical touch. The Old Testament book Song of Solomon makes it clear that physical touch between a husband and wife can be beautiful, intimacy building, and celebrated. The verse above is just one example of the book's poetry celebrating physical expressions of love.

For some people, both men and women, physical touch is their primary love language. If you don't give them tender touch, they may not feel loved even though you are speaking other love languages. If this describes your spouse, make sure you work on meaningful touch.

Father, thank you for the gift of physical touch. Help me to communicate my love to my spouse by the way I touch him or her.

LEARNING THE LANGUAGE OF TOUCH

His left arm is under my head, and his right arm embraces me.

SONG OF SOLOMON 2:6

TO THE PERSON whose primary love language is physical touch, nothing is more important than tender touches. To touch my body is to touch me. To withdraw from my body is to distance yourself from me emotionally. In our society, shaking hands is a way of communicating openness and social politeness. When on rare occasions one person refuses to shake hands with another, it communicates that things are not right in their relationship. The same principle applies in marriage. Withdraw from your spouse physically, and you are withdrawing emotionally.

Touches may be explicit and call for your full attention, such as a back rub or sexual foreplay. Or they may be implicit and require only a moment, such as putting your hand on her shoulder as you pour a cup of coffee or rubbing your body against him as you pass in the kitchen. Once you discover that physical touch is the primary love language of your husband or wife, you are limited only by your imagination. Kiss when you get in the car. It may greatly enhance your travels. Give him a hug before you go shopping, and you may hear less griping when you return. Try new touches in new places and listen for feedback on whether or not it is pleasurable. Remember, your spouse has the final word; you are learning to speak his or her language.

Lord Jesus, please help me to learn how my spouse wants to be touched. My love is so strong, and I want to communicate that.

TOUCH TO COMFORT

For everything there is a season, a time for every activity under heaven. . . .
A time to cry and a time to laugh. A time to grieve and a time to dance. A
time to scatter stones and a time to gather stones. A time to embrace and a
time to turn away. ECCLESIASTES 3:1, 4-5

ALMOST INSTINCTIVELY in a time of crisis, we hug one another. Why? In a crisis, more than anything, we need to feel loved. We cannot always change events, but we can survive if we feel loved.

All marriages will experience crises. The death of parents is inevitable. Automobile accidents injure thousands each year. Disease is no respecter of persons. Disappointments are a part of life. The most important thing you can do for your spouse in a time of crisis is to love him or her. Especially if your spouse's primary love language is physical touch, nothing is more important than holding her as she cries or putting a hand on his shoulder as he makes a difficult decision. Your words may mean little to a person who is hurt or in shock, but your physical touch will communicate that you care.

Ecclesiastes 3 reminds us that there's a time for everything, and crises provide unique opportunities for expressing love. Tender touches will be remembered long after the crisis has past, but your failure to touch may never be forgotten. Physical touch is a powerful love language. In a time of crisis, a hug is worth more than a thousand words.

Heavenly Father, when we face a difficult situation as a couple, help me to reach out to my spouse with loving touch. May my touch bring comfort.

PROCESSING ANGER

Turn from your rage! Do not lose your temper—it only leads to harm.

PSALM 37:8

WHEN WAS THE LAST TIME you experienced anger toward your spouse, and how did you handle it? In the next few days, I want to give you a five-step program for handling anger in a positive way.

The first step is admitting to yourself that you are angry. "That's obvious," you might reply. "Anyone would know that I am angry." Perhaps, but the question is, are *you* conscious of your anger? Anger comes on so suddenly that often you may be caught up in a verbal or physical response before you consciously acknowledge what is going on inside you.

The Scriptures never say that anger is wrong, but multiple passages talk about the importance of controlling anger. Psalm 37 speaks about avoiding rage and not losing your temper, which can harm others. When you realize you are angry, I suggest that you say these words out loud: "I am angry about this. Now what am I going to do?" You have placed the issue on the table, and you have distinguished the difference between what you are feeling—your anger—and the action you are going to take. You have set the stage for applying reason to your anger rather than simply being controlled by your emotions. This is the first step in processing anger positively.

} *Father, I get angry more than I like to admit. Please help me as I try to deal with it the right way. Guard me from losing my temper and hurting the one I love most.*

CHANGING ANGER PATTERNS

An angry person starts fights; a hot-tempered person commits all kinds of sin.

PROVERBS 29:22

HOW DO I KEEP from sinning when I am angry? That is the challenge given in Ephesians 4:26, which says, "Be angry, and do not sin" (NKJV). King Solomon echoes the same sentiment in Proverbs 29 when he reminds us that a hot temper can lead to many kinds of sin. We've all seen evidence of that, whether the sin is hurtful, cutting words; physical violence; or reckless behavior. There is a better way.

Yesterday we looked at the first step for handling anger in a positive way: Consciously acknowledge to yourself that you are angry. Today we look at step two: Restrain your immediate response. Don't jump to action; think. Most of us follow the patterns we learned in childhood, and those patterns tend to cluster around two extremes—verbal or physical venting on the one hand, or withdrawal and silence on the other. Both are destructive.

How do you change these patterns? How do you restrain your immediate response? Some do it by counting to ten or one hundred. Others do it by taking deep breaths or going for a walk. One woman told me that when she gets angry, she waters her flowers. She said, "The first summer I tried this I almost drowned my petunias." Yes, you can break old patterns. Find a plan that works for you and learn to restrain your negative responses to anger.

Lord Jesus, when I get angry, I often lose my temper and hurt my mate by lashing out verbally. I know that's destructive to our relationship. Please help me to retrain myself to respond differently.

FINDING THE SOURCE OF ANGER

If another believer sins against you, go privately and point out the offense.
If the other person listens and confesses it, you have won that person back.

MATTHEW 18:15

IN THE PAST DAYS, we've looked at two steps to controlling your anger: Admit to yourself that you are angry, and restrain your immediate response. Today we'll look at step three: Locate the focus of your anger. If you are angry with your spouse, step back and ask yourself, *Why am I angry? Is it what my spouse has said or done? Is it the way he is talking? Is it the way she is looking at me?*

The bottom line in locating the focus of your anger is to pinpoint what your spouse did or failed to do that you consider to be wrong. Has your spouse sinned against you in some way? If no sin was committed, then your anger is distorted. You didn't get your way, so you are angry. That is childish. It's time to grow up and realize that in marriage, you don't always get what you want. However, if your mate *has* genuinely sinned against you, then it's time for a calm and loving confrontation. Follow the example Jesus set forth in Matthew 18 by making the confrontation private and direct, and be willing to listen as well as talk. Locating the focus of your anger will help you determine whether your anger is distorted or appropriate.

Father, I need wisdom to determine why I'm getting angry. Please don't let my emotion cloud my thinking. Help me to differentiate clearly between anger that has a justifiable cause and anger that does not. I pray for positive communication between myself and my mate.

BECOMING SLOW TO ANGER

Understand this, my dear brothers and sisters: You must all be quick to listen, slow to speak, and slow to get angry. Human anger does not produce the righteousness God desires. JAMES 1:19-20

AS WE'VE BEEN DISCUSSING, the way you handle anger can be detrimental to your marriage. Today we look at step four in controlling your anger: Analyze your options. Now that you know why you are angry, you can decide how you are going to respond.

There are many things that you might do, some of which are extremely harmful. You could give your spouse a tongue-lashing. Some people move into physically abusive territory and shake or even hit the other person. God hates that kind of violence; in fact, Psalm 11:5 says that he hates those who love violence. The apostle James encouraged his readers to be slow to anger because of this very issue—that anger often results in unrighteous actions, which are not what God desires for us. You need to set aside those sinful responses and take a more positive approach.

Whatever you contemplate doing, you must answer two questions. First, is the action I'm considering positive? That is, does it have the potential for dealing with the wrong that was committed and making things better? Second, is the action I'm considering loving? Is it designed to benefit the person at whom I am angry? If the answer to these two questions is yes, then you are ready for the final step.

Father, forgive me for the times when I am quick to get angry and sin in my anger. Please give me strength as I try to make better decisions about how I will respond.

HANDLING ANGER CONSTRUCTIVELY

Get rid of all bitterness, rage, anger, harsh words, and slander, as well as all types of evil behavior. Instead, be kind to each other, tenderhearted, forgiving one another, just as God through Christ has forgiven you. EPHESIANS 4:31-32

IN THE PAST DAYS, we've looked at a five-step program for handling anger: Admit to yourself that you are angry; restrain your immediate response; locate the focus of your anger; analyze your options. Today we're ready for step five: Take constructive action.

As I see it, there are two possibilities. The first is to lovingly confront the person with whom you are angry. The second is to consciously decide to overlook the matter. It's what the Bible calls forbearance. The book of Romans talks about God's mercy and forbearance in not counting our sins against us. Forbearance is the best option when you realize that your anger is distorted and has grown out of selfishness. If that's the case, you release your anger to God with a prayer: "Father, forgive me for being so selfish." Then you let it go. You may also choose to let go of offenses that are real but which you have blown out of proportion.

On the other hand, when your spouse has sinned against you, the clear biblical teaching is that you lovingly confront. "I realize I may not have all the facts, but I'm feeling angry and really need to talk with you. Is this a good time to talk?" Then you lay the matter before your spouse and seek reconciliation. In this case, anger has served a good purpose, and the relationship is restored.

Father, thank you that anger can serve a positive purpose. Help us as a couple to move from anger to resolution, so that our relationship may grow stronger.

SEEKING HIS KINGDOM

The one thing I ask of the LORD—the thing I seek most—is to live in the house of the LORD all the days of my life, delighting in the LORD's perfections and meditating in his Temple. PSALM 27:4

A PRIORITY IS SOMETHING we believe to be important. When we list priorities, we are listing those things we believe to be of great value in life.

Most Christians would agree that priority number one is our relationship and fellowship with God. Nothing is more important. In fact, our relationship with God influences the rest of our priorities. If God is the author of life, then nothing is more important than knowing him. If God has spoken, then nothing is more important than hearing his voice. If God loves, nothing can bring greater joy than responding to his love. In Psalm 27:4, the psalmist voiced his highest desire: to seek God's face and be in his presence. Jesus said, "Seek first the kingdom of God and His righteousness" (Matthew 6:33, NKJV).

Can you honestly say that seeking the Kingdom of God is your first priority? If so, that will have a profound impact on the way you approach your marriage. To follow God's guidelines for marriage, as in all of life, will be your burning desire.

Father, I know that your Kingdom should be my first priority, but too often that's not reflected in the way I live. Please forgive me. Help me to seek your Kingdom above all. May I have your perspective on every aspect of my life, including the way I think about marriage.

PRIORITIZING FAMILY

"At last!" the man exclaimed. "This one is bone from my bone, and flesh from my flesh! She will be called 'woman,' because she was taken from 'man.'" This explains why a man leaves his father and mother and is joined to his wife, and the two are united into one. GENESIS 2:23-24

IS YOUR FAMILY one of your top priorities? When we recognize that God established marriage and family as the most basic unit of society, family becomes extremely important. In fact, Psalm 68:6 tells us that in his compassion, "God places the lonely in families."

Within family relationships, we recognize that the marriage relationship is more fundamental than the parent-child relationship. The above verses from Genesis 2 show just how unique the husband-wife relationship is. Not only was the first woman created from the man's rib, but no other human relationship is described with such terms as "cleaving" or "becoming one." Marriage is a lifelong, intimate relationship. By contrast, most children will eventually leave their parents and establish their own families.

If family is one of my top priorities, how will that affect the way I spend my time, money, and energy? When I serve my wife, I am also doing something for my children. I'm setting an example that I hope they will remember when they get married. One of the most important things you can do for your children is to love and serve your spouse. Nothing creates a more secure environment for children than seeing Mom and Dad loving each other. And nothing else cements your marriage relationship quite so well.

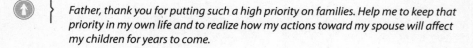

Father, thank you for putting such a high priority on families. Help me to keep that priority in my own life and to realize how my actions toward my spouse will affect my children for years to come.

TAKING CARE OF YOURSELF

Don't you know that you yourselves are God's temple and that God's Spirit lives in you? . . . God's temple is sacred, and you are that temple.

1 CORINTHIANS 3:16-17 (NIV)

A WIFE SAID TO ME RECENTLY, "I'm so busy with my family, my job, and my church that I feel like I don't have any time for me." Is this wife being self-centered? Not at all. She is trying to balance her priorities. Believing that we are made in God's image and that our bodies are the temple of the Holy Spirit, most Christians would agree that among their list of priorities should be caring for their own physical, emotional, and spiritual well-being. Paul writes in 1 Corinthians 3 that as believers, we are God's sacred temple because the Holy Spirit lives in us. The desire to be a fitting temple should provide motivation to take care of ourselves. Quoting Old Testament law, Jesus told his hearers that we are to love our neighbor as we love ourselves (see Matthew 22:39). The Christian who does not give adequate attention to his own needs will not long love and serve his neighbor.

In marriage, we must help each other find time for personal development. The husband who takes responsibility for the children while his wife takes a walk or reads a book is being a spiritual leader. He is looking out for his wife's well-being. When the wife returns the favor, she is serving God by serving her husband. Helping each other find time for self-renewal physically, emotionally, and spiritually is an important element of a growing marriage.

Lord God, I am in awe that the Holy Spirit resides in me. I know that I can never be a worthy temple without your help, so I pray that you will cleanse me. Help me to take the necessary time for myself so that I may be rejuvenated physically, emotionally, and spiritually. Show me how to provide that for my spouse as well.

SUPPORT ONE ANOTHER

The body is a unit, though it is made up of many parts; and though all its parts are many, they form one body. So it is with Christ.

1 CORINTHIANS 12:12 (NIV)

MOST OF US WOULD rank marriage, family, and vocation at the top of our priorities. But how to balance them in terms of time and energy is sometimes elusive. Let me share an idea. Call a family meeting, and with a calendar on the table, list the important events in the life of each family member this month. This may include doctor appointments, church activities, job responsibilities, and if you have children, piano recitals, school events, and sports events. Make copies of the monthly calendar for each member of the family.

With your spouse, decide which events require your attendance, then seek diligently to work out your schedule so that you can attend them. Many employers are willing to allow flexibility when they see your commitment to your family. Also, challenge each person to pray for family members on the day of their special events.

The Bible is clear that although members of the body of Christ have different talents and play different roles, we are bound together as one in Christ. That's true with the church, and it's true with a believing family. As you work on this calendar, remind your children that, even though each person in your family is different, you can and should support each other well. Balance is the key, and you can do it.

Father, thank you for my family. Thank you for the reminder that while we are all individuals, we are one in you. Help us to show that kind of "oneness" support to each other as we seek to balance our activities.

LISTENING WITH EMPATHY

The heart of the discerning acquires knowledge; the ears of the wise seek it out.

PROVERBS 18:15 (NIV)

THE ABILITY TO SPEAK and to *listen* are two of the more profound gifts of God. Nothing is more fundamental to a relationship than talking and listening. Open communication is the lifeblood that keeps a marriage in the spring and summer seasons—times of optimism and enjoyment. Conversely, failure to communicate is what brings on fall and winter—times of discouragement and negativity.

It sounds so simple. The problem is that many of us tend to be judgmental listeners. We evaluate what we hear based on our own view of the situation, and we respond by pronouncing our judgment. And then we wonder why our spouse doesn't talk more.

For most of us, effective listening requires a significant change of attitude. We must shift from *egocentric* listening (viewing the conversation through our own eyes) to *empathetic* listening (viewing the conversation through our partner's eyes). The goal is to discover how our spouse perceives the situation and how he or she feels. Proverbs 18:15 equates wisdom with careful listening and seeking for knowledge. In a relationship, this often means seeking knowledge about our spouse. Words are a key to the other person's heart, and listening with the intention to understand enhances conversation.

Lord Jesus, I want to be an empathetic listener rather than a judgmental one. Please help me to concentrate on my spouse when we're talking rather than on myself. Bless our conversations.

COMMUNICATING WITHOUT ARGUING

The words of the godly are like sterling silver. . . . The words of the godly encourage many. PROVERBS 10:20-21

HOW DO WE TALK without arguing? It begins with a resolution: I will not condemn your thoughts, but I will try to understand them. When you respond to your loved one, your words can be encouraging or discouraging. For example, compare "That's an interesting thought. Would you like to explain that further?" with "That's the most ludicrous thing I've ever heard. How could you think that?" Which is more likely to elicit further sharing from your spouse?

The book of Job contains many negative conversational examples. In Job 8:1-2, Job's supposed friend Bildad responds harshly to Job, who has been pouring out his heart about his difficult situation. Bildad's words ("How long will you go on like this? You sound like a blustering wind.") contrast sharply with King Solomon's descriptions of the words of the godly, which are valuable and encouraging.

Here are some conversation starters to help you develop deeper communication:

- ❧ Read the same article in the local newspaper and share your thoughts with each other.

- ❧ Watch a movie or television program and answer these questions: Was there a message in this movie? What did you find objectionable? What did you find most interesting?

- ❧ Read a book on any subject, one chapter per week, and tell each other one idea you found intriguing or helpful in the chapter.

With any of these options, concentrate on understanding each other rather than trying to prove your point or be "right." Intimacy is developed by positive conversations. These kinds of intentional discussions, when practiced over a period of time, will stimulate intellectual intimacy, which may well lead to emotional and sexual intimacy. Good communication is a key to a strong marriage.

Father, forgive me for the times when my words have been more like Bildad's than like King Solomon's. I pray that as a couple we may grow in our ability to have conversations without arguing. May these help us understand each other better.

AFFIRMING IN DISAGREEMENT

A gentle answer deflects anger, but harsh words make tempers flare.

PROVERBS 15:1

DO YOU KNOW HOW to affirm your spouse even when you disagree? It's a big step in learning how to have meaningful conversations. Take this example: A wife has shared that she is hurt by something her husband has done, and he responds, "I appreciate your sharing your ideas and feelings with me. Now I can understand why you could feel so hurt. If I were in your shoes, I'm sure I would feel the same way. I want you to know that I love you very much, and it hurts me to see you upset. I appreciate your being open with me." This husband has learned the art of affirming his wife even though he may not agree with her perception.

Of course, he has a perspective and will eventually share it, but first, he wants his wife to know that he understands what she is saying and can identify with her pain. He is not condemning her interpretation, nor is he telling her that she should not feel upset. In fact, he is acknowledging that if he were in her shoes, he would feel the same way. And he would—because if he had her personality and perception, then he would feel what she feels.

Harsh words or judgment will frequently provoke anger. But giving a gentle answer, as King Solomon says in the above proverb, encourages a thoughtful response. This affirmation of feelings creates a positive climate where the offended person can now hear the other person's side.

Father, let me make it my goal to give a gentle answer to my spouse. Please give me the humility to acknowledge his or her feelings without immediately needing to point out my perspective.

OUR NEED TO LOVE AND BE LOVED

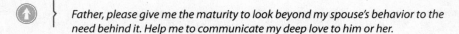

How precious is your unfailing love, O God! All humanity finds shelter in the shadow of your wings. PSALM 36:7

HUMAN BEHAVIOR IS MOTIVATED by certain physical, emotional, and spiritual needs. If you don't understand your spouse's needs, you will never understand his or her behavior. In the next few days, we will look at some of those needs. Today we focus on the need for love.

The need to love and be loved is the most fundamental of our needs. The desire to love accounts for the charitable side of humans. We feel good about ourselves when we are loving others. On the other hand, much of our behavior is motivated by the desire to *receive* love. We feel loved when we are convinced that someone genuinely cares about our well-being. The psalmist reiterates this human need to feel love in the verse above when he thanks God for his unfailing love. The image of people taking shelter in the Lord, like chicks huddling under their mother's wings, touches us deeply because that need to be cared for is so significant.

When your spouse complains that you don't give her enough time, she is crying for love. When your spouse says, "I don't ever do anything right," he is begging for affirming words. Argue about the *behavior* and you will stimulate more negative behavior. Look *behind* the behavior to discover the emotional need. Meet that need, and you will eliminate the negative behavior. Love seeks to meet needs.

Father, please give me the maturity to look beyond my spouse's behavior to the need behind it. Help me to communicate my deep love to him or her.

ALLOWING FREEDOM

He is so rich in kindness and grace that he purchased our freedom with the blood of his Son and forgave our sins. EPHESIANS 1:7

ONE OF GOD'S great gifts is the gift of freedom. As the verse above states, God has given us the ultimate freedom by releasing us from the bonds of sin. We have great freedom in Christ, and this call to freedom is a part of who we are.

This desire for freedom is so strong that whenever we feel that someone is trying to control us—particularly someone we love—we tend to become defensive and angry. We need to give each other freedom: to read a book, to watch a sports event, to go shopping, to take a nap, to consider a new vocation. When we try to control our loved one's behavior, we threaten his or her freedom and stimulate anger.

Ever wonder why, when you accuse your spouse of wasting time, he or she tends to "come out fighting"? You have threatened her freedom. She feels like you are trying to control her behavior. It is fine to *request* behavior change, but requests are far different from demands. Demands come across as controlling; requests give information. Try a respectful request: "Could you please take out the garbage? That would make me really happy." He may or he may not, but at least he won't feel like you are trying to control him.

Lord Jesus, thank you for the freedom you offer us because of your sacrifice. Help us as a couple to offer freedom to each other as well, rather than trying to control each other.

SEEKING SIGNIFICANCE

They will be my people, and I will be their God. And I will give them one heart and one purpose: to worship me forever. JEREMIAH 32:38-39

WE ALL HAVE a need for significance. There is within each of us the desire to do something bigger than ourselves. We want to accomplish something that will impact the world and give us a sense of fulfillment and satisfaction. This desire is given to us by God, who wants us to find our ultimate significance in him. As this verse from Jeremiah makes clear, he has created us with the purpose of serving and worshiping him.

This need for significance is sometimes behind the driven nature of the workaholic. Many times this drive for significance is heightened by childhood experiences. The father who tells his son that he will never amount to anything may make it difficult for his son to ever feel significant. As a result, the son may spend a lifetime trying to prove his father wrong. He may, in fact, accomplish much—yet never feel significant.

Understanding this motivation will greatly enhance the efforts of someone who is married to a workaholic. To praise the workaholic for her accomplishments is far more productive than to condemn her for devoting too much time to work. Affirmation is productive. Condemnation is destructive.

Father, please give me compassion and understanding for my spouse, who works so hard in an attempt to feel significant. Help me to affirm him or her. Help us also to remember that our ultimate significance is not something we have to attain, because you give it to us.

OUR NEED FOR REST

On the seventh day God had finished his work of creation, so he rested from all his work. GENESIS 2:2

PHYSICALLY, MENTALLY, and emotionally, humans are designed with the need for rhythm between work and play. The old saying "All work and no play makes Jack a dull boy" reflects a fundamental human need for recreation or relaxation. This need is reflected in the second chapter of the Bible, where we learn that after Creation was completed, the Lord rested from his work. As people made in God's image, is it surprising that we also have this need?

Look at your own and your spouse's behavior, and you will see that at least some of your actions are motivated by this desire for recreation and relaxation. The methods of meeting this need are colored by our personality and preferences.

Why does Eric come home from work, click on the TV, and enjoy his favorite drink before engaging in conversation with his wife? Because he wants to relax before he makes the effort to relate to her. Or why does Ashley stop at the gym before she comes home and interacts with her family? Consciously or unconsciously, she is seeking to meet her need for relaxation. If we understand our spouse's need, we can try to find a way to get the love we need and still allow our partner the freedom to meet his or her own needs. We, too, must find our own way of relaxing—whether it's reading, exercising, watching TV, or pursuing a hobby—or we will lose our emotional stability. The wise spouse encourages recreation and relaxation.

Father, thank you for the need to rest and relax. Too often, I view this as a waste of time, but I know it's an important need that you have given us. Help me not to criticize my spouse for relaxing, but to view it as a positive thing for refreshment.

CHOOSING TO LOVE

Choose today whom you will serve. . . . But as for me and my family, we will serve the LORD. JOSHUA 24:15

RECENTLY, A WOMAN SAID TO ME, "How can we speak each other's love language when we are full of hurt, anger, and resentment over past failures?" The answer to that question lies in the essential nature of our humanity. We are creatures of choice. That means that we have the capacity to make poor choices and wise choices, in spite of our emotions.

When the Israelites were settling in the Promised Land, their leader, Joshua, instructed them to choose their path carefully. Would they serve the gods of the culture they had left (Egypt) or the gods of the culture they were joining (Canaan)? Or would they choose to serve the Lord God who had brought them to this place? The people had made poor choices in the wilderness, but now they had a new chance to respond. They followed Joshua's lead and chose to follow the Lord.

Having made poor choices in the past doesn't mean that we must continue to make them in the future. In our relationships, we can say, "I'm sorry. I know I have hurt you, but I would like to make the future different. I would like to love you and meet your needs." Confessing past failures and expressing a desire to make the future better is a choice. I have seen marriages rescued from the brink of divorce when couples make the choice to love and then learn to speak each other's love language.

Hurts are not to be denied. They are to be replaced with expressions of love. When we choose to love in spite of our feelings, we find negative feelings will dissipate, and feelings of intimacy return. Loving acts create loving feelings.

Father, thank you for giving us the ability to choose to love. Help me to make the right choices in my relationship with my spouse, not choices that are based only on emotion or past problems. Let me replace the hurts between us as a couple with expressions of love.

LOVE AS ACTION

Love is patient and kind. Love is not jealous or boastful or proud or rude. It does not demand its own way. It is not irritable, and it keeps no record of being wronged. It does not rejoice about injustice but rejoices whenever the truth wins out. Love never gives up, never loses faith, is always hopeful, and endures through every circumstance. 1 CORINTHIANS 13:4-7

A MAN NAMED BRENT confided in me: "I just don't love her anymore. I haven't loved her for a long time. I don't want to hurt her, but I don't enjoy being with her anymore. I don't know what happened. I wish it were different, but I don't have any feelings for her."

Brent was thinking and feeling what thousands of people have thought and felt through the years. It's the "I don't love her anymore" mind-set that gives men and women the freedom—at least in their minds—to seek love with someone else.

It's worth taking another look at the apostle Paul's famous "definition" of love in 1 Corinthians 13. In this passage, which is read at many weddings, the focus is all on attitude and action—not on feelings. For example, enduring through every circumstance and not demanding our own way pretty much require that we're not overly focused on our emotions. But when we act in a loving way, often the emotions will follow.

Unfortunately, Brent had never made the distinction between the two stages of romantic love. In stage one, the feelings are euphoric and without effort. In stage two, action is the key, and the feelings come only when we speak each other's love language. Can Brent's marriage be saved? Yes, if he and his wife will confess past failures and agree to speak love in a language the other person understands. In stage two, loving actions precede loving feelings.

Lord Jesus, thank you for this reminder that true, godly love is more about the way I act than about the way I feel. Sometimes it's hard to act in a loving way when I don't feel like doing it. But please give me the will and the courage to express my love to my mate.

WHEN IT DOESN'T COME NATURALLY

This is my commandment: Love each other in the same way I have loved you. There is no greater love than to lay down one's life for one's friends.

JOHN 15:12-13

I'M OFTEN ASKED, "What if your spouse's love language is something that doesn't come naturally for you?" Maybe his love language is *physical touch*, and you're just not a toucher. Or *gifts*, but gifts are not important to you. Perhaps her language is *quality time*, but sitting on the couch and talking for twenty minutes is your worst nightmare. He wants *words of affirmation*, but words don't come easily for you. Or she prefers *acts of service*, but you don't find satisfaction in keeping the house organized. So what are you to do?

You learn to speak your partner's language. If it doesn't come naturally for you, learning to speak it is an even greater expression of love because it shows effort and a willingness to learn. This speaks volumes to your spouse. Also, keep in mind that your love language may not come naturally for your loved one. Your spouse has to work just as hard to speak your language as you do to speak his or her language. That's what love is all about.

Jesus made it clear that we are to love each other as he loved us—and that is with the highest degree of sacrifice. Few of us are called to literally lay down our lives for others, but we are called to lay down our lives in small ways every day. Love is giving. Choosing to speak love in a language that is meaningful to your spouse is a great investment of your time and energy.

Lord Jesus, thank you for demonstrating for us the greatest kind of love. I'm in awe of your willingness to lay down your life for me. Thank you. Please help me to respond with a humble willingness to lay down my life for my spouse, even in smaller ways such as communicating in his or her love language.

PUTTING YOUR SPOUSE FIRST

"A man leaves his father and mother and is joined to his wife, and the two are united into one." Since they are no longer two but one, let no one split apart what God has joined together. MATTHEW 19:5-6

NO COUPLE WILL REACH their full potential in marriage without "leaving parents." This has practical implications in the area of decision making because your parents may have suggestions about many aspects of your life. Each suggestion should be taken seriously, but in the final analysis, you and your spouse must decide for yourselves.

Once you are married, you should no longer make decisions on the basis of what will make your parents happy, but on the basis of what is best for your spouse. This means that the time may come when a husband must say to his mother, "Mom, you know that I love you very much, but you also know that I am now married. I cannot always do what you want me to do. I want to continue the warm relationship that we have had through the years, but my first commitment must be to my wife. I hope you understand."

A husband must not allow his mother to control his life after he is married. This is not the biblical pattern. Instead, Jesus taught that a husband and wife become one when they marry—and no one should come between them to split them apart. The marriage relationship becomes your first priority. You must treat your parents respectfully while first and foremost remaining committed to your spouse.

Heavenly Father, I love my parents and want to please them, but I know that sometimes this can cause me to put their opinion above my spouse's. Please help me to remember that my decisions must be primarily about what is best for my spouse, not what is best for my parents.

HONORING IN THE FACE OF DISRESPECT

Get rid of all bitterness, rage, anger, harsh words, and slander, as well as all
types of evil behavior. Instead, be kind to each other, tenderhearted, forgiving
one another, just as God through Christ has forgiven you. EPHESIANS 4:31-32

HONORING PARENTS after we are married implies that we will speak kindly
to them. When the apostle Paul was writing to Timothy, who was a very young
pastor at the time, he admonished, "Never speak harshly to an older man, but
appeal to him respectfully as you would to your own father" (1 Timothy 5:1).
We are to be understanding and sympathetic. Certainly we are to speak the
truth, but it must always be in love (see Ephesians 4:15). Often, the way we say
something is just as important as what we say.

The command of Ephesians 4:31-32, as shown above, must be taken seriously in our relationships with parents and in-laws. We are to avoid harsh
words and out-of-control anger but instead treat each other kindly, with forgiveness.

There is no place for yelling and screaming at our parents or in-laws.
The law of kindness must prevail, even if they are not following it themselves.
If they are out of control, that is the time for us to keep our cool and listen.
We don't have to be doormats, but the Bible makes it clear that we must be
responsible for the way we speak to others. That includes our spouse—and
also our parents.

> *Father, you have called us to honor our parents no matter what the circumstances.*
> *Please give me the self-control and grace to speak respectfully to my parents and*
> *in-laws at all times.*

OTHERS ABOVE SELF

Don't be concerned for your own good but for the good of others.

1 CORINTHIANS 10:24

MOST COUNSELORS AGREE that one of the greatest problems in marriage is decision making. Visions of democracy dance in the minds of many newly married couples, but when there are only two voting members, democracy often results in deadlock. How does a couple move beyond deadlock? The answer is found in one word: *love.*

Love always asks the question, What is best for you? As Paul wrote in 1 Corinthians, believers need to be primarily concerned about what is beneficial for others rather than just what will help or please themselves. Love does not demand its own way. Love seeks to bring pleasure to the one loved. That is why Christians should have less trouble making decisions than non-Christians. We are called to be lovers. When I love my wife, I will not seek to force my will upon her for selfish purposes. Rather, I will consider what is in her best interests.

Putting my spouse, the one I love, above myself is such a simple concept, Lord, yet it's so difficult. I need your help. As we make decisions as a couple, help us not to demand but to offer. Help me to be loving in the way I make choices.

HEADSHIP WITHOUT A HELPER

The Lord God said, "It is not good for the man to be alone. I will make a helper who is just right for him." GENESIS 2:18

THE SCRIPTURAL IDEA of the husband being the head of the wife has been one of the most exploited concepts of the Bible. Christian husbands, full of self-will, have made all kinds of foolish demands of their wives under the authority of "the Bible says." Headship does not mean that the husband has the right to make all the decisions and inform the wife of what is going to be done.

The wife is called to be a "helper," according to Genesis 2:18. Without her, the man would be alone—which God says outright would not be good. Her help is clearly necessary and valuable. Yet how can she be a helper if she has no opportunity to share her ideas? Wise King Solomon wrote, "Two people are better off than one" (Ecclesiastes 4:9). That is certainly true in decision making. Why would a husband want to make a decision limited to his own wisdom when God has given him a helper?

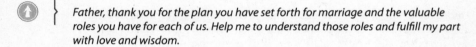

Father, thank you for the plan you have set forth for marriage and the valuable roles you have for each of us. Help me to understand those roles and fulfill my part with love and wisdom.

SUBMISSION AND RESPECT

Submit to one another out of reverence for Christ. For wives, this means submit to your husbands as to the Lord. . . . Husbands, this means love your wives, just as Christ loved the church. He gave up his life for her.

EPHESIANS 5:21-22, 25

MANY WIVES SHUDDER when they hear the pastor say, "Turn in your Bible to Ephesians 5:22." They know that's the verse that says, "Wives, submit to your husbands as to the Lord" (NIV). *But you don't know my husband,* they think. I sometimes imagine that God responds, *But you don't understand submission.* Submission is not a command that applies only to females. In fact, Ephesians 5:21 instructs us to "submit to one another" because of our love for Christ.

Both the instruction to husbands about loving and the instruction to wives about submitting call for an attitude of service. Submission does not mean that the wife must do all the giving. The husband is to give his life for her. Nor does it mean that she cannot express her ideas. The goal of Paul's instructions is unity, which requires both to have an attitude of service.

Father, I see that you have given my spouse and me equally challenging tasks. We need your help to fulfill them. Please help us to love and serve each other as you would have us do.

SEASONS OF MARRIAGE

Both day and night belong to you [Lord]; you made the starlight and the sun. You set the boundaries of the earth, and you made both summer and winter. PSALM 74:16-17

THE BIBLE TELLS US that God has created all the boundaries of the earth, including the rotation around the sun, which causes seasonal changes. The seasons come and go: winter, spring, summer, and fall. So do the seasons of marriage. Relationships are perpetually in a state of transition, continually moving from one season to another. But the seasons of marriage don't always follow the order of nature. You may be in a spring marriage today and in a winter marriage next month. What do the seasons of marriage look like?

Sometimes we find ourselves in winter—discouraged, detached, and dissatisfied. Other times we experience springtime with its openness, hope, and anticipation. On still other occasions, we bask in the warmth of summer— comfortable, relaxed, enjoying life. And then comes fall with its uncertainty, negligence, and apprehension. The cycle repeats itself many times throughout the life of a marriage, just as the seasons repeat themselves in nature.

In the next few days, we will look at these recurring seasons of marriage and help you identify which season your marriage is in. I will also suggest ways to enhance the seasons of marriage. You're never "stuck" in one season; you can make positive changes.

Lord, you have created different seasons of the earth, and we can see different seasons of our lives. But I know you did not create us to be in cold, wintry relationships. Encourage us as a couple to renew the hope and optimism we have for our relationship.

FIGHTING WINTER

The heartfelt counsel of a friend is as sweet as perfume and incense.

PROVERBS 27:9

TELL ME YOUR EMOTIONS, your attitudes, and your behavior toward your spouse, and I'll tell you the season of your marriage. Today we focus on the winter marriage.

What are the emotions of winter? Hurt, anger, disappointment, loneliness, and rejection. What are the attitudes of a winter marriage? In a word, negativity. You might hear things such as, "I'm so discouraged with my marriage." "It's such a frustration." "I don't know if we're going to be able to work things out."

What are the actions in a winter marriage? Speaking harshly or not speaking at all, destructive and perhaps violent behavior. In the winter season of marriage, couples are unwilling to negotiate differences. Conversations turn to arguments. There is no sense of togetherness. The marriage is like two people living in separate igloos.

The good news is that a winter marriage often makes couples desperate enough to break out of their suffering and seek the help of a counselor or pastor. The book of Proverbs refers to heartfelt counsel from someone who cares for us as very sweet. Good advice is highly valuable, and often the perspective of someone outside the relationship is critical for people who really want to change. Those who seek help will find it.

Father, when our relationship is in trouble, filled with rejection and discouragement, help us to find a wise adviser. Give us the grace and energy to work on rejuvenating the love between us.

SEEDS FOR SPRING

Remember this—a farmer who plants only a few seeds will get a small crop. But the one who plants generously will get a generous crop.

2 CORINTHIANS 9:6

A SPRING MARRIAGE is filled with hope, anticipation, optimism, gratitude, love, and trust. Does that sound exciting? It is! Some of you are saying, "I remember the early days of our marriage when we were in spring." I want to suggest that you can have spring again and again. A healthy marriage will have many spring seasons throughout the years.

How do couples create this kind of climate? By making plans and communicating openly. Those who want to live in a spring relationship are willing to seek the help of a counselor or read a relevant book. Spring is a time of new beginnings, when the streams of communication are flowing. A couple feels a sense of excitement about life together. They have great hopes for the future, and they are planting seeds from which they hope to reap a harvest of happiness. The above verse from 2 Corinthians gives us this promise: If we plant generously, we will experience a good return on our work. Those who plant seeds will see the flowers of spring.

Father, I remember times of spring in my marriage, and I want that again. Please rekindle in us a sense of excitement and optimism. Help us to put in the time and effort to plant seeds in our relationship—that we may reap a good return.

RELAXATION OF SUMMER

"Don't sin by letting anger control you." Don't let the sun go down while you are still angry, for anger gives a foothold to the devil. EPHESIANS 4:26-27

IN A SUMMER MARRIAGE, there are feelings of happiness, satisfaction, accomplishment, and connection. There is a deep level of trust and a commitment to growth. Life is more relaxed, and communication is constructive. A couple in this stage is likely attending marriage conferences periodically, reading books, and growing spiritually.

The climate of a summer marriage is comfortable, supportive, and understanding. The couple resolves conflicts in a positive manner. Having accepted their differences, they seek to turn them into assets, utilizing their differences to help each other. In summer, husbands and wives have a growing sense of togetherness.

There is one downside to summer: There are yellow jackets. They live underground and represent those unresolved issues that have been pushed beneath the surface in order to have peace. Remember the wise instruction in Ephesians to deal with anger right away. Letting things fester, even in the name of peacemaking, only makes things worse. Ultimately, you must deal with the yellow jackets, or your summer marriage will be headed toward fall.

Father, thank you for a comfortable, positive relationship with my spouse. Even though I am grateful for the peace between us, let me not seek that at the expense of genuine resolution of our problems. Help me to deal with them lovingly.

WAKE-UP CALL OF FALL

We put our hope in the LORD. He is our help and our shield. In him our hearts rejoice, for we trust in his holy name. Let your unfailing love surround us, LORD, for our hope is in you alone. PSALM 33:20-22

IN THE FALL where I live in North Carolina, the leaves begin to change colors and eventually fall off the trees. That is what happens in a fall marriage. It may look good on the outside, but it is actually falling apart. In the fall season, couples sense that something is happening, but they're not sure what. One or both spouses begin to feel neglected. They are disengaging emotionally.

In a fall marriage, you begin to feel sadness, apprehension, discouragement, fear, and eventually resentment. You have neglected your relationship and have drifted apart. There is a growing concern, uncertainty, and a tendency to blame each other.

The fall season of marriage is a wake-up call to seek help: See a counselor or pastor, read a book, or attend a class. Unlike the real seasons, marriages can move from fall to spring without going through winter, but you must take action to make that happen. If you do not take action, you will soon be in the coldness of winter.

The Bible reassures us that there is always hope. Trust in the Lord as your help, and let his love surround you and encourage you that better days can be ahead.

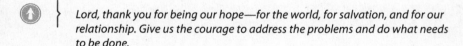

Lord, thank you for being our hope—for the world, for salvation, and for our relationship. Give us the courage to address the problems and do what needs to be done.

COVENANT MARRIAGE

Wherever you go, I will go; wherever you live, I will live. Your people will be my people, and your God will be my God. Wherever you die, I will die, and there I will be buried. RUTH 1:16-17

IS MARRIAGE A CONTRACT or a covenant? It's both, but the emphasis is on covenant. Why? Because most contracts apply to a limited amount of time—for example, a three-year contract to lease a car. Unfortunately, many people enter marriage with a contract mentality, thinking, *If it doesn't work, we can get a divorce.* Consequently, some research indicates that one-half of all marriages end within two years.

Covenants, on the other hand, are intended to be permanent, as we see in multiple places in the Bible. God made a covenant with Noah that extended to "all generations" (see Genesis 9). He did the same with Abraham (see Genesis 17). Covenants between two humans were also seen as permanent. For example, Ruth told her widowed mother-in-law, Naomi, that she would go wherever Naomi went and stay with her, adopting her culture and her religion, even until death. That beautiful statement of commitment is the language of covenant marriage. In fact, it's similar to what we say in most marriage ceremonies: "For better or for worse, for richer or for poorer, in sickness and in health, so long as we both shall live."

Christian marriage is viewed as a lifelong covenant. It is this commitment to marriage that helps us through the rough spots of life. If we have a contract mentality, then we bail out when things get tough. Perhaps it's time to remind yourself that you are committed to a covenant marriage.

Lord God, I am amazed that you entered into permanent covenants with sinful humans. You have made clear that marriage should be a permanent covenant as well. When my spouse and I are frustrated in our relationship, please remind us of our commitment. May it be an encouragement and a joy to us.

COVENANT LOVE

My sheep listen to my voice; I know them, and they follow me. I give them eternal life, and they will never perish. No one can snatch them away from me.

JOHN 10:27-28

IN YESTERDAY'S DEVOTION, we noted that contracts are temporary, but covenants are permanent. What is another difference between a covenant marriage and a contract marriage? Contracts are conditional: *I will do this if you will do that.* For example, the bank allows you to drive your car so long as you make the payments. Stop the payments, and the car goes back to the lender. Some couples view marriage in the same way. *If you keep your end of the bargain, then I'll keep mine.* This is a cheap view of marriage.

Covenant marriage is based on unconditional love. I am committed to my spouse's well-being, no matter what. Isn't that the kind of love God has for us? When we accept Christ, we become his children. We may be disobedient, but we are still his. He will not disown us. He will hold us accountable, but he will not walk out on us. In John 10, Jesus compares himself to a shepherd who sacrifices himself for his sheep. He gives his sheep—believers—eternal life, and no one can separate them from him, no matter how hard they try. That's a picture of covenant.

This is the pattern for Christian marriage. We must be committed to seek our spouse's well-being, no matter what he or she does. Certainly we will seek to hold each other accountable for sinful behavior, but we will not abandon our marriage because we are each other's best source of help. Covenant says, "I will always seek your best interests."

Lord Jesus, thank you for loving us unconditionally. Even when we do the things that real sheep do—run away, act foolishly, ignore your voice—you hold on to us and love us. May that picture inspire me as I try to love my spouse unconditionally. Renew our love and commitment, Father, I pray.

COVENANT AND RECONCILIATION

At that time I will plant a crop of Israelites and raise them for myself. I will show love to those I called "Not loved." And to those I called "Not my people," I will say, "Now you are my people." And they will reply, "You are our God!"

HOSEA 2:23

COVENANT MARRIAGE requires confrontation and forgiveness. We make major promises when we get married, but sometimes we fail. Failures will not destroy a marriage, but failing to deal with failures will. The proper response to a failure is to admit it and ask forgiveness.

This is the way God treats us. He says, "If you violate my covenant, you will suffer, but I will not take my love from you. Nor will I betray my faithfulness." God will not smile upon our failure. He lets us suffer the consequences, but he continues to love us, and he seeks reconciliation. The verses above are some of the beautiful, heartfelt words from the book of Hosea. The Lord was frustrated and angry with the Israelites, who repeatedly turned away from him and worshiped idols instead. Several passages in the book detail the consequences the people would suffer because they refused to listen—but those passages are then followed up with wonderful promises like those we see here. The Lord always seeks reconciliation. He is ready to welcome us with open arms.

The same should be true in marriage. We cannot condone a spouse's sinful behavior, but we can lovingly confront with a desire to forgive and reconcile. When your spouse says, "I'm sorry. I know I was wrong. Will you forgive me?" the covenant response is always, "Yes, I want to renew our covenant relationship." Love always seeks reconciliation.

Father, thank you for the powerful example you show us through the book of Hosea. If you can repeatedly forgive and welcome us back to you, how much more can I forgive and reconcile with my spouse? Please help me to remember this important part of a covenant marriage.

ENCOURAGING A QUIET PERSON TO TALK

Wise words bring many benefits, and hard work brings rewards. . . . The wise listen to others. PROVERBS 12:14-15

WHEN IT COMES TO TALKING, there are two personality types. The first is what I call the Dead Sea personality. Just as the Dead Sea in Israel receives water from the Jordan River but has no outlet, so many people can receive all kinds of experiences throughout the day. They store these in their minds and have little compulsion to share.

Then there is the personality that I call the Babbling Brook. Whatever information comes in the eyes or ears of this person quickly comes out the mouth. Often these two types of people marry each other. Can they have a happy marriage? Yes, if they understand their personality differences and seek to grow.

Chances are the Babbling Brook will be complaining, "My mate won't talk. I don't ever know what he's thinking. I feel like we are becoming strangers." How do you get a quiet person to talk?

Two suggestions: First, ask specific questions. The worst thing you can ever say to a Dead Sea personality is, "I wish you'd talk more." That statement is overwhelming, and it comes across as condemnation. It's far better to ask a specific question, because even the quietest person will generally respond.

Another suggestion is to stop the flow of your own words. If you want another person to talk more, you have to talk less. Leave little pools of silence. Remember, King Solomon wrote that "The wise listen to others." If you find yourself talking too much and your spouse talking too little, follow the advice of the apostle James and be "quick to listen, slow to speak" (James 1:19). Your marriage will benefit.

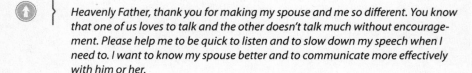

Heavenly Father, thank you for making my spouse and me so different. You know that one of us loves to talk and the other doesn't talk much without encouragement. Please help me to be quick to listen and to slow down my speech when I need to. I want to know my spouse better and to communicate more effectively with him or her.

BREAKING FREE OF FEAR

Now all glory to God, who is able, through his mighty power at work within us, to accomplish infinitely more than we might ask or think. EPHESIANS 3:20

YESTERDAY WE DISCUSSED the fact that personality is often a factor when one spouse won't talk. Today I want to address another common reason: fear. Perhaps in childhood, perhaps in a former marriage, or perhaps in your marriage your spouse has discovered that if he shares his true thoughts and feelings, it will likely cause an explosion. Not liking explosions, he clams up.

How do you overcome this shutdown? I suggest you begin with loving confrontation. Bring up the matter kindly. For example, you might say, "I want us to have a growing marriage, and I think you want the same. I feel that in the past when you have shared your ideas, you have experienced my wrath, or maybe a parent's or someone else's anger. I don't know about them, but I know that is not what I want. I am asking God to help me hear you. So could we begin by sharing just one event that has happened in our lives each day? I think this will get us on a positive track." Your spouse will likely be relieved that you have brought up the topic and will be willing to try again. Remember, the Bible makes clear that change is possible. The Lord can do more than we can even imagine, so he can certainly turn our communication patterns around.

Father, please forgive me for the times when I have shut down my spouse by responding in anger. I pray for help to identify times when I do this. Please touch my spouse's heart so that he or she will be willing to try again.

RESPECTFUL COMMUNICATION

Respect everyone, and love your Christian brothers and sisters. 1 PETER 2:17

I'VE HEARD many people say, "My spouse won't talk with me." If this describes your marriage, the question is, why? One reason some spouses go silent is negative communication patterns. Here are some questions to help you think about your own patterns. Consider whether you often come across as negative or complaining.

- Do I listen to my spouse when he talks, or do I cut him off and give my responses?

- Do I allow my partner space when she needs it, or do I force the issue of communication, even at those times when she needs to be alone?

- Do I maintain confidences, or do I broadcast our private conversations to others?

- Do I openly share my own needs and desires in the form of requests rather than demands?

- Do I give my spouse the freedom to have opinions that differ from my own, or am I quick to "set him straight"?

If you answer yes to the second half of any of these questions, it may be time to change your communication patterns. It's all about treating your spouse (and all believers) with respect and love, as 1 Peter 2:17 directs. Doing so may loosen the tongue of a silent spouse.

Father, please forgive me for the times I have been disrespectful to my spouse in the way I talk. I have not listened, been demanding and controlling, and breached confidences. I know that kind of behavior is not loving. I pray that you would help me commit to a new, better way of communicating.

COMMUNICATING LOVE

Live a life filled with love, following the example of Christ. He loved us and offered himself as a sacrifice for us, a pleasing aroma to God. EPHESIANS 5:2

WHAT WOULD YOU LIKE your spouse to do for you? Your answer to this question will probably reveal your primary love language. If your answer is clean out the garage, paint the bedroom, vacuum the floors, wash dishes, or walk the dog, then your primary love language is acts of service. If you would really like your spouse to hold your hand when you go for a walk, your primary love language is probably physical touch. When you know which of the five love languages most connects with you and your spouse, you know what needs to happen to really make both of you feel loved.

Before you start preaching to your spouse about speaking your love language, stop and ask yourself, "Does my spouse feel loved by me?" You might even ask your spouse, "On a scale of 0 to 10, how full is your love tank? That is, how much do you feel loved by me?" If the answer is anything less than 10, ask, "What could I do to help fill it?" Whatever your spouse suggests, do it to the best of your ability. After all, in Ephesians 5, Paul challenges us to "live a life filled with love." When we follow Christ's example and offer love freely to each other, good things happen. As you learn to speak your spouse's love language, chances are, your spouse will learn to speak yours.

Lord, I want to please you through my acts of love and service to my husband or wife. Help me to focus my energies on him or her, not on myself. Enrich our marriage through expressions of love.

JOY THROUGH SERVICE

The commandments of the LORD are right, bringing joy to the heart. The commands of the LORD are clear, giving insight for living. PSALM 19:8

WHAT IF YOUR SIGNIFICANT other's love language is acts of service? What if you discover that the thing that really makes her feel loved is your taking out the garbage, washing the dishes, or doing the laundry? One husband said, "I'd say that she is probably not going to feel loved." Well, that's one approach, but the more biblical approach is to learn to serve your spouse.

It may not be easy for you to learn to speak the language of acts of service. I remember one wife who told me, "I'll have to admit, there were some trying and humorous times in those early weeks when my husband began to help me around the house. The first time he did the laundry, he used undiluted bleach instead of regular detergent. Our blue towels came out with white polka dots. But he was loving me in my language, and my love tank was filling up. Now he knows how to do everything around the house and is always helping me. We have much more time together because I don't have to work all the time. Believe me, I have learned to speak his love language too. We are a happy couple."

The Lord loves it when we serve each other in love and put each other's needs above our own. When we follow his commands, joy often follows—as mentioned in the psalm above and as evident in this couple's example. Learn to speak your spouse's love language, and you, too, can have a growing, thriving relationship.

Father, following your commands brings joy. Thank you for the love and rejuvenation that can come when we serve each other and communicate love to each other. I pray for the grace to do that willingly.

DON'T GIVE UP!

Love never gives up, never loses faith, is always hopeful, and endures through every circumstance. 1 CORINTHIANS 13:7

I'VE BEEN COUNSELING people with marital struggles for more than thirty years. Often they come alone because their spouse will not come with them. And often they have no hope. They are living in very difficult marriages.

I am under no illusion that I can provide a magic formula to bring healing to all such marriages. However, I do believe that in every troubled relationship, one partner can take positive steps that have the potential to change the emotional climate between the two of them. The first step is to decide not to give up. Read a book, talk with a counselor or pastor, or share with a trusted friend, but don't give up. According to the verse above—taken from the apostle Paul's famous "love chapter"—when you don't give up, don't lose faith, maintain hope, and endure, you're practicing love the way God defines it. That brings great encouragement. After all, nothing is impossible with God.

Father, I believe that anything is possible for you. When my relationship seems so difficult—or even beyond repair—I come to you, the healer. Please rekindle my hope and breathe new life into our marriage.

LOVE BRINGS CHANGE

Above all, clothe yourselves with love, which binds us all together in perfect harmony. COLOSSIANS 3:14

CONTROL IS A SIGNIFICANT ISSUE in some relationships. One wife who was struggling with a controlling husband told me, "I feel like I'm a bird in a cage. Actually, I feel like a hamster in a cage—I don't have wings anymore. I don't want a divorce, but I don't know how much longer I can go on living under such pressure." This wife has lost her freedom and is feeling the pain of incarceration.

Is there hope? Yes, and it begins by believing that things can change. Can her husband change? Yes! Can she help stimulate that change? Yes! Her most powerful influence is love. The apostle Paul writes in Colossians 3 that we should seek love above all else. Why? Because love has the power to unite people, to bind them together even more closely. That's a powerful influence in a marriage.

In this woman's situation, two kinds of love are needed. First comes soft or tender love. She needs to learn to speak her husband's love language and seek to meet his need for emotional love. Second is tough love. She can say, "I love you too much to sit here and do nothing while you destroy our marriage." Then she must lay out some ground rules and consequences—in effect, tell him what she will do until he takes steps to change his behavior.

When a spouse first feels tender love, he is then able to receive tough love.

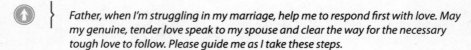

Father, when I'm struggling in my marriage, help me to respond first with love. May my genuine, tender love speak to my spouse and clear the way for the necessary tough love to follow. Please guide me as I take these steps.

SEEKING COMPANIONSHIP, AVOIDING LONELINESS

Live happily with the woman you love through all the . . . days of life that God has given you under the sun. The wife God gives you is your reward for all your earthly toil. ECCLESIASTES 9:9

ONE OF THE BENEFITS of being married is companionship. A loving, supportive spouse is not only good for your emotional health, but also for your physical health. Some time ago, a research project involving ten thousand married men, forty years of age or older, found that those who had loving, supportive wives had significantly fewer heart problems. An intimate relationship in marriage enhances physical health.

However, loneliness within the marital relationship is detrimental to health. Marriage is designed by God to provide companionship. God said of Adam, "It is not good for the man to be alone. I will make a helper who is just right for him" (Genesis 2:18). Essentially, companions share life together. Thus when a married couple communicates with each other daily, they develop a sense of companionship. They are committed to each other. They stand together as they face the uncertainties of life. Something about having a companion makes life more bearable. That was God's plan. King Solomon wrote in Ecclesiastes that a wife—and, by extension, a husband—is a gift from God that refreshes us from the toil of daily life.

So as a couple, talk and listen to each other and build your relationship. Don't allow loneliness to rob your health.

Lord Jesus, thank you for the gift of marriage and the companionship it can bring. I want to bring friendship and partnership to my spouse, not loneliness. Please help us to strengthen our relationship more and more.

WHEN YOUR SPOUSE IS ANGRY

A gentle answer deflects anger, but harsh words make tempers flare.

PROVERBS 15:1

HOW SHOULD YOU RESPOND if your spouse is angry? It's natural to respond in kind, with angry words. But as Proverbs 15:1 reminds us, that will only lead to more argument. If you want to deflect the anger and get to the root of the situation, the first step is to listen. Why is your spouse angry? What have you done to cause hurt? Maybe it's simply a misunderstanding, but you can't know that until you listen. So if your spouse is angry, the best thing you can do is to stop everything and ask, "Honey, why are you angry with me?" Listen to the response.

The second step is to listen again. Ask questions to make sure you know what is being communicated. You might say, "Is this what you are saying? You're angry because you left your shirts on the chair for me to take to the cleaners, and when you came home tonight, you saw them still lying on the chair." "That's right," your mate says, "and you promised to take them to the cleaners. I don't understand that."

The third step is to listen. That's right—do it one more time. "Honey, are you saying that I disappointed you by not taking your shirts to the cleaners?" "Yes, and I don't have a shirt to wear tomorrow. I don't know what I'm going to do." Ah, now you are ready for step four, which I'll share in tomorrow's devotion.

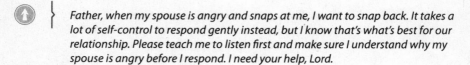

Father, when my spouse is angry and snaps at me, I want to snap back. It takes a lot of self-control to respond gently instead, but I know that's what's best for our relationship. Please teach me to listen first and make sure I understand why my spouse is angry before I respond. I need your help, Lord.

RESPONDING TO ANGER

Listen closely to what I am about to say. Hear me out. JOB 13:17

REMEMBER THE FIRST THREE STEPS to responding to an angry spouse? Listen. Listen. Listen. Until you listen to your spouse three times, you will not have a clear picture of why he is angry. When you ask questions and listen intently, your spouse knows that you are taking him seriously. The story of Job in the Bible shows Job experiencing great physical suffering and intense emotions. The longer he talked without feeling someone was listening, the angrier and more frustrated he became. A friend—or spouse—who listens effectively can have a significant impact.

The fourth step is to try to understand your spouse's plight. That is, put yourself in his shoes and try to look at the world through his eyes. It's true that what happened may not have made you mad. But given your spouse's personality, can you understand why he would be upset?

Once you've gained new understanding, step five is to express that understanding. For example, "Honey, when I try to look at this through your eyes, I can understand why you are angry. If I were in your shoes, I would probably be angry also. It makes sense to me now." Wow. You have just ceased to be the enemy. You are now a friend, and friends can help friends solve problems.

Lord God, when my spouse is angry, I don't want to become his or her adversary. Instead, please help me to listen, understand, and communicate that understanding so that I can be my spouse's friend. Please give me the forbearance and humility to work with my spouse to find a solution to the problem we're facing.

FINDING A SOLUTION

Make allowance for each other's faults, and forgive anyone who offends you. Remember, the Lord forgave you, so you must forgive others.

COLOSSIANS 3:13

AS WE'VE DISCUSSED in the past few days, when you respond to an angry spouse, you need to listen and empathize to understand the reason for the anger. Once you've done that, you are ready for step six: Share your perspective. You almost certainly see the situation differently, and it's appropriate for you to communicate that. For example, "Honey, let me tell you what I had in mind when I said that." Or, "Let me tell you what I was thinking when I did that." Chances are, your spouse will be able to hear your explanation because you have created a friendly atmosphere by going through steps one through five.

Finally, step seven is to seek resolution. The question now is, "How can we solve this problem?" Two adults who have heard each other out can now find a solution. If genuine wrong has been committed, then there can be confession and forgiveness, as well as discussion about how to keep it from happening again. Colossians 3:13 reminds believers that forgiving each other is not optional. You need to give each other grace. If misunderstanding was at the root of the anger, you should discuss how you might handle this differently in the future.

Every angry episode in a marriage should be a learning experience, and now you have a plan to make it happen.

Lord Jesus, thank you that anger need not destroy our relationship. As my spouse and I try to respond calmly to each other's anger, help us to work together to find a solution. When we experience conflict, may we learn from it and come up with a better way to handle it next time.

PARENTING AS A TEAM

As iron sharpens iron, so a friend sharpens a friend. PROVERBS 27:17

IS IT POSSIBLE for two parents who have very different approaches to child rearing to find a meeting of the minds? The answer is an unqualified yes. I've been there. In my marriage, we discovered that I tended to be the quiet, calm, "let's talk about it" parent. My wife, Karolyn, tended to be a "take action now" kind of parent. It took us a while to realize what was happening, analyze our patterns, and admit to each other our basic tendencies.

Eventually, though, we began to concentrate on the question, What is best for our children? We found that we could work together as a team and that, in fact, we must. Our basic tendencies did not change, but we did learn to temper them. I learned how to take responsible action and to blend words and actions. Karolyn learned to think before she moved.

The well-known proverb above is often applied to friendships or accountability groups. But it applies just as well—or better—to marriage. When we recognize that our spouse has different gifts and approaches that can balance ours, we are "sharpened." For those who have children, accepting our differences and learning how to complement each other makes for good parenting and a growing marriage.

Lord Jesus, thank you for the blessing of our children. I pray that you will help us to approach parenting as a couple. We have different approaches and strengths, and that's okay. Please give us the wisdom to blend those approaches in the best way and to work well as a team.

MELDING WORDS AND ACTIONS

Fathers, do not provoke your children to anger by the way you treat them. Rather, bring them up with the discipline and instruction that comes from the Lord. EPHESIANS 6:4

IF YOU HAVE CHILDREN, you know that the two wheels on which the chariot of parenting rolls are *teaching* and *training*. Teaching generally uses words to communicate with the child, and training uses actions. It is not uncommon for one parent to emphasize words and the other actions. One will want to talk the child into obedience, while the other will simply make the child obey. Both approaches have value, but when taken to an extreme, each has its problems. One can lead to verbal abuse and the other to physical abuse.

The Bible is clear that good parenting should not "provoke . . . children to anger" or, as another translation states, "exasperate" them (NIV). While this verse from Ephesians is directed to fathers, it certainly applies to both parents, either of whom can anger a child by unfair, disrespectful, or unnecessarily harsh treatment. The better approach is to bring words and actions together. Tell the child exactly what is expected and what the results of disobedience will be. Then if the child does not obey, kindly but firmly apply the consequences. When you are consistent, your child will learn obedience.

Rather than being competitors in parenting, why not team up and combine your skills to make helpful rules and determine consequences? The positive result is that both of you will know what to do if the child disobeys, and you'll be consistent. Of course, all of this works best when the child feels loved by both parents. Parenting is a team sport.

Lord, thank you for the chance to parent with my spouse as part of a team. Help us to work together to come up with the best approach for our children—one that doesn't exasperate them but helps mold them into the people you want them to be. Thank you for the family you have given us.

DEMOLISHING THE WALL

Confess your sins to each other and pray for each other so that you may be healed. The earnest prayer of a righteous person has great power and produces wonderful results. JAMES 5:16

MANY COUPLES ARE at a stalemate because they have allowed a wall to develop between them. Walls are erected a block at a time. Each block represents one partner's failure in a particular matter. It may be as small as failing to carry out the garbage or as large as failing to meet sexual needs. The one committing the failure often ignores it instead of dealing with it. Excuses are offered, such as, "After all, what does she expect? I'm doing my part." Or, "Why doesn't he think of my needs?"

Often, one failure after another is ignored until a long, high, thick wall develops between two people who started out "in love." Communication grinds to a halt, and only resentment remains.

Would you like to demolish the wall in your relationship? I can tell you how. You do it by tearing down those blocks of failure, one by one. Admit your failures as specifically as possible and ask your spouse to forgive you. If you begin to tear down the wall from your side, you make it easier for your spouse to begin demolition from the other side.

James 5:16 makes it clear that believers should confess their sins to each other. How much more true that is within the context of marriage, where those sins have directly affected the other person. Be willing to admit when you were wrong. If both of you are willing to tear down the wall of separation, you can clear away the rubble and build a beautiful relationship.

Thank you, Lord, for new beginnings. Please help us to be willing to tear down the old hurts, confess our failures, and begin again with forgiveness. Thank you for your constant forgiveness.

A CLEAR CONSCIENCE

Cling to your faith in Christ, and keep your conscience clear. 1 TIMOTHY 1:19

IN ACTS 24:16, the apostle Paul shared a principle that guided his own life: "I always try to maintain a clear conscience before God and all people." In his case, that was in large part because he wanted nothing to hinder his witness as he spread the good news about Christ. That's a great reason for us as well, but keeping a clear conscience is also good for your mental health and your relational health. Unfortunately, all of us are flawed. We sometimes fail to keep God's commands. You don't have to be perfect to have a good marriage, but you do have to deal with your failures.

How do you clear your conscience before God? By confessing your sins to him. How do you get a clear conscience before people? By confessing your sins to the person you sinned against. In marriage, that is your spouse.

I'm often asked, "But what if my spouse isn't willing to forgive me?" That is not your problem. Your responsibility is to admit your mistake and ask forgiveness. You have not taken the first step until you have confessed your own failures. Then your spouse has a choice: to forgive or not to forgive. At any rate, your conscience is clear, and you can now ask God to help you be a part of the solution rather than a part of the problem.

> *Father, thank you that I can always confess my sins to you. Your forgiveness is an incredible gift. Help me to confess my sins to my spouse as well and keep my conscience clear.*

ACCEPTING RESPONSIBILITY

We are each responsible for our own conduct. GALATIANS 6:5

WHY ARE WE SO QUICK to blame our loved one when things aren't going well in our relationship? Unfortunately, it's human nature, going all the way back to Adam and Eve. (See Genesis 3 for some blatant blame-shifting between the two of them.) But Galatians 6:5 reminds us that each of us is responsible for our own choices and behavior, and that includes our part in a relationship.

May I suggest a better approach? Try the following steps:

1. I realize that my marriage is not what it should be.

2. I stop blaming my mate and ask God to show me where I am at fault.

3. I confess my sin and accept God's forgiveness, according to 1 John 1:9.

4. I ask God to fill me with his Spirit and give me the power to make constructive changes in my life.

5. I go to my mate, confess my failures, and ask forgiveness.

6. In God's power, I go on to change my behavior, words, and attitudes, according to the principles that I discover in Scripture.

This is God's plan, and it works. Blaming your spouse stimulates resentment and antagonism. Admitting your own failures and letting God change your behavior creates a new and positive climate in your marriage. It is the road to a growing marriage.

Father, you know how easily I slip into blaming my spouse for the things that are wrong in our relationship. Please forgive me. Help me instead to take full responsibility for my own wrongs. Show me clearly where I have failed, and help me to change. I know I can do it only in your power.

DEALING WITH YOURSELF FIRST

Why worry about a speck in your friend's eye when you have a log in your own? How can you think of saying to your friend, "Let me help you get rid of that speck in your eye," when you can't see past the log in your own eye? Hypocrite! First get rid of the log in your own eye; then you will see well enough to deal with the speck in your friend's eye. MATTHEW 7:3-5

IN THE PAST FEW DEVOTIONS, we have discussed taking responsibility for our own failures rather than blaming our spouse. I do not mean that we should never discuss the faults of our mate. As a couple, we are trying to learn how to work together as a team. This means that if I think my spouse is treating me unfairly, I should, in love, share my feelings. But that's only appropriate after I have first dealt with my own failures.

This is what Jesus taught in the verses above from Matthew 7. When we cast blame on our mate without first examining ourselves, we're likely not seeing past our own faults—and as a result, it becomes impossible to see the problem clearly. Whenever a relationship breaks down, both people are a part of the breakdown. One may bear more responsibility than the other, but either can move to restore the relationship. We must each deal with the wrong we personally bear.

Be willing to take the first step. Don't sit around blaming your spouse, and don't waste time waiting for him or her to confess. If you honestly confess your part, that may be the stimulus that triggers confession on the part of your mate. The first step is the most important one.

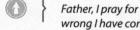

Father, I pray for the humility and courage to take the first step. Help me to see the wrong I have contributed to a situation and confess that, without waiting for my spouse to act first. Please bless our efforts.

CARING ENOUGH TO CONFRONT

[The Lord] said to me, "The sins of the people of Israel and Judah are very, very great. The entire land is full of murder; the city is filled with injustice."

EZEKIEL 9:9

SOME THINGS ARE NOT PERMISSIBLE in a marriage. Physical abuse, sexual unfaithfulness, abuse of children, alcoholism, or drug addiction require loving action. In fact, we are not loving if we accept such behavior as a way of life. Why? Because love is always concerned about the other person's well-being, and such behavior destroys both the individual and the marriage. Love must confront. That's tough love, and that's real love.

In the Bible, confronting is often seen as redemptive. Certainly the Old Testament prophets were frequently directed by God to confront Israel with her sin, as we see in the above verse from Ezekiel. The prophet's tone often sounds harsh to us, but the purpose of showing the people how far they had fallen was to encourage them back to a right relationship with God.

On an interpersonal level, Jesus said, "If another believer sins against you, go privately and point out the offense" (Matthew 18:15). The purpose of confronting is so that the relationship might be restored. If there is genuine repentance and change, then there can be genuine forgiveness, and the marriage can be rebuilt. Without confrontation and repentance, however, the behavior will continue. Tough love is caring enough to confront.

Father, confrontation is hard for me. But I can learn from your Word that some things cannot be tolerated because they are causing too much hurt and damage. Please give me wisdom to know when I should confront my spouse—and how I should react if he or she confronts me about my own behavior.

WHEN IT'S TIME FOR TOUGH LOVE

I wrote that letter in great anguish, with a troubled heart and many tears. I didn't want to grieve you, but I wanted to let you know how much love I have for you. 2 CORINTHIANS 2:4

THERE IS NEVER a time to stop loving your spouse, but there is a time to change the way you express that love. If your spouse has developed a pattern of chronic destructive behavior—and has refused to change even though you have sought to meet his or her needs—it may be time to apply tough love. The apostle Paul had to use tough love with the church at Corinth. Because they had tolerated a sinful situation within the church, he rebuked them—not because he didn't care about them, as he makes clear in the above verse. Rather, he loved them so much that he wanted them to stop what was harmful and make better choices.

Tough love says to an abusive spouse, "I love you too much to help you do wrong. I will not sit here and let you destroy yourself and me by cursing me every night. I cannot make you stop that behavior, but I will not be here to receive it tonight. If you want to make our marriage better, then I am open. But I won't be a part of letting you destroy me."

Your attitude is not to be one of abandonment but of love. Love for a spouse involves caring so much for the person's well-being that you refuse to play into the sick behavior. Many people are healed when someone loves them enough to stand up to their destructive actions.

> *Lord God, I pray for wisdom to discern when tough love is needed in our relationship. Please help us to love each other enough to confront destructive behavior.*

GENTLE WORDS

A gentle answer deflects anger, but harsh words make tempers flare.

PROVERBS 15:1

POSITIVE WORDS are powerful tools in building a strong marriage. When my wife compliments me on something, it makes me want to do more. When she criticizes me, it makes me want to defend myself and fight back. If you want to see your spouse blossom, try giving a compliment every day for thirty days and see what happens.

Have you ever noticed that when you speak softly, your spouse seems to calm down, and when you speak harshly, your spouse tends to get louder? We influence each other not only by what we say, but by how we say it. Screaming is a learned behavior, and it can be unlearned. We don't have to yell at each other. The above verse from Proverbs tells us what we instinctively know: Harsh words lead to more anger, but gentle words can defuse the situation. It's all in how we say it.

If you have a problem that you need to discuss with your spouse, write out what you want to say. Stand in front of a mirror and make your presentation in a soft voice. Then ask God to help you use the same tone of voice when you talk to your spouse. You may not be perfect the first time, but you will learn to speak the truth in love and gentleness.

Dear Lord, I want to affirm my spouse by the things I say as well as the way I say them. Please help me to remember that kindness will always go further than criticism. Guard me from yelling or screaming at my spouse; please show me the way to speak with gentleness and kindness.

ENCOURAGING WORDS

Wise words satisfy like a good meal; the right words bring satisfaction.
The tongue can bring death or life. PROVERBS 18:20-21

THIS PROVERB IS TRUE: "The tongue can bring death or life." You can kill your spouse's spirit with negative words, and you can give life through positive words. Encouraging words should be the norm in your marriage. You can't treat encouragement like a fire extinguisher, pulling it out only when you really need it and then putting it away again. Encouragement needs to be a way of life.

Encouraging words grow out of an attitude of kindness. When I choose to be kind to my spouse, to look for her positive qualities, and to do things that will make her life easier, then positive words begin to show up in my vocabulary. Complaining, cutting remarks grow out of a negative attitude. If I focus on the worst in my spouse and think about what she should be doing for me, then I become negative. I will destroy my spouse with my negative words.

I encourage you to give your spouse life by choosing positive, affirming words. The Bible tells us that wise or helpful words bring satisfaction. Proverbs 20:15 compares the value of wise words to gold and many rubies. Encouragement can work wonders in a relationship. Look for something good in your spouse and express your appreciation. Do it today—and every day.

Heavenly Father, thank you for the gift of encouragement. I want to be an encourager in my marriage; I want to bring satisfaction and hope with what I say, rather than discouragement or frustration. Please help me as I try to develop the habit of sharing positive words.

LEARNING TO ENCOURAGE

Let everything you say be good and helpful, so that your words will be an encouragement to those who hear them. EPHESIANS 4:29

NOT EVERYONE IS A BORN encourager, so I want to give you some practical ideas on how to increase your word power. First, *keep it simple.* Some people feel that in order to encourage, they must speak flowery words. I've sometimes called this Hallmark-itis. It's far better to use simple, straightforward words that sound like you. Your spouse will appreciate your genuine effort to express encouragement.

Second, *mean what you say.* Affirming does not mean lying or exaggerating to make your spouse feel better about himself. If you're not being sincere, you'll know it and your spouse will know it, so what's the point? Better a small compliment that is sincere than a long accolade that is all fluff.

Third, *keep the focus on your spouse, not on yourself.* If your spouse tends to reflect a compliment back to you by saying, "Oh, you're far better than I in that area," gently turn the compliment back to her. The affirmation process is not about you but about the other person.

The Bible makes it clear that believers are to encourage one another. Ephesians 4:29 gives us a significant challenge—to let everything we say be good and helpful so that others may be encouraged. Doing so with your spouse will bring optimism and blessing to your marriage.

Lord God, as I seek to grow in encouraging my spouse, please help me to remember these three ideas. I want to make encouraging words a habit, because I know that is pleasing to you and that it will help our relationship as a couple to grow.

LEARNING AFFIRMATION

Dear brothers and sisters, I close my letter with these last words: Be joyful.
Grow to maturity. Encourage each other. Live in harmony and peace. Then
the God of love and peace will be with you. 2 CORINTHIANS 13:11

TODAY, I WANT TO GIVE two further guidelines for learning to speak affirming words. First, *don't give backhanded encouragement.* That is, don't smother your comments in sarcasm. For example, "It took you almost two whole days to finish that bag of Oreos. I admire your willpower." It should go without saying, but comments like these are not affirming. Leave off the "zingers" if you want to affirm.

Second, *don't get upset if your spouse's response doesn't live up to your expectations.* Remember, everyone responds to compliments in a different way. Sure, it would be great if your spouse responded to your affirmation with a smile and a hug, but you may get that "What are you talking about?" look instead. This is especially true if you and your spouse are new to this affirmation business. The good news is that the more you give compliments, the better response you'll get.

At the end of 2 Corinthians, Paul gives a list of short directives to his listeners. Right in the midst of those is encouraging each other. It's a biblical mandate, it's something that pleases God, and it will strengthen your marriage. Take your first step today.

Father, thank you for the encouragement I receive from your Word. Please help me as I seek to change my words from negative to positive. Show me the best way to affirm my spouse so that he or she may be encouraged and feel sure of my love.

FOCUSED ATTENTION

Love each other with genuine affection, and take delight in honoring each other. ROMANS 12:10

IT HAS BEEN MY OBSERVATION that many husbands simply do not understand the needs of their wives. Some husbands believe that if they work a steady job and bring home a decent salary, they have fulfilled their role as husband. They have little concept of a wife's emotional and social needs. Consequently, they make no effort to meet those needs. (I can hear some of you wives saying, "Yes!" as you read this.)

But I have also observed that many wives do not understand their husbands' needs. Some wives believe that if they take care of the children and work with their husbands to keep food on the table and keep the house in some semblance of order, they are being good wives. They have little concept of their husbands' need for admiration and affection.

Often it's just a matter of focus. Why is it that when we were dating, we focused so much time and attention on each other, but after a few years of marriage, we focus on everything else? The fact is, we desperately need each other. The Bible calls us not only to love each other but to take delight in it! I want to call you to refocus attention on your spouse.

Father, you know how much my spouse and I need each other. You created us that way. Please help us to be aware of each other's needs and to take delight in meeting them.

TOTAL COMMITMENT

[Joshua said,] "Fear the LORD and serve him wholeheartedly. Put away forever the idols your ancestors worshiped when they lived beyond the Euphrates River and in Egypt. Serve the LORD alone." JOSHUA 24:14

MOST WOMEN HAVE an emotional need for security. It is first a physical need—to be safe from danger inside and outside of the home—but her greatest security need is often for assurance that her husband is committed to her.

The husband who threatens his wife with divorce or makes offhanded comments such as, "You'd be better off with someone else" or "I think I'll find someone else" is playing into a dysfunctional pattern.

When Joshua was leading the Israelites to the Promised Land, he challenged them to be totally committed to the Lord. They could no longer serve the God of Israel and still try to worship their old idols. They needed to make a choice. We face a similar question when we come to marriage. Will we put aside any thoughts or comments about divorce and be totally committed to our spouse?

The wise husband will make every effort to communicate to his wife that whatever happens, he is with her. If there are disagreements, he will take the time to listen, understand, and seek resolution. If she suffers physical or emotional pain, he will be by her side. Every wife should be able to say, "I know that my husband is with me, no matter what happens. He is committed to our marriage." Every husband needs the same commitment from his wife.

> *Lord God, I know that I need to be totally committed to my spouse. He or she is a gift that you have given me, and I am thankful. Please help me to show my commitment through my words and my actions so my spouse will feel secure in my support.*

FIVE LEVELS OF COMMUNICATION

Let your conversation be gracious and attractive so that you will have the right response for everyone. COLOSSIANS 4:6

I'VE IDENTIFIED FIVE levels of communication that occur in a relationship. You might picture these five levels as five ascending steps, each leading us to a higher level of communication. Today we start with the bottom step. I call this Hallway Talk because it's the kind of talk you share in passing as you walk down the hallway. For example: "Hi, how are you doing?" "Fine, how are you?" "Fine, thank you." By now you have passed each other, and the conversation is over.

This level of communication is common in marriage, but it is rarely satisfying. Several years ago, a young wife whose husband was an airline pilot said to me, "My husband is gone three days and then home three days. That's his work schedule. He comes home after three days away, and I say to him, 'How did things go?' He says, 'Fine.' Three days apart and all I get is 'Fine.'"

Do you understand her frustration? Some couples go for days speaking only on this level—and they should not be surprised at the lack of intimacy in their relationship. In Colossians 4, Paul writes about the way we should speak. The New International Version describes it as "full of grace, seasoned with salt." In other words, our communication as a couple should not be bland and trite but meaningful. Without that, we will not be satisfied. In the next days, we'll look at other steps on the communication ladder.

Father, forgive me for the times when I have been so lost in my own world that I have offered my spouse nothing but meaningless conversation. Please help us to enter into a deeper, richer discourse.

JUST THE FACTS

Everyone enjoys a fitting reply; it is wonderful to say the right thing at the right time! PROVERBS 15:23

YESTERDAY WE LOOKED at the first and least meaningful level of communication: Hallway Talk. Today we take a step up the communication ladder to Reporter Talk. This communication involves only the facts: who, what, when, where, and how.

For example, imagine that Emma says to her husband, Rich, "I talked with Grace this morning, and she told me that Michael has been sick for six days. The doctor is recommending that he go to the hospital on Friday for tests." Her husband responds, "Hmmm." Then he asks, "Did Jimmy find the dog?" "Yes," Emma answers. "One of the neighbors had him locked up in his backyard. Jimmy heard him barking this afternoon and rescued him." The husband nods, walks out the door, and begins to mow the grass.

On this level of communication, we are simply sharing information. There's no expression of feelings or opinions. Some couples limit almost all of their communication to this level and think that they have really good communication. It's true that lots of words may be exchanged. But in reality, there is little intimacy built by Reporter Talk, because we're sharing nothing of ourselves. What a contrast to the "fitting reply" Solomon mentioned in Proverbs 15:23. Our goal should be to engage deeply with each other.

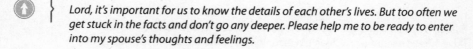

Lord, it's important for us to know the details of each other's lives. But too often we get stuck in the facts and don't go any deeper. Please help me to be ready to enter into my spouse's thoughts and feelings.

EXCHANGING OPINIONS

The heart of the discerning acquires knowledge; the ears of the wise seek it out.

PROVERBS 18:15 (NIV)

STEP ONE on the communication ladder was Hallway Talk, and step two was Reporter Talk. Today we take step three: Intellectual Talk. This kind of communication says, "Do you know what I think?"

Here's an example. Imagine Olivia says to her husband, John, "I heard today that George has cataracts." Her husband responds, "I think he should go see Dr. Gillespie. I hear he's the best in town." "I don't know," his wife responds. "I've heard that Dr. Black is good. He's younger and has the latest techniques." "I'd go for the experience of Dr. Gillespie," her husband responds. Then they move to another topic of conversation.

After the basic information was shared (George has cataracts), they both shared their ideas on the subject. Typically, when people talk on this level, they watch for the other person's response. If one person gets defensive, the other person will likely bring the conversation to a close or retreat to a safer subject.

This kind of conversation allows us to express our opinions, but it doesn't go much further than that because we're not really interacting with each other's ideas. As the above proverb says, the wise and discerning seek out knowledge—they are not content with what they know. We need to seek out knowledge from our spouse.

Lord Jesus, please teach me to listen and learn. I pray that as a couple we will be able to share our ideas and discuss them in a deeper way. May our communication strengthen our relationship.

SHARING EMOTIONS

Understand this, my dear brothers and sisters: You must all be quick to listen, slow to speak, and slow to get angry. JAMES 1:19

AS WE'VE DISCUSSED, communication has five levels. The fourth level is Emotional Talk, which says, "Let me tell you how I feel." Now we are getting to high-level communication. Some will find it far more difficult to share their feelings than to share their ideas because feelings are much more personal. Many couples do little communication on this level because they fear that their feelings will be rejected.

Take this example: Peter says, "I'm beginning to feel that you don't like me." His wife, Rachel, may become defensive. Her response may be either to start crying and withdraw, or else to express her anger verbally and tell Peter how foolish he is to feel that way. It's never appropriate or helpful to tell someone how he or she should feel.

An alternative, healthy response would be, "I'm sorry to hear that. I had no idea you were feeling that way. Tell me about it." If she encourages Peter in emotional talk, they can deal with the problem. If not, their talk reverts to a lower level and growth stops.

Emotional Talk is a normal part of a healthy marriage. If it feels threatening to you, try to modify your initial response. As James reminds us, we should be quick to listen and slow to speak. If you feel yourself becoming defensive in reaction to your spouse's emotions, ask a question. Listen. Calmly consider what has been said. Remember that having the openness to discuss emotions is one way for your relationship to grow.

Heavenly Father, forgive me for those times when I shut my spouse down with my own defensiveness. Please help me to listen and encourage discussion of our emotions. May that be fruitful in our relationship.

HONEST COMMUNICATION

[Love] does not demand its own way. It is not irritable, and it keeps no record of being wronged. It does not rejoice about injustice but rejoices whenever the truth wins out. 1 CORINTHIANS 13:5-6

TODAY WE COME to the apex of communication. I call it Honest Talk, because this level allows us to speak the truth in love. We are honest but not condemning, open but not demanding our own way. Honest Talk allows each of us the freedom to think differently and to feel differently. We try to understand each other and look for ways to grow together in spite of our differences. This kind of communication mirrors parts of Paul's definition of love from 1 Corinthians 13. When we speak honestly, we are being kind, we are rejoicing in the truth, and we are not demanding that the conversation go our way. Deeper love and intimacy are our highest goals.

If this sounds easy, let me assure you it is not. If it sounds impossible, let me also assure you it is not. Though it is true that many couples experience little communication on this level, more and more couples are finding that with God's help, this kind of open and loving communication leads to a deep sense of intimacy in their marriage.

Often this kind of communication is enhanced when the couple becomes a part of a marriage enrichment group that meets regularly and helps each other learn communication skills. Consider checking in your church or community to find such a group. Join it and move up the communication ladder.

Father, thank you for this picture of loving communication. Please help me as I try to emulate honest communication today. May I be truthful, patient, and loving as I talk to my spouse.

HANDLING FINANCES TOGETHER

I appeal to you, dear brothers and sisters, by the authority of our Lord Jesus Christ, to live in harmony with each other. Let there be no divisions in the church. Rather, be of one mind, united in thought and purpose.

1 CORINTHIANS 1:10

HOW ARE YOU HANDLING your money? Before marriage, you probably simply bought what you wanted. But once two people merge their finances, that pattern can no longer continue. After marriage, there are two people spending money, and if both of you buy what you want, you will likely be in trouble very shortly. You don't necessarily have to ask each other every time you want to spend a dollar, but you do need a plan to make sure that you don't overspend.

Obviously, certain amounts must be set aside for the rent or house payment, utilities, gas for the car, groceries, and other bills. Also, I hope you will begin by agreeing on what you will give to God each month. But once the regular payments and gifts are set aside, you will know how much expendable money is available. Then you can decide how much to save and how much to spend. Let me share an idea: Every week, each of you should get a certain amount of money that you can use as you please. (The amount will depend upon how much discretionary money is available.) The rest of the money, you agree to spend together.

The apostle Paul reminds us that we should be "of one mind, united in thought and purpose." As couples, we need to work toward this goal in all areas of our relationship, including money. Strive toward harmony as you figure out how to spend your money. Working together on your finances can be fun and exceedingly rewarding.

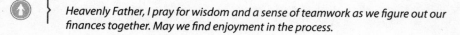

Heavenly Father, I pray for wisdom and a sense of teamwork as we figure out our finances together. May we find enjoyment in the process.

PLANNING YOUR FINANCES

The plans of the diligent lead to profit as surely as haste leads to poverty.

PROVERBS 21:5 (NIV)

THE WORD *BUDGET* FRIGHTENS some couples who don't want to feel tied down. The fact is, they are already on one. A budget is simply a plan for handling your money. Some people's plan is to spend it all the day they get it. The stores stay open late to help you do that. Some people's plan is to spend it all before they get it. Then all you have to do is mail off payments each month. Both of these methods can bring stress to a marriage. The question is not, Do you have a budget? The question is, Could you have a better budget?

King Solomon made a wise observation in the above verse from Proverbs. I don't think he was claiming that wealth is within reach for anyone who makes plans. I do think he was stating a fact of life: If you plan and make deliberate choices, the results will be better than if you simply go with the flow. That's certainly true of our finances. Planning is part of good stewardship and being wise with our resources.

If you have never put your budget on paper, I don't suggest that you do that today. Instead, keep records for two months. Record all the money you spend and what you spend it for, all the money you give away, and all the money you save. At the end of two months, you will have your budget on paper—at least, you will have a record of your budget for the past two months. Then you can examine it and ask, "Do we like our budget? If we continue on this plan, where will we be in two years?"

If you find that you don't like the way you've been allocating your money, then together you can change it. A workable budget is a genuine asset to a growing marriage.

Lord Jesus, it's amazing how money can slip through our fingers if we're not careful. We want to be better stewards of what you've given us. Please grant us the discipline to make and maintain a wise budget.

GIVING IT AWAY

Seek the Kingdom of God above all else, and live righteously, and he will give you everything you need. MATTHEW 6:33

THERE ARE ONLY THREE things you can do with money: spend it, save it, or give it away. I want to suggest that the place to start is by giving it away. In Matthew 6:33, Jesus told his hearers to seek God's Kingdom "above all else," and God would supply their needs. In the context of his words, "all else" referred to food, clothing, and shelter. The Lord knows that we need these things, and he will meet our needs if we put him first.

King Solomon was never more on target than when he said, "Honor the LORD with your wealth and with the best part of everything you produce. Then he will fill your barns with grain, and your vats will overflow with good wine" (Proverbs 3:9-10). Ever wonder why the barn is empty—why we're struggling financially? Maybe because we have not honored God with the firstfruits, meaning the best part of what we have. Please don't give to God out of what you have left over on Saturday night. Instead, make a commitment as a couple to give to God off the top as a symbol that all you have belongs to him. Agree together on an amount or percentage of your income that you will give to your local church or other ministries, and give it joyfully. This generosity will give you a sense of unity and will bless your marriage.

Father, we want to do the right thing with our money. Please help us to seek your Kingdom first and make that our primary concern. We trust you, Lord, and we want to show that trust with our finances.

TAKING WISE PRECAUTIONS

A prudent person foresees danger and takes precautions. The simpleton goes blindly on and suffers the consequences. PROVERBS 22:3

DID YOU KNOW that appliances are not eternal? Refrigerators die, usually when you're on vacation at Myrtle Beach. And did you know that when your refrigerator dies, it will cost you several hundred dollars to replace it? Are you saving for the death of your refrigerator?

As Proverbs 22:3 says, being wise involves looking ahead and taking precautions. A regular savings plan is wise stewardship. Please notice that I said "regular." Saving ten dollars every week is better than saving whatever you happen to have left over at the end of the week. If you plan, you'll come out ahead. For painless saving that doesn't depend on you to remember, you might investigate automatic deductions from your checking account to a savings or investment account.

Give to God first, pay yourself second (save), and then live on the rest. You may have to lower your standard of living to follow this plan, but that's not a bad idea. The Bible says, "In the house of the wise are stores of choice food and oil, but a foolish man devours all he has" (Proverbs 21:20, NIV). Problems occur in life. Cars break down, homes need repair, kids get sick. If these events create a financial strain, they will bring even more stress to your relationship than they would otherwise. Be wise and start a regular savings plan. Being prepared for the unexpected is one step toward a growing marriage.

I know, Father, that unexpected expenses can be a source of tension in my marriage. Please help us to be disciplined enough to save for the future, knowing that saving is good stewardship and will prepare us for whatever is ahead. Thank you that the future is in your hands.

SETTING GOALS FOR MARRIAGE

Forgetting the past and looking forward to what lies ahead, I press on to reach the end of the race and receive the heavenly prize for which God, through Christ Jesus, is calling us. PHILIPPIANS 3:13-14

ONE OF THE BARRIERS to a growing marriage is lack of time. One wife said, "I'd like to have a good marriage, but I'm not sure I have time." Many people can identify. After all, there are meals to be cooked, children to be reared, lawns to be mowed, and employers to be pleased. How do we find time to do all of this and still have time for each other? I'd like to share some ideas on overcoming the time barrier.

First, we must set goals. We do this in business, so why not in marriage? How often would the two of you like to go out for dinner? How often would you like to go on a weekend trip or take a walk in the park? How often would you like to experience sexual intercourse? What are the kinds of activities that would keep your marriage alive? Would you like to have a "daily sharing time" in which the two of you share your day with each other? If so, how much time would you like to invest in this? How can you pray for each other or be a spiritual encouragement to each other? These are the kinds of questions that lead to setting meaningful goals.

In Philippians 3, the apostle Paul wrote about his own ultimate goal: reaching the end of the race—in other words, the end of his life of service to God—and winning the prize of God's approval. He set everything else aside to make that his primary object. That single-mindedness would do us good in our marriages as well. Remember, setting goals is the first step to overcoming the barrier of time, because our goals continually remind us of what's really most important.

Heavenly Father, it's easy for me to waste time with things that don't really matter. But then I realize how far I am from the things that are most important. Please help us as a couple to come up with the right goals. I want to commit to doing what is best for our relationship.

FOCUSING ON THE GOAL

Look straight ahead, and fix your eyes on what lies before you. Mark out a straight path for your feet; stay on the safe path. Don't get sidetracked; keep your feet from following evil. PROVERBS 4:25-27

IRONIC, ISN'T IT, that with all the "time savers" of modern technology, we seem to have even less time for each other? Microwaves, remote controls, dishwashers, and computers were supposed to save us valuable time. But what happened to all that extra time? Apparently, it got gobbled up by other activities. Can we reclaim some of that time for our marriages? The answer is yes, *if* we set goals and make time to reach those goals.

The passage above from Proverbs 4 shows King Solomon's advice for meeting goals. Essentially, it comes down to knowing where you're going, setting a straight path to get there, and not getting sidetracked. That's the approach we need to take if we're going to meet our goals for marriage.

How do we make time? By eliminating some of the good things we are doing so that we will have time for the best. Life's meaning is not found in money, sports, shopping, academic success, or career achievement, as good as some of those things are. It is found in relationships—first with God, and then with people. If you are married, nothing is more important than your marital relationship. It is the framework in which God wants you to invest your life and experience his love. The husband is told to "love" his wife, and she is instructed to "honor" him. How better to love and honor than to make time for each other?

Father, thank you for the goals we've been able to set for our relationship. I pray for the wisdom and self-control to keep looking straight ahead at the goal. Let us not be distracted by other things that could keep us from meeting our goal, even if they're good things. Please show us how to straighten out our priorities.

PRACTICAL TOOLS FOR MAKING TIME

So be careful how you live. Don't live like fools, but like those who are wise. Make the most of every opportunity. EPHESIANS 5:15-16

I DON'T KNOW ANYTHING that pays greater dividends than investing time in your marriage. It will affect your physical, mental, and spiritual health and the health of your spouse and children. It will also bring glory to the God who instituted marriage. In the past few days, we've been talking about setting goals and making time for each other. I want to suggest two more things that will help you meet those goals: delegating other responsibilities and scheduling time with your spouse.

When you consider delegating responsibilities, start with your children. How about making them responsible for washing dishes, clothes, and dogs? Or, if it's financially feasible, you can hire a neighborhood teen to mow your lawn or vacuum the carpet. Whatever you can pass off to others gives you more time to invest in your marriage. When your spouse says, "You know, I like the way we're becoming friends again," you'll know your investment is paying off.

The second suggestion is to reflect your priorities in your schedule. If your goal is to have dinner out at least once a week, do you have it on the calendar for this week? How about next week? If you don't schedule things, they are not likely to happen. I encourage you to sit down together with your calendars and write down all the times you plan to spend together, big and small. When you write your spouse into your schedule, you communicate that he or she is important to you. You are making the most of every opportunity, as the Scriptures suggest, and you're on the road to overcoming the barrier of time.

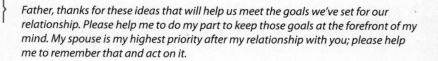

Father, thanks for these ideas that will help us meet the goals we've set for our relationship. Please help me to do my part to keep those goals at the forefront of my mind. My spouse is my highest priority after my relationship with you; please help me to remember that and act on it.

SPEAKING LOVE THROUGH GIFTS

*"Let [Rebekah] be the wife of your master's son, as the LORD has directed."
When Abraham's servant heard their answer, he bowed down to the ground
and worshiped the LORD. Then he brought out silver and gold jewelry and
clothing and presented them to Rebekah. He also gave expensive presents to
her brother and mother.* GENESIS 24:51-53

MY ACADEMIC BACKGROUND is anthropology. In all the cultures around
the world that anthropologists have studied, they have never discovered a
culture where gift giving is not a part of the love and marriage process. The
biblical account of Rebekah's engagement to Isaac clearly shows this custom.
Once she and her family had agreed that she would be Isaac's wife, Abraham's
servant gave her costly gifts to show his master's sincerity and respect. Giving
gifts as an expression of love is universal. A gift is a visible token that says, "I
was thinking about you."

Receiving gifts is some people's primary love language. Nothing speaks
louder of a spouse's devotion. Unfortunately, these people are often married
to others who don't speak this love language very well.

A man may have given gifts before marriage because he thought that
was a part of courtship, but after marriage the gift giving stopped. Perhaps he
expresses love in other ways, but he ceases to give gifts. I remember the wife
who said, "My husband tells me that he loves me, but to me, words are cheap.
'I love you. I love you.' I'm sick of words. Where are the gifts?" Her husband's
words may be sincere, but he's speaking the wrong love language. For his wife,
one gift is worth a thousand words.

If that's true of your spouse as well, make sure you're finding an appropriate way to express your love.

*Lord God, sometimes I forget how much a small gesture can mean to my spouse—
even if his or her primary love language isn't gifts. Please help me to be thoughtful
and to show him or her how much I care.*

EVIDENCE OF LOVE

When [the wise men] saw the star, they were filled with joy! They entered the house and saw the child with his mother, Mary, and they bowed down and worshiped him. Then they opened their treasure chests and gave him gifts of gold, frankincense, and myrrh. MATTHEW 2:10-11

WHEN IS THE LAST TIME you gave your spouse a gift? What did you give? If you can't answer those questions, a gift is long overdue. Gift giving is one of the five fundamental languages of love. A gift to your spouse is visible evidence of your loving thoughts.

The most famous gifts in the Bible are undoubtedly the gifts from the wise men to the baby Jesus. These men brought costly gifts of gold and expensive spices, and in doing so they honored Jesus and showed that they believed him to be a king. I'm sure Mary and Joseph were awed by these beautiful things and the love for their son they signified.

The gift need not be expensive. Guys, you can get flowers free. Just go out in your yard and pick one. That's what your children do. No flowers in your yard? Try your neighbors' yard. Ask them; they'll give you a flower.

However, if you can afford to buy gifts, don't give free flowers. Why not invest some of your money in your marriage? Give your spouse something you know will be appreciated. If you're not certain, ask! Explain that you want to do something nice, and ask for a list of some things your spouse would like to have. That's valuable information. Use it to build your relationship.

Father, thank you for the example of the wise men, who brought the best they had to show their love for Jesus. Help me to do my best to express love to my spouse through thoughtful, meaningful gifts.

MAKING DECISIONS TOGETHER

Trust in the LORD with all your heart; do not depend on your own under-standing. Seek his will in all you do, and he will show you which path to take.

PROVERBS 3:5-6

CAN WE DEVELOP a method of decision making that doesn't include argu-ing? I think the answer is yes, but this doesn't imply dictatorship. The husband who rules with a "rod of iron" or the wife who insists on having the last word might get compliance, but they will not attain unity. Unity requires that we treat each other with respect. We understand that we will not always agree, but when we disagree, we will respect each other's ideas, even if we don't fully understand them.

"Two people are better off than one," the Bible says (Ecclesiastes 4:9), but how can that be apparent if one person acts alone? Most of the poor decisions made in marriages are made in isolation. If I make a decision without con-sulting my wife, I am limited to my own wisdom. How tragic. God instituted marriage as a partnership where two people work together as a team. When we pool our wisdom, we are far more likely to make a wise decision.

The Bible clearly instructs us not to depend, or "lean," on our own limited understanding, as we see in Proverbs 3. Certainly as a couple, above all, we need to ask God for wisdom as we make decisions. As we do that, both part-ners' insights are necessary and valuable.

Life is hard. Why go it alone? Treat your spouse as a valued partner. Rec-ognize that God gave you a wealth of wisdom when he gave you a spouse.

Father, thank you for the gift of my spouse and for the wisdom he or she represents. When we make decisions, please keep me from either taking over or abdicating all responsibility. Help us to talk together, reason well, and make wise decisions.

COMING TO AGREEMENT

May God, who gives this patience and encouragement, help you live in complete harmony with each other, as is fitting for followers of Christ Jesus.

ROMANS 15:5

WHAT SHOULD WE DO when we don't agree on a decision? I believe we should wait. If the decision can wait, why would you want to go ahead with something on which the two of you do not agree? And most decisions can wait until tomorrow, next week, or maybe even next month. While you are waiting, both of you should be praying for God's direction. You might ask the advice of a friend. Perhaps tomorrow you will be able to reach an agreement. If not, continue to wait. I believe you should wait as long as you can. Being in agreement is more important than the decision itself.

The apostle Paul prayed that God would help believers live in unity and harmony. That's important for a church and even more important for a marriage. When one spouse makes a decision without the other's agreement, disharmony mars the relationship.

Here is one example: I know some guys who have bought motorcycles that their wives never agreed to. And do you know what they find out about five weeks down the road? It's hard to sleep with a motorcycle. Being in agreement is more important than the decision. Wouldn't it be better to wait and pray to find unity? Once you've reached an understanding, you can ride the motorcycle together. Or, you can agree that life lived in unity is more important than speeding down the road on a motorcycle. Agreement is worth the wait.

Lord Jesus, I pray for harmony in our marriage. As we need to make decisions, I want to commit to waiting until we reach agreement rather than going ahead with what I want. Please give us wisdom and unity.

DEALING WITH IRRESPONSIBILITY

Pay careful attention to your own work, for then you will get the satisfaction of a job well done, and you won't need to compare yourself to anyone else. For we are each responsible for our own conduct. GALATIANS 6:4-5

WHY ARE SOME HUSBANDS and wives irresponsible? When we get married, we expect that our spouse will carry his or her part of the load. But if your spouse won't work, shows no interest in parenting, and ignores you, you have a problem. The Bible makes it clear that each of us should be responsible for our own behavior and our own work, as we see in the above passage. Marriage partners are on the same team, but if one half of the team isn't contributing, the team doesn't function. If that's your situation and you want to help your spouse, you must first understand the source of the behavior. Let me suggest some possibilities:

1. An irresponsible spouse may be following the model of a parent.

2. An irresponsible spouse may be rebelling against the model of a parent. Perhaps he watched his mother control his father's every move, and he vows that won't happen to him.

3. An irresponsible spouse may have developed a self-centered attitude. The world revolves around her.

4. An irresponsible spouse's behavior may be an expression of resentment toward her mate. His words or actions have stimulated hurt and anger. She can't verbalize it, but it shows up in her behavior.

How do you discover the source of your spouse's behavior? You ask questions. Not direct questions such as, "Why are you so irresponsible?" but probing questions such as, "What kind of relationship did you have with your father?" Or, "In what ways have my words or actions hurt you most?" When you begin that dialogue and receive honest responses, you are on the road to understanding your spouse. That's the first step to dealing with irresponsibility.

Father God, you know that when I see irresponsibility in my spouse, it frustrates me, and I don't always respond well. Please help me to take a step back and do my best to understand the root cause of this behavior. Show me the right questions to ask, and give me ears to hear the answers.

WORKING FOR CHANGE

Anyone who belongs to Christ has become a new person. The old life is gone; a new life has begun! 2 CORINTHIANS 5:17

LIVING WITH AN IRRESPONSIBLE spouse is not fun. However, watching an irresponsible spouse change and grow can be great fun. In yesterday's devotion, I suggested that the first step to helping is to find out why your spouse is irresponsible. Today, I want to suggest that the next step is to acknowledge your own failures in the past.

If you want to see change in your spouse, it is always best to begin by changing yourself. You know, and your spouse knows, that you have not been perfect. When you confess your own failures to yourself, to God, and then to your spouse, you are paving the road to growth for both of you. The apostle Paul makes clear in 2 Corinthians 5:17 that those who belong to Christ are beginning new lives. Never forget that God has the power to transform your own heart as well as your spouse's. When you begin with what you can control—yourself—and ask God to change you, changes in your spouse will not be far behind.

Consider saying this to your spouse: "I know I've been critical of you. I've realized that in many ways I have failed to be the Christian spouse I should have been. I know I haven't always given you the encouragement you needed. I hope that you will forgive me. I want the future to be different." With that communication, you have immediately changed the climate between the two of you. You have opened the door to growth.

Lord, I am grateful that you are in the business of changing lives. Though it's tempting to think that only my spouse needs to change, I know that's not true. Please help me to be willing to change as well. Show me how to be a better husband or wife, and grant me the humility to confess my wrongs to my spouse without first demanding change from him or her.

EXPRESSING LOVE BRINGS
ABOUT CHANGE

[The prodigal son] returned home to his father. And while he was still a long way off, his father saw him coming. Filled with love and compassion, he ran to his son, embraced him, and kissed him. LUKE 15:20

HOW DO YOU STIMULATE GROWTH when you are married to an irresponsible spouse? You can have a positive influence on your spouse *if* you take the right approach.

We've talked about locating the source of your spouse's behavior. Ask questions to try to determine why he or she is irresponsible. Next I talked about opening the door to change by admitting your own failures and asking for forgiveness. Today, I want to encourage you to seek to meet your spouse's need for emotional love. You may be thinking, *Wait a minute. I'm the one who doesn't feel loved.* I understand, but you are also the more responsible one. You're the one who wants to see change.

If you speak the primary love language of your spouse, you are taking a positive step in stimulating change. Why? Because a person who feels loved and secure is much more open to change. Didn't Jesus love us when we were unlovely? He died for us while we were still mired in our sin (see Romans 5:8). Doesn't the Bible say that we love him because he first loved us (see 1 John 4:19)? A beautiful example of this comes in the Prodigal Son's story found in Luke 15. When the son returned home after squandering all of his money, the father ran toward him and embraced him even before he knew the status of the son's heart. In the same way, loving your spouse *before* seeing any change is one of the most powerful steps you can take in stimulating transformation.

Lord, thank you for the example of the father of the Prodigal Son. He embraced his son literally and figuratively even before he knew whether or not his son was going to change. Please help me to respond that way to my spouse. May I express love without expecting anything else first.

MAY 22

HAVING THE ATTITUDE
OF CHRIST

You must have the same attitude that Christ Jesus had. Though he was God,
he did not think of equality with God as something to cling to. Instead, he gave
up his divine privileges; he took the humble position of a slave and was born
as a human being. When he appeared in human form, he humbled himself in
obedience to God and died a criminal's death on a cross. PHILIPPIANS 2:5-8

HOW DOES MY RELATIONSHIP with God affect my marriage? Profoundly!
By nature, I'm self-centered. I carry that attitude into my marriage. So when I
don't get my way, I argue or sulk. That doesn't lead to a growing marriage. My
attitude must change, and that's where God comes into the picture. He is in
the business of changing attitudes.

The apostle Paul says, "You must have the same attitude that Christ Jesus
had." What was his attitude? He was willing to step from heaven to earth to
identify with us—something that one translation describes as "becoming
nothing." Once he became a man, he was willing to step down even further
and die for us. Jesus' attitude is first and foremost an attitude of sacrificial love
and service. If that attitude is in me, I will have a growing marriage.

My research has shown that not a single wife in the history of this nation
has ever murdered her husband while he was washing the dishes. Not one!
That's a bit tongue-in-cheek, but it ought to tell us something.

Developing this attitude of service may seem impossible, but it's not.
Never underestimate God's power to transform a willing individual.

Lord Jesus, I am amazed at your attitude of humble servanthood. I can't even under-
stand what it must have been like for you to set aside so much to become a limited
human—and to die for us. Thank you, Lord. I need your transformation to have this
same attitude. Please give me a willing heart.

GOD'S POWER OF TRANSFORMATION

Jesus said, "Come to me, all of you who are weary and carry heavy burdens, and I will give you rest. Take my yoke upon you. Let me teach you, because I am humble and gentle at heart, and you will find rest for your souls. For my yoke is easy to bear, and the burden I give you is light." MATTHEW 11:28-30

DOES GOD MAKE A DIFFERENCE in marriage? Thousands of couples will testify that he made a difference in theirs. How does this transformation happen? First of all, we must establish a relationship with God. This means that we must come to him and acknowledge that we have walked our own way and broken his laws. We tell him that we need forgiveness and we want to turn from our sins.

He stands with open arms and says, "Come to me, all of you who are weary and carry heavy burdens, and I will give you rest." That's a beautiful and astounding invitation. If we are willing to come to him, he will not only forgive us but also send his Spirit to live inside us.

The Holy Spirit is the one who changes our attitudes. When he is in control of our lives, we begin to look at things differently. He shows us that people are more important than things and that serving others is more important than being served. He works within us to produce wonderful character qualities such as love, patience, kindness, and gentleness (see Galatians 5:22-23). He alone can effect such substantial change in the way we think and act.

Do you see how these new attitudes would transform your relationship? Nothing holds greater potential for changing your marriage than asking God to come into your life, forgive your sins, and let you see the world the way he sees it.

Father God, thank you for inviting us to come to you. I am so grateful for your forgiveness, your teaching, and your Holy Spirit, which lives in me and directs me. I need your transformation. Please help me to allow you to change me.

TRUTH LEADS TO FREEDOM

If you abide in My word, you are My disciples indeed. And you shall know the truth, and the truth shall make you free. JOHN 8:31-32 (NKJV)

THE WAY YOU PERCEIVE yourself greatly affects your marriage. Some people grew up thinking of themselves as failures. The message they heard from their parents was, "You're not good enough." This perception keeps them in bondage. Their attitude is, *Why try? I'll fail anyway.* When these people fall in love and get married, they bring this distorted self-perception into the marriage.

I can tell you that such a person's spouse will be greatly frustrated. Often, someone who thinks of himself as a failure will expect his spouse to build him up, but it doesn't take long for the spouse to discover that such efforts are futile.

If you recognize yourself as having a distorted self-perception, please realize that your spouse cannot change the way you see yourself. Only you can do that.

So where do you start? In John 8, Jesus said that the truth will make you free—free from sin, and free from wrong patterns of thinking. What is the truth about you, according to God's Word? You are made in God's image (see Genesis 1:27), highly valued by him (see Matthew 10:31, among many other references), and especially gifted to serve in his Kingdom (see 1 Corinthians 12; Hebrews 13:20-21).

Believe the truth about yourself. Discover your abilities, and give them to God. He will make you a success. When you do this, you will free your spouse from having to battle the way you view yourself—and you will free yourself from negative thinking.

> *Lord God, I often see myself as a failure or worthless. I cling to my spouse for affirmation, but then I don't believe his or her words. I realize how destructive this is. Please help me to see myself as you see me. Your love gives me great value. Please set me free from the lies I have believed.*

ADMITTING MISTAKES

Where there is no counsel, the people fall; but in the multitude of counselors there is safety. PROVERBS 11:14 (NKJV)

HAVE YOU EVER HEARD THIS? "You're the one with the problem. I don't need counseling." The person who thinks he's always right is mistaken. None of us are perfect. All of us need help. The book of Proverbs says that "in the multitude of counselors there is safety." Why? Because other people can often bring clearer perspective to our problems. The person who refuses to seek counsel and tries to handle things on his own is often insecure. He thinks that to admit that he made a mistake is to prove that he is inadequate, and that is his greatest fear. Perhaps his father told him he would never make it, and he is trying hard to prove his father wrong.

How can you help, if you are married to this person? Give unconditional love. Speak her primary love language often. Brag on her in front of your friends, both in her presence and behind her back. Focus on her accomplishments. When she knows she is secure in your love, perhaps she will be able to admit that she's not perfect. When she does, let her know how much you admire her for admitting her failures. When she sees that her success is not dependent on being perfect, she can relax and become the person God has made her to be.

Father, it's sometimes hard for me to admit my own mistakes. Please help me to realize that pretending I'm perfect doesn't make the problems go away but just makes things worse. When my spouse struggles with this, show me how to respond lovingly in a way that builds him or her up. Help me to love unconditionally, not based on what he or she does.

CHANGING SELF-PERCEPTIONS

Don't copy the behavior and customs of this world, but let God transform you into a new person by changing the way you think. ROMANS 12:2

HOW WOULD YOU DESCRIBE yourself? How would you describe your spouse? Are you optimistic or pessimistic; negative or positive; critical or complimentary? Is your spouse extroverted or introverted; talkative or quiet; patient or impatient? The way you perceive yourself and the way you perceive your spouse will make a difference in your behavior and, consequently, in your marriage.

We usually speak of these characteristics as personality traits. Unfortunately, we have been led to believe that they are set in concrete by the age of five or six and that we cannot change them. The good news is that we don't have to be controlled by these perceptions. The message of the Bible is that we *can* change, with God's help. Romans 12:2 makes clear that if we're willing, God will transform us. He can change us at a heart level by altering the very way we think.

Here's one way to start: If you perceive yourself as being negative and critical, then practice the art of giving compliments. You might begin by giving *yourself* a compliment. Find something you did well, then stop long enough to say, "Hey, I did a good job with that." If you give yourself one compliment every day, before long you will change your self-perception. Do the same for your spouse, and watch him or her begin to live up to your compliments too.

You can change your self-perceptions—and the way you interact with your spouse—for the better.

> *Father, thank you for having the power to transform us from the inside out. I want to change the way I view myself and the negative ways I interact with my spouse. I don't want to be stuck in the same patterns. Please change me. Help me to be willing to take those first steps.*

FOLLOWING GOD'S EXAMPLE OF TEAMWORK

God decided in advance to adopt us into his own family by bringing us to himself through Jesus Christ. This is what he wanted to do, and it gave him great pleasure. . . . And when you believed in Christ, he identified you as his own by giving you the Holy Spirit, whom he promised long ago.

EPHESIANS 1:5, 13

IT SEEMS TO ME that if we could understand God better, we could understand marriage better. Ever notice how God the Father, God the Son, and God the Holy Spirit work together as a team? Read the first chapter of Ephesians and observe how the Father planned our salvation, the Son shed his blood to effect our salvation, and the Holy Spirit sealed our salvation. God is one within the mystery of the Trinity, and this unity is expressed in the diversity of roles needed to accomplish one goal, our salvation.

The Scriptures say that, in marriage, the husband and wife are to become one flesh. However, this unity does not mean that we are clones of each other. No, we are two distinct creatures who work together as a team to accomplish one goal—God's will for our lives. In mundane things such as washing clothes and mopping floors, or in exciting things such as volunteering in a soup kitchen or leading a Bible study, we complement each other. The husband who takes care of the children while his wife leads a Bible study is sharing with her in ministry. Indeed, two become one when they work together as a team.

Father, I am grateful for your example of teamwork. I can't fully understand the Trinity, but I know that your three persons work together in perfect unity. I pray for that kind of unity within my relationship with my spouse. Help us to function smoothly as a team, being generous with each other and keeping our end goal in mind. May our marriage glorify you as we do your will.

LAYING THE GROUNDWORK OF TEAMWORK

I planted the seed in your hearts, and Apollos watered it, but it was God who made it grow. It's not important who does the planting, or who does the watering. What's important is that God makes the seed grow. The one who plants and the one who waters work together with the same purpose. And both will be rewarded for their own hard work. For we are both God's workers.

1 CORINTHIANS 3:6-9

TEAMWORK IS THE ESSENTIAL ingredient to a successful marriage. Think about the first command God gave Adam and Eve: to be fruitful and multiply. This command required teamwork; of course, neither a man nor a woman can make a baby alone. As teamwork is required in this basic biological goal, it is also required in the rest of marriage.

The apostle Paul wrote about the concept of teamwork in 1 Corinthians 3. He was responding to some new believers who were being divisive by proclaiming their allegiance to either Paul or Apollos. He reminded the Corinthians that it doesn't matter who completes what task if both people have the same goal. He and Apollos both did their part to share the gospel, and they left the outcome in God's hands. That's teamwork.

The concept of teamwork is especially helpful when it comes to processing daily life. Cooking meals, washing dishes, paying bills, sweeping, mopping, mowing, trimming, and driving are all things that must be done to maintain life. Who is going to do what, and how often? are the questions that lead to teamwork. If you settle these issues early on, you will save yourselves a lot of conflict later. It's certainly undesirable to wake up months or years into the marriage and realize that you have spent a lot of time fighting when you could have been spent it in productive activity.

Household tasks are not determined by gender. Some men are better cooks than their wives. Some women are better at math than their husbands and should handle the finances. You are teammates, not competitors. Why not work out a team plan that utilizes your best gifts? Remember, you're not enemies. You're on the same team.

Heavenly Father, it's easy for me to become competitive with my spouse. I'm concerned about who's doing more and focus too much on what is fair. Instead, show me how to be a good teammate. Help us to work together for the common goal of making our family run smoothly.

TRUE GREATNESS

[Jesus] sat down, called the twelve disciples over to him, and said, "Whoever wants to be first must take last place and be the servant of everyone else."

MARK 9:35

SLAVERY HARDENS THE HEART and creates anger, bitterness, and resentment. That is why wives who are forced to serve their husbands seldom truly love their husbands. It is hard to love someone who is treating you like a slave. When people serve others because they are forced to do so, they lose the freedom to serve genuinely.

Scripture calls for service that is freely given, not out of fear, but out of choice. It comes out of the personal discovery that "it is more blessed to give than to receive" (Acts 20:35). This kind of service is the hallmark of true greatness. Jesus said that in his Kingdom, the greatest leader would be the greatest servant.

Serving our spouse is a way of practicing the teachings of Jesus. If service does not begin in marriage, where will it begin? Jesus said that every time we serve one of his creatures, we are serving him (see Matthew 25:40). This lifts our service to an even more noble level. Every time I vacuum floors for my wife, I am serving Jesus. Bring on the vacuum.

Lord Jesus, thank you for reminding us that when we serve each other, we are really serving you. Please help us to develop a humble attitude of service toward each other.

SERVING, NOT DEMANDING

[Jesus] began to wash the disciples' feet, drying them with the towel he had around him. . . . [He said,] "Since I, your Lord and Teacher, have washed your feet, you ought to wash each other's feet. I have given you an example to follow. Do as I have done to you." JOHN 13:5, 14-15

IN EVERY VOCATION, those who excel are those who have a genuine desire to serve others. The most notable physicians view their vocation as a calling to serve the sick and diseased. Truly great politicians see themselves as "public servants." The greatest of all educators seek to help students reach their full potential.

It is no different in the family. Great husbands are men who view their role as helping their wives accomplish their objectives. And great wives are those who give themselves to helping their husbands succeed. In giving their lives to each other, they both become winners.

Holding on to your rights and demanding that your spouse serve you is exactly the opposite of what the Bible teaches. The Scriptures say, "Give, and you will receive" (Luke 6:38), not "Demand and people will do what you demand." The fact is, most people do not respond well to demands—but few people will reject loving service. Service follows the example of Jesus and is the hallmark of greatness.

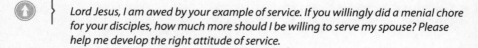

Lord Jesus, I am awed by your example of service. If you willingly did a menial chore for your disciples, how much more should I be willing to serve my spouse? Please help me develop the right attitude of service.

COMBATING THE SILENT TREATMENT

Ahab went home angry and sullen because of Naboth's answer. The king went to bed with his face to the wall and refused to eat! 1 KINGS 21:4

JILL TOLD HER HUSBAND, Mike, that she wanted to spend a weekend at the beach with the women who worked in her office. Mike responded with silence. No explosions, no loud words, no arguing, no nothing—just silence. He had been silent for four days when Jill came to my office for help.

I made three guesses:

1. This was not the first time Mike had given her the "silent treatment."

2. Mike was very unhappy about the idea of Jill going to the beach with her friends.

3. Jill was not meeting Mike's emotional need for love.

I later learned I was right in all three guesses.

Let me assure you that if you want a healthy marriage, you must not settle for silence. If you are the partner who has stopped talking, you need to realize that you are shooting yourself in the foot and sabotaging your marriage. Being silent may be better than lashing out in anger, but as a long-term solution it rarely helps anything. One rather vivid biblical example of the silent treatment comes from King Ahab, a notoriously evil king of Israel. When a man named Naboth wouldn't sell his vineyard to the king, Ahab went home and lay on his bed with his face to the wall—definitely not a productive response.

If you are the person receiving the silent treatment, the first lesson is to understand that when your spouse stops talking, there is always a reason, and usually more than one. If you want your spouse to talk, you must *think* more and *talk* less. Criticizing your loved one for not talking will likely prolong the silence.

Father, forgive me for the times when I stop talking to my spouse out of anger. Please show me a better way to respond. And when my spouse is silent to me, please show me how to listen better and figure out the reason.

THE REASONS BEHIND THE SILENCE

Even if my father and mother abandon me, the LORD will hold me close. Teach me how to live, O LORD. Lead me along the right path. PSALM 27:10-11

WHEN YOUR SPOUSE gives you the "silent treatment," there are always reasons. Usually there's a contemporary reason, an emotional reason, and a historical reason. The *contemporary reason* is whatever has just happened that the spouse finds objectionable. For Mike, in our example from yesterday, it was Jill's announcement that she was going to spend the weekend at the beach with her women friends.

The *emotional reason* involves the deeper feelings triggered by the event. In our example, Mike did not feel secure in Jill's love. He reasoned, *If she loved me, she would want to be with me—not go away for the weekend.*

The *historical reason* often involves patterns of communication. Mike had learned the "silent treatment" in his childhood. His parents would not allow him to argue with them, so when he felt hurt or angry, he learned to be silent. If you learned negative patterns from your parents, I encourage you to remember that you are not stuck in them. The Lord can renew your mind and teach you new ways, as the passage above reminds us.

If you have been given the "silent treatment" by your spouse, here are the three questions you need to answer to address the three possible reasons for the situation:

- What have I just done or failed to do that my spouse might have found objectionable?

- Does my spouse feel secure in my love? Have I been speaking the right love language lately and connecting with his emotions?

- What do I know about my spouse's history or childhood that might help me understand his silence?

Tomorrow we will talk about a strategy for breaking the silence.

Heavenly Father, you know how deep-seated some of our communication patterns are. Please show us the way to new, better ways of talking and dealing with problems. Thank you for teaching us.

BREAKING THE SILENCE

Be an example to all believers in what you say, in the way you live, in your love, your faith, and your purity. 1 TIMOTHY 4:12

WHEN YOUR SPOUSE gives you the "silent treatment," you may feel helpless. But you're not. You can help break the silence. However, you don't do it by criticizing your spouse for not talking. Instead, you do it by trying to understand what is going on inside your loved one and addressing those issues.

I can hear someone saying, "But how can I know what is going on inside him if he won't talk?" The answer is to *think*. Think about your spouse's emotional needs. When our emotional needs are not met, we act badly, and silence is one form the misbehavior can take.

Jill addressed the issue when she said to her husband, "Mike, I realize that I have not been speaking your love language lately. I'm really sorry about that. I got so busy that I forgot the main thing—I love you. I think that your silence is probably related to the fact that you feel neglected by me. If so, could we agree that next time this happens, you will simply say, 'My love tank is empty. I need to know that you love me'? I promise you I'll respond, because I do love you."

You guessed it. In response to that loving, honest request, Mike started talking. As the above verse mentions, our words should be above reproach, and our love should be evident. When that's the case, we will have a positive effect on others.

Lord, please give me the maturity, the self-control, and the wisdom to respond lovingly to my spouse when he or she has stopped talking to me. Show me how to address the core issue of his or her emotional needs. Heal our relationship.

THE BONDING POWER OF SEX

Marriage should be honored by all, and the marriage bed kept pure.

HEBREWS 13:4 (NIV)

THE BOOK OF GENESIS says that when a husband and wife have sexual intercourse, they become "one flesh" (Genesis 2:24, NIV). In other words, their two lives are bonded together. Sex is the consummating act of marriage. We have a public wedding ceremony and a private consummation of the public commitment. Sexual intercourse is the physical expression of the inward union of two lives.

In the ancient Hebrew Scriptures and in the New Testament writings, sexual intercourse is always assumed to be reserved for marriage. That is not an arbitrary denunciation of sex outside of marriage but simply an effort to be true to the nature of sexual intercourse. Such deep bonding is inappropriate outside a loving, lifetime commitment between a husband and a wife. The author of the book of Hebrews talked about keeping the marriage bed pure— in other words, keeping sexual intercourse as a special thing only between a husband and wife.

Sex is not simply a matter of joining two bodies that were uniquely made for each other. It touches on intellectual, emotional, social, and spiritual bonding as well. Sex was God's idea, and marriage is the context in which it finds ultimate meaning.

Heavenly Father, thank you for the gift of sex in my marriage. I am grateful for the physical, emotional, and spiritual bonding that results from our sexual relationship. I pray for your grace to keep this bond strong and pure.

STUDYING YOUR SPOUSE

The husband should fulfill his wife's sexual needs, and the wife should fulfill her husband's needs. 1 CORINTHIANS 7:3

WE MUST UNDERSTAND male-female differences if we are going to discover God's ideal for sexual intimacy. The husband's emphasis is most often on the physical aspects: the seeing, the touching, the feeling. The wife, on the other hand, typically emphasizes the emotional aspect. Feeling loved, cared for, and treated tenderly will pave the road to sexual intimacy for her.

The apostle Paul's words make clear that as a couple, our goal must be to meet each other's sexual needs. That takes some deliberate work. The husband must learn to focus on his wife's emotional need for love. The wife must understand the physical and visual aspect of her husband's sexual desires. As in all other areas of marriage, this requires learning. If the couple focuses on making the sexual experience an act of love, each seeking to pleasure the other, they will find fulfilling sexual intimacy. But if they simply "do what comes naturally," they will find sexual frustration.

It should be obvious that we cannot separate sexual intimacy from emotional, intellectual, social, and spiritual intimacy. We can study them separately, but in the context of human relationships, they can never be compartmentalized.

The sense of closeness, of being one, of finding mutual satisfaction is reserved for the couple who is willing to do the hard work of learning about each other. Love can be learned, and sexual intimacy is one of the results.

Lord Jesus, it's easy to fall into selfishness when it comes to sex. As a couple, please help us to focus on each other. May our desire to please each other increase, and may that strengthen our relationship.

EMBRACING DIFFERENCES

Your love delights me, my treasure, my bride. Your love is better than wine,
your perfume more fragrant than spices. . . . You are my private garden, my
treasure, my bride, a secluded spring, a hidden fountain.

SONG OF SOLOMON 4:10, 12

MEN AND WOMEN ARE SIMILAR, yet vastly different. That was God's design in many areas, including the sexual. Men are stimulated by sight. Simply watching his wife undress in the shadows of the bedroom light may prepare a man for sex. (I'm sorry, men. Our wives can watch us undress and be unmoved. I mean, the thought never even crosses their minds.)

Women tend to be far more stimulated by tender touch, affirming words, and acts of thoughtfulness. That is why many wives have said, "Sex doesn't begin in the bedroom. It begins in the kitchen. It doesn't start at night; it starts in the morning." The way she is treated and spoken to throughout the day will have a profound effect upon her desire for sexual intimacy in the evening.

The above passage from the Song of Solomon beautifully demonstrates the delight that can come from recognizing that your spouse is full of secrets to discover. Differences don't have to be frustrating; they can be entrancing as well. I'm convinced that if husbands would follow the biblical admonition to "dwell with [their wives] according to knowledge" (1 Peter 3:7, KJV), they would discover the sexual intimacy that God designed marriage to provide.

> *Father, thank you for the differences between my spouse and me. I pray that you*
> *would give us the patience to study each other, to understand how the other*
> *responds sexually, and to treat each other with love.*

SEEING AS THE LORD SEES

Let the Spirit renew your thoughts and attitudes. Put on your new nature, created to be like God—truly righteous and holy. EPHESIANS 4:23-24

ATTITUDE HAS TO DO with the way I choose to think about things. It results from my focus. Two men looked through prison bars—one saw mud, the other stars. Two people were in a troubled marriage—one cursed, the other prayed. The difference is attitude.

Negative thinking tends to beget more negative thinking. Focus on how terrible the situation is, and it will begin to seem even worse. Focus on one positive thing, and another will appear. In the darkest night of a troubled marriage, there is always a flickering light. Focus on that light, and it will eventually flood the room.

Maintaining a positive attitude in a troubled marriage may seem impossible, but as Christians, we have outside help. The above passage from Ephesians 4 talks about allowing the Holy Spirit to renew our thoughts and attitudes. When we have been redeemed, we have a new nature and are no longer slaves to the old way of thinking. If we ask the Lord, he will develop a new attitude in us. Consider praying this way: "Lord, help me to see my marriage the way you see it. Help me to view my spouse the way you view him or her. Help me to think the thoughts that you have toward him or her." When you begin to see your spouse as a person beloved of God—a valuable person for whom Christ died—you will begin to develop a positive attitude.

Father, I often struggle with my attitude. I don't want to be a slave to negative thinking, focusing only on the worst. Please transform my thinking. Show me how to focus on the good things. Give me wisdom to see my spouse and my marriage the way you see them. Please develop more love and optimism in me, for the good of my marriage.

MAINTAINING A POSITIVE ATTITUDE

Don't worry about anything; instead, pray about everything. Tell God what you need, and thank him for all he has done. Then you will experience God's peace, which exceeds anything we can understand. . . . Fix your thoughts on what is true, and honorable, and right, and pure, and lovely, and admirable. Think about things that are excellent and worthy of praise. PHILIPPIANS 4:6-8

TRYING TO KEEP a positive attitude is not a new idea. It is found clearly in the first-century writing of Paul the apostle. He encouraged the church at Philippi to pray about problems rather than worry about them. Why? Because worry leads to anxiety and negativity, while prayer leads to peace and a more positive outlook. Then Paul revealed the key to having a positive attitude: think about positive things—things that are "excellent and worthy of praise."

We are responsible for the way we think. Even in the worst marital situation, we choose our attitude. Maintaining a positive attitude requires prayer. As Paul said, we can bring our requests to God. We can tell him what we need and be thankful for what he has already done. Will God always do what we ask? No, but what does happen is that as we release worry and express gratitude, God's peace descends on our minds and hearts. God calms our emotions and directs our thoughts.

When we find ourselves struggling with an aspect of our marriage, let's try to develop a more optimistic perspective. With a positive attitude, we become a part of the solution, rather than a part of the problem.

Father, thank you for letting us bring anything to you in prayer. Help me to release my worries to you, knowing that you are in control. When I thank you for what you have already done, I'm reminded of how you have acted for me in the past, and I can be more positive about the future. Please encourage the right attitude in me.

ATTITUDE INFLUENCES BEHAVIOR

Always be joyful. Never stop praying. Be thankful in all circumstances, for this is God's will for you who belong to Christ Jesus. 1 THESSALONIANS 5:16-18

ONE REASON MY ATTITUDES are so important is that they affect my actions—that is, my behavior and words. If I have a pessimistic, defeatist, negative attitude, it will be expressed in negative words and behavior. The reality is that I may not be able to control my environment. Perhaps I have experienced such difficulties as sickness, an alcoholic spouse, a teenager on drugs, a mother who abandoned me, a father who abused me, a spouse who is irresponsible, aging parents, and so on. Any one of those situations can be overwhelming. But it's crucial to realize that *I am* responsible for *what I do* within my environment. And my attitude will greatly influence my behavior.

First Thessalonians 5 gives us some key steps to developing a positive attitude: be joyful, keep praying, and be thankful in all circumstances. As we talked about in yesterday's reading, being thankful can renew our perspective, reminding us of what God has already done for us and encouraging us that he will help in the future.

If you want to know your attitude, look at your words and behavior. If your words are critical and negative, then you have a negative attitude. If your behavior is designed to hurt or get back at your spouse, then you have a negative attitude. Paul gives straightforward counsel in Philippians 2:14: "Do everything without complaining and arguing." Following this advice and guarding your attitude are the most powerful things you can do to affect your behavior. And your behavior greatly influences your marriage.

Heavenly Father, when I have a bad attitude, it comes out in the way I talk to my spouse. Please forgive me for my sharp words and negativity. I want to set a goal to avoid complaining or arguing. Instead, please help me to rejoice, pray, and be thankful. I know the resulting positive attitude will bless my spouse and strengthen our marriage.

INTERCESSORY PRAYER

I pray for you constantly, asking God, the glorious Father of our Lord Jesus Christ, to give you spiritual wisdom and insight so that you might grow in your knowledge of God. EPHESIANS 1:16-17

MARTIN LUTHER SAID, "As it is the business of tailors to make clothes and cobblers to mend shoes, so it is the business of Christians to pray." Intercession is one ministry which requires no special spiritual gift. All Christians are equipped to pray.

Not only is intercessory prayer a ministry, it is also a responsibility. The prophet Samuel told the Israelites, "I will certainly not sin against the LORD by ending my prayers for you" (1 Samuel 12:23). The apostle Paul began many of his epistles by telling his readers how frequently he prayed for them. Prayer is one of the means that God has chosen to let us cooperate with him in getting his work done. It is a ministry that husbands and wives can do together. They can pray for each other as well as for their children, their parents, their pastor and church, other ministries, and world missions.

If you don't have a daily prayer time with your spouse, why not start today? Ask your spouse to spend five minutes praying with you. If you don't want to pray out loud, then pray silently. Take the first step in learning the ministry of intercessory prayer.

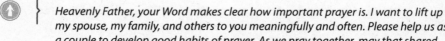

Heavenly Father, your Word makes clear how important prayer is. I want to lift up my spouse, my family, and others to you meaningfully and often. Please help us as a couple to develop good habits of prayer. As we pray together, may that shared experience and our shared desires for your will to be done draw us closer together.

WHY PRAY?

If my people who are called by my name will humble themselves and pray and seek my face and turn from their wicked ways, I will hear from heaven and will forgive their sins and restore their land. 2 CHRONICLES 7:14

AUTHOR AND BIBLE PROFESSOR Harold Lindsell once said, "Why should we expect God to do *without* prayer what he has promised to do *if* we pray?" The Bible contains many calls to prayer, including God's words to Solomon, as recorded in 2 Chronicles 7. If the people humbled themselves and prayed after they sinned, God would hear them, forgive them, and restore them. His invitation to us is clear: "Ask me and I will tell you remarkable secrets you do not know about things to come" (Jeremiah 33:3). The author of Hebrews tells us to "come boldly" to God's throne, where we will receive mercy and grace (4:16).

We come to God as our Father, knowing that he wants to do good things for his children. But we must be ready to receive them. Thus he says, "Keep on asking, and you will receive what you ask for" (Matthew 7:7). Now, granted, God does not do everything that we request. He loves us too much and is too wise to do that. If what we request is not for our ultimate good, then he will do something better. His will is always right.

Couples who learn to pray together are simply responding to God's invitation. He wants to be involved in your marriage. Praying together is one way of acknowledging that you want his presence and his power. Through prayer, he can change your attitudes and your behavior. Remember, God is love, and he can teach you how to love each other. "Keep on asking."

Lord, I am amazed that you so often invite us to pray—to communicate with you, the Lord of the universe! I am grateful for the love and guidance you offer. Please help my spouse and me to take the time to pray together. May we "come boldly" to you and through our prayers be brought closer to each other and closer to you.

AVOIDING DIVORCE

So guard your heart; remain loyal to the wife of your youth. MALACHI 2:15

THROUGH THE YEARS, I have counseled enough divorced persons to know that while divorce removes some pressures, it creates a host of others. If you are considering divorce, reflect on the following facts: Only a small percentage of divorced individuals claim to have found greater happiness in a second or third marriage. In fact, whereas the divorce rate in first marriages is 40 percent, the divorce rate in second marriages is 60 percent and in third marriages, 75 percent. The hope of the grass being greener on the other side of the fence is a myth.

I am not naive enough to suggest that divorce can be eliminated from the human landscape. I am simply saying that far too many couples have opted for divorce too soon and at too great a price. Divorce should be the last possible alternative. It should be preceded by every effort at reconciling differences, dealing with issues, and solving problems. I believe that many divorced couples could have reconciled if they had sought and found proper help.

Don't settle for the myth that there is no hope for your marriage. Given the right information and the proper support, you can be a positive change agent in your relationship. Follow God's advice as given in Malachi 2, and guard your heart. Remain faithful to your spouse, and seek help.

Heavenly Father, there are moments when divorce seems tempting. But I know it's never an easy solution; it's a path filled with pain and difficulty. Please give me a rock-solid commitment to my spouse, no matter what. Show me how to express love to my spouse and how to effect change in our relationship.

CHOOSING LOVE

Now I am giving you a new commandment: Love each other. Just as I have loved you, you should love each other. JOHN 13:34

THE FIVE LOVE LANGUAGES, a book I wrote several years ago, has helped hundreds of thousands of couples rediscover warm emotional feelings for each other. Now, this did not happen because someone decided, "I'm going to have warm feelings toward my spouse again." It began when one person decided, "I'm going to express love to my spouse *in spite of the fact* that I don't have warm feelings toward him or her." That person learned the love language that spoke most deeply to his or her spouse and spoke it regularly.

What happened? The person who was receiving such love began to have warm feelings toward the spouse who was loving. In time, the recipient reciprocated and learned to speak the other's love language. Now both of them have warm feelings for each other.

Emotional love can be rediscovered. The key is learning your spouse's love language and choosing to speak it regularly. Warm feelings result from loving actions. Jesus commanded his disciples—and, by extension, all believers—to love each other as he loved them. His love is not measured in warm feelings, although I have no doubt those are present. Rather, we know Jesus loves us because of what he did for us. Love is a choice, and when we make that choice, we emulate our Savior.

Lord Jesus, thank you for loving me so much that you died on the cross to save me. You are the ultimate example of love. Please help me to make the choice to love my spouse. As I act lovingly, I know that loving feelings will come.

LOVING THROUGH HURT

You have heard the law that says, "Love your neighbor" and hate your enemy. But I say, love your enemies! Pray for those who persecute you! In that way, you will be acting as true children of your Father in heaven.

MATTHEW 5:43-45

HOW CAN WE EXPRESS love to our spouse when we are full of hurt, anger, and resentment over past failures? The answer to that question lies in the essential nature of our humanity. We are creatures of choice. In the past, both of you have likely made some poor choices. I can hear someone saying, "True, but my spouse has made more poor choices than I have." Perhaps you are right, but remember the words of Jesus: "Love your enemies, bless those who curse you" (Matthew 5:44, NKJV).

Why would Jesus say this? Because love is the most powerful weapon to change the heart of another person. The Bible says, "We love each other because he loved us first" (1 John 4:19). Someone must choose to love, in spite of past failures. When we do that, we're acting the way God acts—or, as Jesus says, acting as "true children of [our] Father in heaven." What a wonderful thought.

When we express love using someone's primary love language, that person is "touched" emotionally. This emotional touch makes it easier for a spouse to admit past failures and to change behavior. Love doesn't erase the past, but it makes the future different.

Father, thank you for loving us even when we didn't love you. Please help me to take that as my model. Give me the courage to love my spouse first, regardless of the failures we've experienced in the past. Transform our relationship and our future.

MEETING EMOTIONAL NEEDS

Husbands ought to love their wives as their own bodies. He who loves his wife loves himself. EPHESIANS 5:28 (NIV)

MEETING MY WIFE'S emotional need for love is a choice I make every day. If I know her primary love language and choose to speak it, her deepest emotional need will be met and she will feel secure in my love. If she does the same for me, my emotional needs are met, and both of us live with a full "love tank."

In this state of emotional contentment, both of us can give our creative energies to many wholesome projects outside the marriage while we continue to keep our relationship exciting and growing.

How do you create this kind of marriage? It all begins with the choice to love. I recognize that as a husband, God has given me the responsibility of meeting my wife's need for love. Paul's words in Ephesians 5 make that clear. I am not only to love my wife, but to love her as I love my own body. That's a tall order, but with the Holy Spirit's help, I choose to accept that responsibility. Then I learn how to speak her primary love language and I choose to speak it regularly. What happens? My wife's attitude and feelings toward me become positive. Now she reciprocates, and my need for love is also met. Love is a choice.

Heavenly Father, you have given us high standards for loving each other. We need your help to make the right choices to love. Please refresh us with your Holy Spirit and rejuvenate our relationship.

SPEAKING ANOTHER'S LOVE LANGUAGE

Let love be your highest goal! 1 CORINTHIANS 14:1

WHAT IF SPEAKING your spouse's love language doesn't come naturally for you? The answer is simple: You *learn* to speak it.

My wife's love language is acts of service. One of the things I do regularly for her as an act of love is to vacuum the house. Do you think that vacuuming floors comes naturally for me? When I was a kid, my mother made me vacuum. On Saturdays, I couldn't play ball until I vacuumed the whole house. In those days, I said to myself, *If I ever get out of here, there's one thing I'm never going to do: vacuum!*

You couldn't pay me enough to vacuum the house. There is only one reason I do it: *love.* You see, when an action doesn't come naturally to you, doing it is a greater expression of love. My wife knows that every time I vacuum the house, it's nothing but 100 percent pure, unadulterated love, and I get credit for the whole thing. The Bible reminds us that love should be our highest goal. We can make it an attainable goal by speaking our spouse's love language, even when it's not our own.

And how do I benefit? I get the pleasure of living with a wife who has a full love tank. What a way to live!

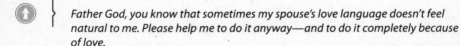

> *Father God, you know that sometimes my spouse's love language doesn't feel natural to me. Please help me to do it anyway—and to do it completely because of love.*

RAISING OUR CHILDREN FOR INDEPENDENCE

The father of godly children has cause for joy. What a pleasure to have children who are wise. PROVERBS 23:24

MOTHER-IN-LAW JOKES ABOUND, but the fact is, if you have children, and if you live long enough, you will likely become a mother-in-law or a father-in-law. I've reached that stage of life, and believe me, it's not that bad. How do we become good in-laws?

It helps to remember our objective in child rearing. From the moment of their birth until their marriage, we have been training our children for independence. We want them to be able to stand on their own two feet and operate as mature people under God. If we've done our job well, we have taught them how to cook meals, wash dishes, make beds, mow the lawn, buy clothes, save money, and make responsible decisions. We have taught them respect for authority and the value of the individual. In short, we have sought to bring them to maturity.

We hope that by the time of their marriage, we have helped them move from a state of complete dependence on us as infants, to complete independence as adults. Once they have arrived at the adult stage, and particularly once they are married, our relationship with them must change. It's a joy to see our children as mature, godly adults—a joy that King Solomon must have shared, as we see in the verse above. We pray for them to reach this point, but when they do, it takes some flexibility and release on our part. In the next days, we'll explore how to make the transition.

Father, thank you for my children. I know that I need to rear them so that one day they will be independent—whether that day is close or still far away. When the time comes, please help me to let go and be a respectful parent of an adult.

BECOMING AN IN-LAW

I could have no greater joy than to hear that my children are following the truth. 3 JOHN 1:4

IF YOUR SON or daughter has married, overnight you have become a mother-in-law or a father-in-law. What do you do now? Let's start with the basics: As parents of married children, we must now view them as adults. We must never again impose our will upon them; we must respect them as equals. Oh, for some of us that's hard. We have been parents for so long, and we think we know what is best for them. We want so much to tell them what they should do.

Resist the urge. If you maintain the parent-child mode of operation, you will become a "thorn in their flesh." You may find your son or daughter pulling away from you or your son- or daughter-in-law becoming hostile.

Rule #1 for in-laws is to treat the young couple as adults. You have reared them to be independent; now let them experience their independence. Will they make some mistakes? Probably, but they will learn maturity in the process. Their attaining maturity is far more important than your keeping them from making a few mistakes. Celebrate their independence.

Lord God, as my children get older, please help me give them the respect they deserve. Teach me when and how to let go. Help us as a couple to love them respectfully.

MAINTAINING STRONG IN-LAW RELATIONSHIPS

Get rid of all bitterness, rage, anger, harsh words, and slander, as well as all types of evil behavior. Instead, be kind to each other, tenderhearted, forgiving one another, just as God through Christ has forgiven you.

EPHESIANS 4:31-32

A NEWLY MARRIED COUPLE needs the emotional warmth that comes from a wholesome relationship with both sets of in-laws, and parents need the emotional warmth that comes from the couple. After all, as parents, we have a large investment in our children. But we're not perfect. Sometimes we say things that hurt. Perhaps we didn't mean it the way our children interpreted it, but the relationship is fractured.

Life is too short to live with broken relationships. Confessing our wrongs and asking for forgiveness are fundamental biblical principles that must be applied to in-law relationships as well as to marriage relationships. We do not have to agree with each other in order to have wholesome relationships, but bitterness and resentment are always wrong, as we see clearly in the passage above from Ephesians 4. As believers, we must take the high road when it comes to relationships with our adult children. Our ideals should be kindness, tenderheartedness, and forgiveness.

Mutual freedom and mutual respect should be the guiding principles for parents and their married children.

Father, so many things can threaten our relationships with our parents or our children. Please help us not to take offense easily. When a wrong is committed, please remind us to be kind and forgiving rather than bitter and angry. I know our family relationships will be better for it.

REINING IN DISTORTED ANGER

Naaman became angry and stalked away. "I thought he would certainly come out to meet me!" he said. "I expected him to wave his hand over the leprosy and call on the name of the LORD his God and heal me!" 2 KINGS 5:11

WE OFTEN GET ANGRY about the wrong things. Take this Bible story as an example: Naaman, a military commander from the country of Aram, had been stricken with leprosy. After traveling to Israel to ask Elisha for healing, he became angry when the prophet of God did not come out to see him and speak to him directly. Instead, Elisha sent word that to be healed, Naaman needed to dip seven times in the Jordan River. Naaman felt disrespected because he didn't think Elisha had acknowledged his importance. In his anger he was ready to go home, until a humble servant suggested that his anger was distorted—out of proportion—and misplaced. Naaman repented, did what the prophet suggested, and was healed.

Naaman's pride had been hurt, and we are all too similar. Often we get angry because something our spouse says or does embarrasses us, or something our spouse fails to do irritates us. A husband whose wife is late coming home may start thinking, *I can't depend on her for anything. She doesn't love me. If she loved me, she would not let this happen. She only thinks of herself.* He may be halfway to divorce court before he realizes that his wife is in the hospital. His anger is distorted.

When you are angry, think before you act. Make sure you have all the facts. Pray for wisdom. You may discover that your anger is distorted.

> *Lord Jesus, forgive me for the times when I get ahead of myself in my anger. Please keep me from distorted anger, and show me how to wait to act until I have the truth.*

INFORMATION, NOT CONDEMNATION

Each of us will give a personal account to God. So let's stop condemning each other. Decide instead to live in such a way that you will not cause another believer to stumble and fall. ROMANS 14:12-13

DISTORTED ANGER is that emotion you experience when your spouse doesn't live up to your expectations. What you do with it can make or break your relationship.

Let's take an example: When Beth and Patrick divided the household chores, they agreed that Beth would take responsibility for the laundry. Today, Patrick is angry because Beth forgot to take his shirts to the dry cleaners. What is he going to do?

He could blast her with harsh words: "I can't depend on you for anything. I've never seen anyone so irresponsible." If he takes this approach, things will get worse. If, however, he says, "Sweetie, I'm frustrated. I saw my dirty shirts still lying on the chair. I don't have a clean shirt for tomorrow," then he may hear her say, "Oh, Patrick, I'm so sorry. I was in a rush and forgot them. Don't worry, honey. I'll make sure you have a clean shirt."

The difference? In one statement Patrick shared condemnation. In the other he shared information: "I'm frustrated and don't have a clean shirt for tomorrow." Sharing information is always better than sharing condemnation—not just because it elicits a better response, but also because it follows the Bible's advice. Romans 14 tells believers to stop condemning each other, because harsh condemnation can cause another believer to stumble. When you answer harshly, you may provoke your spouse to anger or discouragement. Sharing information rarely has those negative effects. Try it the next time you feel like your spouse let you down.

Father, it's easy to condemn my spouse without even thinking, but I've seen firsthand how harmful that can be. Help me to practice sharing information instead. Please smooth over our interactions so that they're not characterized by distorted anger.

HELPFUL WORDS

The lips of the godly speak helpful words. PROVERBS 10:32

DISTORTED ANGER is the kind of anger you feel when the person you love disappoints you. One way to deal with it is something I call "negotiating understanding." If you're feeling anger or hurt, it needs to be processed with your spouse in a positive way.

Here's an example. You might begin by saying, "I want to share something with you that is not designed in any way to put you down. I love you, and I want our relationship to be open and genuine, so I feel that I must share some of the struggles I'm having. Over the past few months, I've sometimes felt hurt, disappointed, and neglected. A lot of it focuses around your going to the gym three nights a week. Please understand that I'm not against your efforts to stay in shape. I'm not even asking you to change that. I just want you to know what I'm feeling. Hopefully we can find an answer together."

Those are helpful words and show that your primary goal is finding a solution, not being right. According to Proverbs 10:32, the godly speak helpful words like this. So when you take this approach, you're acting in a way God approves. Such an open, positive approach creates a setting for the two of you to negotiate understanding and find a growing marriage.

> *Lord God, I want my words to be helpful, not hurtful. As we discuss issues as a couple, please give us the desire to find a solution together. Help me to give up the need to be right.*

EXPRESSING REGRET

I confess my sins; I am deeply sorry for what I have done. PSALM 38:18

THERE ARE MULTIPLE LANGUAGES of apology, and one is *regret*. Apology is birthed in the womb of regret. We regret the pain we have caused, the disappointment, the inconvenience, the betrayal of trust. The offended person wants some evidence that we realize how deeply we have hurt him or her. For some people, this is the one thing they listen for in an apology. Without the expression of regret, they do not sense that the apology is adequate.

A simple "I'm sorry" can go a long way toward restoring goodwill, but that kind of apology has more impact when it is specific. For what are you sorry? "I'm sorry that I was late. I know that you pushed yourself to get here on time and then I was not here. I know how frustrating that can be. I feel really bad that I did this to you. The problem was that I didn't start on time. I hope you can forgive me and we can still have a good evening."

Including details reveals the depth of your understanding of the situation and how much you inconvenienced your spouse. When we confess our sins to God, as in the psalm above, we are usually specific about the wrongs we have committed and sincere in expressing our sorrow. We should extend that kind of apology to our spouse as well.

Father, I know that when my spouse expresses sincere regret, it makes a huge difference in how I perceive his or her apology. Please help me to extend that kind of apology to him or her as well so that we can deal with the wrongs between us.

SHIFTING THE BLAME

"Who told you that you were naked?" the Lord *God asked. "Have you eaten from the tree whose fruit I commanded you not to eat?" The man replied, "It was the woman you gave me who gave me the fruit, and I ate it." Then the* Lord *God asked the woman, "What have you done?" "The serpent deceived me," she replied. "That's why I ate it."* GENESIS 3:11-13

REGRET SAYS, "I'm sorry. I feel badly that I hurt you." Sincere regret needs to stand alone. It should never be followed with "But . . ."

One husband told me, "My wife apologizes, then blames her actions on something I did to provoke her. Blaming me does little to make the apology sincere." A wife said, "He apologized but then added that I was acting like a baby and that he had a right to do what he did. What kind of apology is that?" In my opinion, that is not an apology; it's shifting blame.

Shifting blame is easy to do and dates back to the very first humans, Adam and Eve. In the above passage from Genesis 3, we clearly see both of them trying to absolve themselves of guilt. That's not the mature and godly response—and in their case, God saw right through it and held both of them responsible.

When we shift the blame to the other person, we have moved from apology to attack. Blaming and attacking never lead to forgiveness and reconciliation. When you are apologizing, let "I'm sorry" stand alone. Don't continue by making excuses, such as, *"But* if you had not yelled at me, I would not have done it." Leave the *buts* out of your apology and take responsibility for your own actions.

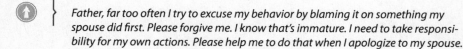

Father, far too often I try to excuse my behavior by blaming it on something my spouse did first. Please forgive me. I know that's immature. I need to take responsibility for my own actions. Please help me to do that when I apologize to my spouse.

REDISCOVERING LOVE

Love is patient and kind. Love is not jealous or boastful or proud or rude. It does not demand its own way. It is not irritable, and it keeps no record of being wronged. It does not rejoice about injustice but rejoices whenever the truth wins out. Love never gives up, never loses faith, is always hopeful, and endures through every circumstance. 1 CORINTHIANS 13:4-7

COUPLES OFTEN COME to me in the midst of marriage difficulty, even at the point of separating. When I ask why they are considering such a step, they share their points of contention and conclude with the statement "We just don't love each other anymore." That is supposed to settle it. They say they have simply "lost" their love, and it's beyond their control. I don't believe that. I'll agree that they may have lost their warm romantic feelings, but real love is another matter.

The Bible makes some strong statements about love within marriage. In Ephesians 5:25, husbands are *commanded* to love their wives. In Titus 2:4, wives are told that they must *learn to love* their husbands. Anything that can be commanded, and anything that can be taught and learned, is not beyond our control.

First Corinthians 13 describes love as being patient and kind, not arrogant or rude. It describes love as refusing to keep a score of wrongs and never holding on to grudges. These words are not describing a feeling. Rather, they are talking about the way we think and behave. We can love each other without having the "tingles" for each other. In fact, the fastest way to see our emotions return is to start loving each other by acting in accordance with the above passage from 1 Corinthians 13.

Heavenly Father, thank you for the beautiful definition of love you gave us through the apostle Paul. It's a challenging one, and sometimes I wonder how I can ever live up to it. Please help me. As I commit to acting on these words, please teach me the right way to love my spouse.

LOVING THROUGH WORDS

Wise words satisfy like a good meal; the right words bring satisfaction. The tongue can bring death or life. PROVERBS 18:20-21

THERE ARE TWO BASIC WAYS to express love in a marriage: words and deeds. Today, we'll look at words. First Corinthians 8:1 says, "Love edifies" (NKJV) or "builds up" (NIV). So if I want to love, I will use words that build up my spouse. "You look nice in that outfit." "Thanks for taking the garbage out." "I loved the meal. Thanks for all your hard work." "I appreciate your walking the dog for me Tuesday night. It was a real help." All of these are expressions of love.

Proverbs 18:21 tells us, "Death and life are in the power of the tongue" (NKJV). Words are powerful. You can kill your spouse's spirit with negative words—words that belittle, disrespect, or embarrass. You can give life with positive words—words that encourage, affirm, or strengthen. I met a woman some time ago who complained that she couldn't think of anything good to say about her husband. I asked, "Does he ever take a shower?" "Yes," she replied. "Then I'd start there," I said. "There are men who don't."

I've never met a person about whom you couldn't find something good to say. And when you say it, something inside the person wants to be better. Say something kind and life giving to your spouse today and see what happens.

> *Lord Jesus, help me to remember that my words are powerful. I want to use them to build up and give life, not to cut down and bring discouragement. Please help me to use my words today to express love to my spouse.*

LOVING THROUGH DEEDS

Dear children, let's not merely say that we love each other; let us show the truth by our actions. 1 JOHN 3:18

IN YESTERDAY'S READING, I suggested that there are two basic ways to express love to your spouse: through words and through deeds. Today we'll look at deeds. As we see in the verse above, the apostle John wrote that we should show our love for each other through actions, not just words. It can be easy to speak words, but our sincerity is proved through what we do. *Do something to show your love.*

Love is kind, the Bible says (see 1 Corinthians 13:4). So to express your love, find something kind and do it. It might be giving him an unexpected gift or washing the car that he drives. It might be offering to stay home with the children while she goes shopping or hiking. Or perhaps it's picking up dinner on the way home when you know she's had a hectic day. How long has it been since you wrote your spouse a love letter?

Love is patient (see 1 Corinthians 13:4). So stop pacing the floor while your spouse is getting ready to go. Sit down, relax, read your Bible, and pray. Love is also courteous. The word means courtlike. So do some of the things you did when you were courting. Reach over and touch his knee or take her hand. Open the door for her. Say please and thank you. Be polite. Express your love by your actions.

Lord, I know that both words and actions are important. Please help me to express my love through the things I say and do. I want to show my spouse how sincere my love is.

EMBRACING DIFFERENCES

The body is a unit, though it is made up of many parts; and though all its parts are many, they form one body. So it is with Christ.

1 CORINTHIANS 12:12 (NIV)

WHAT ARE SOME of the differences between you and your spouse? If you are an optimist, your spouse may be a pessimist. Often, one spouse is quiet; the other is talkative. One tends to be organized with everything in its place; the other spends half a lifetime looking for car keys.

After years of arguing about differences, couples often conclude that they are incompatible. In fact, incompatibility—or "irreconcilable differences"—is often cited as the grounds for divorce. However, after thirty years of counseling married couples, I'm convinced that there are no irreconcilable differences, only people who refuse to reconcile.

In God's mind, our differences are designed to be complementary, not to cause conflicts. The principle is illustrated by the church, as the apostle Paul described in 1 Corinthians 12. Each member performs a different role, yet each is seen as an important part of the body. Believers can accomplish far more when we function as a team. Why can't we get this working in our marriages? It all begins by accepting our differences as an asset rather than a liability. Why not begin by thanking God that you and your spouse aren't exactly alike?

Lord Jesus, thank you for the reminder that your church is stronger because it is made up of many people with different gifts and skills. When I get frustrated with how different my spouse and I are, help me to remember that those differences can make us a better team. Please show us how to celebrate each other's uniqueness.

LEARNING FROM DIFFERENCES

Our bodies have many parts, and God has put each part just where he wants it. How strange a body would be if it had only one part! Yes, there are many parts, but only one body. The eye can never say to the hand, "I don't need you." The head can't say to the feet, "I don't need you." 1 CORINTHIANS 12:18-21

HAVE YOU EVER THANKED God that you and your spouse are very different? Most of the time, we see our differences as irritations. Nathan is by nature a couch potato. His wife, Ashley, is always doing something. In the past, she viewed Nathan as lazy; he viewed her as so nervous she couldn't relax. They often had words over this difference, but most of the time they simply lived with a low-grade resentment toward each other.

Once they discovered that differences were meant to be a blessing and not a curse, they each thanked God for the other. The next step was to ask, "What can we learn from each other?" Ashley learned how to relax and watch a TV show without jumping up to do something else at the same time. Nathan learned to help with the housework so Ashley could have time to relax and not feel guilty. Together they enriched each other's life.

That is what marriage is all about. We are trying to learn how to make the best of our differences. Again, the Bible is clear that the body of Christ benefits from many different people working together. In the church as well as in marriage, we need each other. We can't function without diversity, and that knowledge should lead us to thank God for the differences. Once you've done that, ask him to show each of you what you can learn from the other. You may be surprised at God's answer.

Father, please give me the humility to realize that I can learn from my spouse. Help me to look at our differences as opportunities to grow, not as frustrations. Thank you for making us so different, yet preparing us to fit together perfectly.

ACCEPTING WORTHWHILE ADVICE

"This is not good!" Moses' father-in-law exclaimed.... "This job is too heavy a burden for you to handle all by yourself.... Select from all the people some capable, honest men who fear God and hate bribes. Appoint them as leaders."
... Moses listened to his father-in-law's advice and followed his suggestions.

EXODUS 18:17-18, 21, 24

WHEN WE MARRY, we commit to leaving our parents and cleaving to our spouse. But leaving parents does not mean that we will not consider their suggestions. After all, our parents are older than we are, and perhaps wiser. Your parents or in-laws may have some good advice.

In the book of Exodus, we see that Moses was an overworked administrator until he took the advice of his father-in-law. Jethro observed Moses spending hours judging all the Israelites' disagreements and suggested that Moses was on the fast track to burnout. When he shared the principle of *delegation*, Moses said to himself, *Why didn't I think of that?* That night he talked with his wife about the idea and the next day posted a sign outside his office: *Help Wanted.* Well, not exactly. But he did appoint several managers, to whom he delegated much of his work. It was one of the best decisions Moses ever made, and he got the idea from his father-in-law.

In following Jethro's advice, Moses demonstrated his own maturity. He did not feel compelled to rebel against a good idea simply because it came from his father-in-law. He didn't feel the need to prove his own intelligence. Rather, he was secure enough in his own self-worth that he could accept a good idea, regardless of its source. I hope that you will be as wise as Moses.

Lord Jesus, thank you for the wisdom and experience you have given my parents and my parents-in-law. You know how easy it is for me to discount their suggestions. When they give good advice, please show me how to accept it graciously.

DEALING WITH CONFLICTS INSIDE THE MARRIAGE

If another believer sins against you, go privately and point out the offense.

MATTHEW 18:15

THE PRINCIPLE OF "LEAVING" parents has implications when conflicts arise in a marriage. A young wife who has always leaned heavily on her mother will have a tendency to "run to Mom" when problems arise in her marriage. Any time a conflict arises, she confides in Mom. When this becomes a pattern, before long, her mother has a bitter attitude toward the son-in-law that wreaks havoc on the young couple's relationship. In an extreme case, she may even encourage the daughter to leave her husband.

Remember that "cleaving" to your mate applies in times of conflict as well as in times of peace. If you have conflicts in your marriage—and most of us do—seek to solve them by direct confrontation with your mate. Jesus instructed his disciples that if another believer hurt them, they should go directly to that person. The same principle holds true in marriage. Your first instinct needs to be dealing directly and only with your spouse. Conflict should be a stepping-stone to growth.

If you find that you need outside help, then go to your pastor or a Christian marriage counselor. They are trained and equipped by God to give practical help. They can be objective and help you make wise decisions. By contrast, parents tend to see their own child's side and find it almost impossible to be objective.

Father, when I have a conflict with my spouse, I so often want to pour out my side of the story to someone who will be sympathetic to me. But help me to remember that conflicts in our marriage need to remain between us. I pray for grace to handle the issues that arise.

FOSTERING ONENESS

I want [believers] to be encouraged and knit together by strong ties of love.

COLOSSIANS 2:2

THE SCRIPTURES INDICATE that husbands and wives are to become "one" (see Genesis 2:24). They are to share life to such a degree that they have a sense of unity, or togetherness. In the verse above, the apostle Paul states his vision for believers: that they would be "knit together" or "united in love" (NIV). This is critical for all believers and even more so for marriage partners. Would you describe your marriage like this?

- ⤳ "We are a team."

- ⤳ "We know each other."

- ⤳ "We understand each other."

- ⤳ "We choose to walk in step with each other."

- ⤳ "Our lives are inseparably bound together."

- ⤳ "We are one."

These are the statements of happily married couples. Such togetherness does not happen without a lot of communication. Communication is a two-way street. I talk and you listen; you talk and I listen. It is this simple process that develops understanding and togetherness.

How much time do you spend in conversation with your spouse each day? Do you have a daily sharing time? How consistent are you in keeping this appointment? In the next few devotions, we'll explore ways to enhance communication and increase oneness.

Lord Jesus, I know you desire us to be united as a couple. I pray that we will grow in togetherness, in teamwork, in understanding, and in our sense of oneness. Please show us how to do that.

BECOMING ONE

As the deer longs for streams of water, so I long for you, O God. I thirst for God, the living God. When can I go and stand before him? PSALM 42:1-2

AFTER THE CREATION of Adam and Eve, God said that the two should become one. Becoming "one" does not mean that we lose our personal identities. We retain our personalities, and we still have personal goals and ambitions. We each have our own pursuits; the typical husband and wife spend many hours each day geographically separated from each other. Marital "oneness" is not sameness. It is rather that inner feeling that assures us that we are "together" even when we are apart.

Such oneness is not automatic. Becoming "one" is the result of many shared thoughts, feelings, activities, dreams, frustrations, joys, and sorrows. In short, it is the result of sharing life.

Many couples have found that the secret to growing in oneness is establishing a daily sharing time. Many people have a daily "quiet time" with God for the purpose of getting close to him. As the author of Psalm 42 conveys so beautifully, when we're strong in our relationship with God, we long for him and desire to be near him. It's a bit circular. When we know God, we desire to spend time with him. If we spend time with him, we begin to desire him more. The same thing can be true with our spouse. The more we set aside time to spend together, the more important it becomes to us.

I encourage you to consider having a daily sharing time with your spouse for the purpose of staying close to each other. Set aside time each day to talk and to share your thoughts, emotions, and concerns. Conversation leads to understanding and unity.

Father, I want to long for you as a deer longs for water. And in the same way, I desire a deeper connection with my spouse. Please help me to remember that connection and oneness come with time and effort. Please bless our efforts to set aside time for each other.

GETTING TO KNOW YOU

O Lord, you have searched me and you know me. You know when I sit and when I rise; you perceive my thoughts from afar. PSALM 139:1-2 (NIV)

PSALM 139 MAKES CLEAR that God knows our every thought and even our words before we speak them. The Lord knows us—effortlessly—better than we know ourselves. But it takes effort for a man and woman to know each other. Do you see then why communication is an absolute necessity if we are to understand our spouse?

We cannot know our spouse's thoughts, feelings, or desires unless he or she chooses to tell us and we choose to listen. That is why a daily sharing time is so important in a marriage. We cannot develop a sense of "togetherness" unless we talk regularly with each other.

A daily sharing time is a time set aside each day for the purpose of talking and listening. If you're unsure what to talk about, try this: "Tell me three things that happened in your life today and how you feel about them." It can start with ten minutes and may extend to thirty or longer. The key is not the length but the consistency. I have never seen a truly successful marriage that did not *make* time for communication.

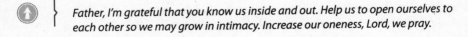

Father, I'm grateful that you know us inside and out. Help us to open ourselves to each other so we may grow in intimacy. Increase our oneness, Lord, we pray.

SEEKING COMPANIONSHIP

Two people are better off than one, for they can help each other succeed. If one person falls, the other can reach out and help. But someone who falls alone is in real trouble. ECCLESIASTES 4:9-10

MARRIAGE WAS DESIGNED by God to meet man's need for companionship. God said of Adam, "It is not good for the man to be alone. I will make a helper who is just right for him" (Genesis 2:18). However, some couples have not found companionship in marriage. They are still alone, cut off, and isolated.

Such loneliness may be painful, but it is doesn't have to last forever. We can overcome loneliness by taking positive action. I suggest taking "baby steps." Don't look at the whole and think about how bad your marriage is. Rather, focus on one step you might take to make it better.

Break through the silence with one act of kindness. Give her a flower, and say, "I was thinking about you today." Look for something he does well, and tell him you appreciate it. Give him a passionate kiss, and say, "I just wanted to remind you of what it was like when we first married. I'm willing to start over if you are." Remember that the Bible is clear about the benefits of companionship, as we read in the book of Ecclesiastes. We are made for each other, and we can support each other in innumerable ways. Keep taking steps toward each other, and loneliness will evaporate.

Father, you know how lonely I feel sometimes. Thank you for giving me my spouse, and thank you for creating us to be companions who can help each other and relieve each other's loneliness. Please give us the courage to take those first steps toward closer companionship.

LONELINESS IN MARRIAGE

Two people lying close together can keep each other warm. But how can one be warm alone? A person standing alone can be attacked and defeated, but two can stand back-to-back and conquer. ECCLESIASTES 4:11-12

THERE ARE TWO TYPES of loneliness: emotional and social. We can experience both of these, even in marriage.

Emotional loneliness is not feeling close to your spouse. You feel like you and your mate don't really know each other. *Social loneliness* is the feeling of isolation that comes when you and your spouse have no shared activities. You don't do anything together.

The cure to emotional loneliness comes not from cursing the darkness but from initiating conversation. Start with simple questions: "Did you eat anything exciting today?" "What was the best moment of your day?" Move to more important questions: "When you think of the future, what could I do to enhance your life?"

The cure to social loneliness is to initiate activities together. Rather than complaining that you don't ever do anything together, plan something that you think your spouse would enjoy and invite him or her to join you. Positive action is always better than negative complaints. The journey of a thousand miles begins with one step—and it is a worthwhile journey. As the book of Ecclesiastes reminds us, there are many reasons why two are better than one. Embrace that concept and seek out deeper companionship with your spouse.

Lord God, I am encouraged by these ideas of things to do to combat the loneliness I feel. Help me to initiate conversations and activities that will bring my spouse and me closer together. I want to take the first step. Thank you for creating us to be companions.

ARE YOU WORKING TOO HARD?

What do you benefit if you gain the whole world but lose your own soul?
Is anything worth more than your soul? MATTHEW 16:26

WORK IS A NOBLE ENDEAVOR. In fact, the Bible says that if a man will not work, neither should he eat (see 2 Thessalonians 3:10).

But can we work too much? Did not God institute the Sabbath, a day of rest every seven days? The Ten Commandments instruct that the seventh day of the week should be a day set apart from regular work and dedicated to the Lord. Why? In imitation of God himself, who rested on the seventh day after creating the universe. Jesus also challenged his disciples in the passage above by asking them to weigh worldly success with spiritual success. "What do you benefit if you gain the whole world but lose your own soul?"

Is vocational success worth losing a marriage? The Scriptures teach that life's meaning is not found in things but in relationships—first, with God, and second, with family and others. This is where life finds real meaning: knowing God and loving family.

Is it possible that you need to readjust your lifestyle? Are you and your spouse growing apart? Could you live with less and be happier if you had more time for each other? Will your children remember you as the parent who worked or the parent who loved?

Lord God, please help me to consider honestly the balance in my life. Am I working so hard for financial or vocational success that I'm ignoring my relationships with you and my family? Help me to find the right priorities—and to have the courage to act on them.

BALANCING WORK AND FAMILY

Live happily with the woman you love through all the . . . days of life that God has given you under the sun. The wife God gives you is your reward for all your earthly toil. ECCLESIASTES 9:9

WHEN WE TALK about work and family and how to balance the two, the answer is not always less work. Sometimes it is integrating the family into your work. For example, does your job allow the opportunity for you and your spouse to have lunch together from time to time? Such lunches can be an oasis in the midst of a dry day.

If your job requires travel, could you take your spouse or one of your children with you? This allows a mini-vacation that you might not otherwise be able to afford. It also exposes your family to your vocation and gives them a little more appreciation for what you do.

Less work and more time at home is not necessarily the answer. Better use of time at home may make all the difference. Do something different tonight with a family member. Get out of the routine. Take initiative.

Such actions say, "I care about this relationship. I want to keep it alive. I enjoy being with you. Let's do something you would like to do." Minimize the television; maximize activity and conversation. According to Ecclesiastes 9:9, the Bible says your spouse is a gift. Hard work is a necessary part of life, but a marriage partner is a reward and a blessing. When you remember that and prioritize accordingly, you will keep your marriage alive and growing.

Lord Jesus, I'm grateful for the gift of my spouse. Please help me to make him or her a priority. Show me creative ways to increase my time with him or her, and ways to make that time meaningful.

HOW *NOT* TO RESPOND TO A CONTROLLING SPOUSE

Respect everyone, and love your Christian brothers and sisters. 1 PETER 2:17

AN OVERLY CONTROLLING SPOUSE is the cause of many a troubled marriage. Living with a controlling spouse kills the spirit. When one spouse treats the other as a child, that person has violated the basic idea of marriage. Marriage is a partnership that must be built on mutual respect. That's a basic building block of any relationship. Two are better than one, the Bible says. But when one makes all the decisions alone, the value of two minds is wasted.

There are two typical ways to respond to a controlling spouse: to argue or to submit. Neither leads to genuine unity. Arguing with a controller is useless because you cannot win. You can extend the argument for two hours, but you will not win; a controlling person will not give in. As an alternative to arguing, some have chosen the road of submission. They think, *I'll go along with my spouse just to keep the peace.* But this renders the person a slave to the controller's demands, and slaves eventually rebel. External peace with internal turmoil is not the biblical idea of marriage.

The biblical idea is two people willingly seeking to meet each other's needs. Mutual love, respect, and consideration are the marks of a Christian marriage. Tomorrow we'll look at a more effective way to respond to a controlling spouse.

Father God, I want our relationship to honor you. Please show me the best way to respond to my spouse when he or she tries to exert too much control, and guard me from trying to control him or her. Help us to be respectful and considerate toward each other always.

COUNTERACTING CONTROL

If you have a gift for showing kindness to others, do it gladly. Don't just pretend to love others. Really love them. Hate what is wrong. Hold tightly to what is good. Love each other with genuine affection, and take delight in honoring each other. ROMANS 12:8-10

CAN A CONTROLLING SPOUSE be influenced to change? The answer is yes. But the approach may surprise you. You don't influence a controller by arguing, nor by submitting silently. Rather, you influence by giving credit for the person's intentions but refusing to be controlled by the person's decisions.

Let's say that without asking your opinion, your husband has bought a new refrigerator. Your response is to feel that your ideas don't matter and that he is treating you like a child. What are you going to do? I suggest that you say to your spouse, "I really appreciate your efforts to help me by getting the new refrigerator. I'm sure you researched it carefully and probably got a good deal on it. However, I wish you had asked for my opinion, since I'm the one who uses it most often. I'd be happy to go with you to select a new refrigerator. So do you want to call the company and ask them not to deliver the one you bought, or do you want me to call?" If he storms off in anger and says he won't call, don't argue with him. The next day, you call the company and make another selection.

Will he change his controlling patterns immediately? Probably not, but eventually, kindness and firmness will lead to change. Follow the advice of the apostle Paul, and focus on kindness, genuine love, and honor. Concentrate on what's good. This kind of treatment will likely foster change in your spouse.

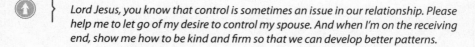

Lord Jesus, you know that control is sometimes an issue in our relationship. Please help me to let go of my desire to control my spouse. And when I'm on the receiving end, show me how to be kind and firm so that we can develop better patterns.

HELPING CHILDREN FEEL LOVED

Always be humble and gentle. Be patient with each other, making allowance for each other's faults because of your love. EPHESIANS 4:2

DO YOUR CHILDREN feel loved? I didn't ask, "Do you love your children?" I know the answer to that. But if you want to make sure your children *feel* loved, it is not enough to be sincere. You also need to speak your child's love language.

For some children, quality time is their primary love language. If you don't give them quality time, they will not feel loved, even if you are giving them words of affirmation, physical touch, gifts, and acts of service. If your children are begging you to do things with them, then quality time is likely their love language. It's easy to get frustrated with the endless requests, but we need to respond with gentleness and patience, as Ephesians 4 reminds us. Bear with your kids, make allowance for their faults, and look for the need behind their behavior. Give them some focused attention, and watch their behavior change.

Lord, you know how much I love my children. I want them to feel that love. Please give me the wisdom to communicate it the best way possible. Help me to have patience when they're asking for something and to see it as a signal for what they really need.

EMOTIONS VS. ACTIONS

*Keep your servant from deliberate sins! Don't let them control me. Then I will
be free of guilt and innocent of great sin. May the words of my mouth and the
meditation of my heart be pleasing to you, O LORD, my rock and my redeemer.*

PSALM 19:13-14

HOW DO EMOTIONS impact a marriage? Emotions are God's gift to enrich
life. Both positive and negative emotions should point us to God. Some Christians have come to distrust emotions because they have seen people who
follow their feelings and hurt everyone around them. But there is a vast difference between an emotion and a decision to do something wrong. Feelings
themselves are not sinful, but the actions people take based on their feelings
often are. In Psalm 19, King David asked God to keep him from deliberate or
"willful" sins (NIV) so that he could be counted innocent. Emotions are not
deliberate; they come on their own. It's what we do with them that can be
right or wrong.

Let's take an example: Even if you're happily married, you may feel an
exciting "tingle" toward a member of the opposite sex who is not your spouse.
The attraction is not sinful, but your actions may be. Take the "tingles" to God.
Thank him for giving you the capacity to experience this emotion, and ask
him to give you wisdom for how to reignite excitement in your marriage so
you can experience it in the proper place. The attraction for someone else is
an indicator that your marriage needs attention.

Let your emotions point you to God. Seek his direction. When you follow his instructions, the emotion has served its highest goal. Emotions are
designed to draw us to God.

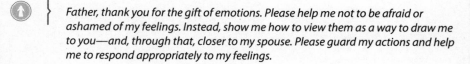

*Father, thank you for the gift of emotions. Please help me not to be afraid or
ashamed of my feelings. Instead, show me how to view them as a way to draw me
to you—and, through that, closer to my spouse. Please guard my actions and help
me to respond appropriately to my feelings.*

ADMITTING NEGATIVE EMOTIONS

Laughter can conceal a heavy heart, but when the laughter ends, the grief remains. PROVERBS 14:13

SOME CHRISTIANS DON'T WANT to accept the fact that they have negative emotions. Anger, fear, disappointment, loneliness, frustration, depression, and sorrow don't fit the stereotype of successful Christian living. We often try to push negative emotions to the back burner and ignore them. That doesn't work very well, as King Solomon noted. We can ignore our negative feelings, but that doesn't make them go away. In fact, ignoring them can actually intensify them.

I believe that it is far more productive to identify and accept our emotions and then seek God's direction regarding what we are feeling. Feelings are like thermometers. They report whether we are hot or cold, whether all is well or not so well. If all is well, we can celebrate by praising God. (There are many biblical examples of this; see Psalm 103 for one.) If emotions indicate that all is not well, we can turn to God for help. (Again, see the Psalms for vivid examples of King David and others bringing strong feelings to God. Psalm 13 is one example.) God will give us wisdom if we need to take action. He can give us comfort if the situation cannot be changed. Always, we should share our emotions with God and seek his guidance.

"Lord, this is how I feel. Now, what do you want me to do about it?" This approach will lead to more insight about yourself, more empathy for your spouse, and more wisdom in your decisions. All this contributes to a growing marriage.

Lord, I am grateful for the Psalms, which show so clearly that you welcome us to express our emotions to you—whether positive or negative. Please help me to do that freely, rather than bottling up my sadness or anger. As you give me comfort and guidance, I know I will act more wisely, and that will benefit my relationship with my spouse.

SETTING ASIDE TIME FOR CONFLICTS

Better a dry crust eaten in peace than a house filled with feasting—and conflict.

PROVERBS 17:1

DO YOU EVER FEEL like you are married to an alien? Early in your relationship you thought you were so compatible. In fact, you agreed on everything. Now perhaps you wonder how you ever got together, because you are so different. Welcome to the world of reality. The fact is, you are married to a human. Humans don't all think the same way and don't all feel the same way. In short, all human relationships include conflicts. The key is to learn constructive methods for reaching resolution when a conflict arises.

Want to solve your conflicts? Here's an idea. Never discuss disagreements "on the run." Rather, set aside time specifically for resolving conflict. I suggest that once a week you have a "conflict resolution session." The rest of the week, try to focus on the things you like about each other. Make positive comments about your spouse. This creates a healthy climate in which to discuss your conflicts.

When you set aside time to deal with conflict, you avoid having your house continually filled with angry words or frustration—a situation King Solomon clearly found unpalatable, based on what we read above. When you allow room for peace, you will work through your conflicts one by one without destroying your relationship. Every resolved conflict brings you and your loved one closer together.

Heavenly Father, I know that conflict between people is inevitable. Please help us to deal with our differences in a way that's helpful, respectful, and deliberate. We want our home to be a place of peace, not a place of continual conflict.

WISE LISTENING

If you listen to constructive criticism, you will be at home among the wise. If you reject discipline, you only harm yourself; but if you listen to correction, you grow in understanding. PROVERBS 15:31-32

FOR THIRTY YEARS, I've been counseling couples and leading marriage-enrichment seminars. I've never met a couple who didn't have conflicts. I've met some who knew how to resolve conflicts, and I've met many who allowed conflicts to destroy their marriage.

In yesterday's devotion, I shared the idea of setting aside time each week for a "conflict resolution session." When you sit down to discuss a conflict, take turns talking. Start with five minutes each. You can have as many turns as needed, but don't interrupt each other with your own ideas. Wait for your turn. According to King Solomon, listening to others—particularly if they have constructive criticism to share with us—makes us wise. When we listen to our spouse, especially in the midst of conflict, we will gain more understanding of ourselves and each other.

You may ask questions to help you understand what your spouse is saying. For example, "Are you saying that you feel disappointed when I play golf on Saturday instead of spending time with you and the children? Are you saying that you would prefer that I not play golf at all?"

After listening, you then have your turn to talk. In this example, you might explain how important golf is to your mental health. Then together you can look for a solution that both of you agree is workable. Listening and seeking to understand each other is crucial in resolving conflicts.

Father, I want to be wise. Please help me to respond the right way when my spouse tells me something I don't necessarily want to hear. Help me to think about what is best for our relationship, not just about my own needs.

FINDING A SOLUTION

I praise you because I am fearfully and wonderfully made; your works are wonderful, I know that full well. PSALM 139:14 (NIV)

ALL COUPLES HAVE CONFLICTS because we are human. Humans are all unique. We all see the world differently. The common mistake is to try to force my spouse to see the world the way I see it. "If she would just think, I know she would agree with me. My way makes sense." The problem is that what makes sense to one person does not always make sense to another. Precision is fine in math and science, but it does not exist in human relationships. As Psalm 139 makes clear, the Lord has made each one of us unique. He formed us and knew us even before we were born. We need to celebrate those differences, not let them frustrate us. We must allow for differences in human perceptions and desires.

Resolving conflicts requires that we treat our spouse's ideas and feelings with respect, not condemnation. The purpose is not to prove our spouse wrong but to find a "meeting of the minds"—a place where the two of us can work together as a team. We don't have to agree in order to resolve a conflict. We simply have to find a workable solution to our differences.

"What would be workable for you?" is a good place to begin. Now we are focusing on resolution rather than differences. Two adults looking for a solution are likely to find one.

Father, this question—What would be workable for you?—is eye opening. How often I waste time trying to convince my spouse that my way is right. Please help me instead to join with him or her in looking for a solution that works for both of us. Thank you for making us both unique.

CREATING SPIRITUAL INTIMACY

Share each other's burdens, and in this way obey the law of Christ.

GALATIANS 6:2

MOST OF THE COUPLES I meet wish that they could share more freely with each other about their spiritual journey. We often speak of emotional intimacy or sexual intimacy, but we seldom talk about spiritual intimacy. Yet this affects all other areas of our relationship.

Just as emotional intimacy comes from sharing our feelings, spiritual intimacy comes from sharing our walk with God. We don't have to be spiritual giants to have spiritual intimacy as a couple, but we must be willing to share with each other where we are spiritually.

The husband who says, "I'm not feeling very close to God today" may not stimulate great joy in his wife's heart, but he does open the possibility for her to enter into his spiritual experience. If she responds with, "Tell me about it," she encourages spiritual intimacy. If, however, she says, "Well, if you don't feel close to God, guess who moved?" she has stopped the flow, and he walks away feeling condemned. The apostle Paul challenged us to share each other's burdens, and those often include feelings of spiritual dryness or difficulty. Spiritual intimacy within a marriage requires a willingness to listen without preaching.

Father, I want to be able to talk with my spouse about my walk with you—and I want to hear about his or her experiences too. Please help us to be kind as we listen to each other and share each other's burdens. Develop spiritual intimacy in us, I pray.

MODELING SPIRITUAL HUNGER

When we get together, I want to encourage you in your faith, but I also want to be encouraged by yours. ROMANS 1:12

HOW DO YOU DEVELOP spiritual intimacy in your relationship? One wife said to me, "I wish that my husband and I could share more about spiritual things. He seems willing to talk about everything else, but when I mention church, God, or the Bible, he clams up and walks away. I don't know what to do, but it's very frustrating." What advice would you give this wife?

Here's what I said: "Don't ever stop talking about spiritual things. Your relationship with God is the most important part of your life. If you don't share this part of yourself, your husband will never know who you are. However, don't expect him to reciprocate, and don't preach him a sermon until he asks for one. Simply share what God is doing in your life. Share a Scripture that helped you make a decision or encouraged you when you were feeling down.

"When you share what your spiritual life is like, you stimulate hunger. When your husband gets spiritually hungry, he will likely want to discuss things with you. At that point, spiritual intimacy will begin."

Encouraging each other in our faith is a valuable goal. Even the apostle Paul wanted to be encouraged by seeing the faith of the Roman believers. When we reach the point of sharing our spiritual successes and struggles, our marriage will be blessed.

> *Father, please help me to be patient with my spouse when he or she does not want to discuss spiritual things. I pray that you would work in our hearts and bring us closer together in this area. Develop our relationships with you as well as our spiritual intimacy with each other.*

ACHIEVING ACTIVE LISTENING

Listen closely to what I am about to say. Hear me out. JOB 13:17

HAS YOUR SPOUSE ever complained, "I just feel like you're not listening to me when I talk"? Quality conversation requires active listening. As we read the book of Job, we see the suffering Job increasingly frustrated with his would-be comforters. Each time they respond, it becomes clear to him that they did not really comprehend what he said. Finally he erupts with, "Hear me out!" That is one frustration you don't want your spouse to share.

Let me offer some suggestions for how to listen effectively.

- Maintain eye contact when your spouse is talking. This keeps your mind from wandering and communicates that your spouse has your full attention.

- Drop all other activities when your spouse is talking. I know that it may be possible for you to watch TV and listen to your spouse at the same time, but the message your spouse is getting is that what he is saying is not very important.

- Listen for feelings and reflect what you hear. "It sounds like you are feeling disappointed because I forgot to take the garbage out this morning." Now your spouse knows that you are listening, and she can go on to clarify her feelings and desires.

- Observe body language. Clenched fists, trembling hands, and tears may give you insight into how strongly your spouse feels about what he or she is saying. The stronger the feeling, the more important it is that you give your spouse your undivided attention.

Lord Jesus, I know I need to listen to my spouse more carefully. I want to communicate that I really understand and that the words I hear are important to me. Please help me today to listen with love and care.

BUILDING INTIMACY THROUGH LISTENING

"You will seek me and find me when you seek me with all your heart. I will be found by you," declares the LORD. JEREMIAH 29:13-14 (NIV)

WHAT ARE THE REWARDS of listening to your spouse? Listening is the doorway into your spouse's heart and mind. God told Israel, "I know the plans I have for you. . . . They are plans for good and not for disaster, to give you a future and a hope" (Jeremiah 29:11). But how was Israel to know what was on God's heart and in God's mind? Verses 13 and 14 make it clear that they would discover the Lord when they sought him wholeheartedly. God wanted Israel to know his thoughts, but Israel had to listen.

What are you doing to seek to know the thoughts and feelings of your spouse? Listening is the key to good communication. Don't condemn your spouse for not talking more. Rather, ask questions, and then listen to the answers. They may be short at first, especially if your spouse is not the talkative type. But once your spouse realizes that you are truly interested, she will eventually share her thoughts. Accept your spouse's thoughts as interesting, challenging, or fascinating and he will talk more.

Listening to God brings you close to his heart. Listening to your spouse brings you the same kind of intimacy.

Heavenly Father, I'm so grateful for your promise that when we seek you wholeheartedly, we will find you. Please help me to devote the same kind of effort to "seeking" and knowing my spouse. Show me how to listen carefully to his or her thoughts and to value them. May this strengthen our relationship.

CAREFUL LISTENING

[Jesus said,] "To those who listen to my teaching, more understanding will be given, and they will have an abundance of knowledge." MATTHEW 13:12

YOU CANNOT OVERESTIMATE the importance of listening to your spouse. Listening says, "I value you and our relationship. I want to know you." You can never have an intimate marriage if you don't know your spouse.

Respecting the other person's ideas, even when they differ from your own, is essential to communication. Few people will continue to communicate if their thoughts are always condemned. Also, responding too quickly gets in the way of effective listening. Listen twice as much as you talk, and you will know your spouse much better. Jesus told his disciples in Matthew 13:12 that listening brings knowledge. The more we listen and the better we listen, the more we understand. That's certainly true of Jesus' teachings, but it also applies to conversations with our spouse.

If your spouse starts talking, take it as a "holy moment." The one you love is about to reveal something. When your spouse begins to reveal his or her inner self, don't do anything to stop the flow. Drop everything else and focus on listening. Nod sympathetically. Smile if your spouse says something funny. Let your eyes show concern if your spouse expresses pain. Ask questions to make sure you're getting the message. Good, active listening stimulates communication.

Lord, I want to listen well to my spouse and gain more and more understanding of this person I love. I know that needs to start with valuing the times when he or she shares thoughts and feelings with me. Please give me the self-discipline to be an active, alert listener so our communication will be stronger and stronger.

WISDOM FOR WIVES

Who can find a virtuous and capable wife? She is more precious than rubies. Her husband can trust her, and she will greatly enrich his life. She brings him good, not harm, all the days of her life. . . . When she speaks, her words are wise, and she gives instructions with kindness. PROVERBS 31:10-12, 26

WHAT'S A WIFE TO DO when her husband refuses to "get with the program"? You have asked him again and again to change. You've told him exactly what you want, but he doesn't budge. So what are you to do?

Let me suggest that you take a different approach. Since he isn't changing, start with yourself. Look carefully at your own behavior and ask yourself, *What have I been doing that I should not be doing? What have I been saying that I should not be saying?* Your answers may include trying to control him, speaking unkindly, or harboring bitterness. Once you've identified them, confess these things to God and then to your husband. Even if your husband is 95 percent of the problem, the place for you to start is with your 5 percent. After all, you *can* change that, and when you do, your marriage will be 5 percent better.

Consider this approach from a wife who tends to treat her husband like hired help: "It was unfair of me to ask you to get rid of that tree stump right after you mowed the lawn. I know I've piled tasks on you before, and I'm sorry. I want you to know that I appreciate the work you did this morning." Whatever his initial response, she has just changed the climate of her marriage.

Strive to be a wife who, like the famous "Proverbs 31 woman," speaks wisely, kindly, and brings good to her husband.

Heavenly Father, please forgive me for the wrong things I have done in my marriage. I sometimes get frustrated with my husband's actions, but I forget that I contribute to the problems in our relationship as well. Please help me to admit my part and start by changing myself. May I bring good to my husband.

WISDOM FOR HUSBANDS

Husbands ought to love their wives as they love their own bodies. For a man who loves his wife actually shows love for himself. EPHESIANS 5:28

WANT TO HAVE a more loving wife? Before criticizing her for all her faults, remember that criticism rarely works to effect positive change. But here are some ideas that do.

First, find something you like about her and express your appreciation. Do it again two days later, and then do it again. When you develop a pattern of compliments, you may be pleasantly surprised with the results.

Second, speak kindly. Don't allow your emotions to dictate your tone of voice. If you have something to say, even if it involves negative feelings, say it as kindly as possible. Remember that the Bible says, "A gentle answer deflects anger, but harsh words make tempers flare" (Proverbs 15:1). Don't stir up anger unnecessarily.

Third, don't give orders. Demands create resentment. Instead of saying, "I want this done today," try asking, "Is there any chance that you could work this into your schedule today? I'd really appreciate it if you can." The way you talk to your wife makes all the difference in the world.

Above all, remember that your responsibility is to love your wife as you love your own body. That means caring for her and treating her respectfully, no matter how she acts or how she responds to you. Let love be your goal, and everything else will fall into place.

Father, loving my wife as I love my own body is a huge challenge that sometimes seems insurmountable. I want to learn more about how to do that. Please help me grow in the way I treat my wife, so that our marriage may become stronger and more intimate.

GIVING LOVE

Love each other with genuine affection, and take delight in honoring each other. ROMANS 12:10

THE DESIRE FOR ROMANTIC LOVE is deeply rooted in our psychological makeup. Almost every popular magazine has at least one article on keeping love alive. So why is it that so few couples seem to have found the secret to a lasting love *after* the wedding? I'm convinced it's because we concentrate on "getting love" rather than "giving love."

As long as you focus on what your spouse should be doing for you, you'll come across as condemning and critical. How about a different approach— one that says, "What can I do to help *you*? How can I make *your* life easier? How can I be a better spouse?" In Romans 12, Paul writes that when we love each other, we should "take delight in honoring each other." Giving to the one we love does not have to be a chore; if our affection is genuine, giving and serving can be a joy. *Giving* love will keep your relationship alive.

> *Father, help me to concentrate on giving love today. May I focus less on what my spouse can give me, and more on what I can give to him or her. Thanks for being the ultimate example of selfless, giving love.*

SEEKING RECONCILIATION

Seek the LORD while you can find him. Call on him now while he is near. Let the wicked change their ways and banish the very thought of doing wrong. Let them turn to the LORD that he may have mercy on them. Yes, turn to our God, for he will forgive generously. ISAIAH 55:6-7

IS THE MARRIAGE OVER if your spouse walks out? The answer is an emphatic *no.* Marital separation means that the marriage needs help. The biblical ideal calls for reconciliation. You may not feel like reconciling, and you may see no hope for reunion. The process may frighten you, but may I challenge you to follow the example of God himself?

Throughout the Bible, God is pictured as having a love relationship with his people—Israel in the Old Testament and the church in the New Testament. On many occasions, God found himself separated from his people because of their sin and stubbornness. In a sense, the entire Bible is a record of God's attempts to be reconciled to his people. Note that God always pleaded for reconciliation on the basis of correcting sinful behavior. Never did God agree to reconcile while Israel continued in sin. In the passage above, the prophet Isaiah passionately called people to turn away from their sins and toward the Lord. God was near, and his forgiveness was available.

There can be no reconciliation without repentance. In a marriage, that means mutual repentance, because the failure has involved both parties. Dealing with your own failures is the first step in seeking reconciliation.

Father, I am thankful for your example of calling for loving reconciliation. I confess my own sins in my marriage. Help me to deal with those first as I seek reconciliation with my spouse.

BELIEVING IN RESTORATION

Now all glory to God, who is able, through his mighty power at work within us, to accomplish infinitely more than we might ask or think. EPHESIANS 3:20

SEPARATION MEANS that the marriage is in trouble. Your dreams of making each other happy have been shattered. The lack of fulfillment you experienced before separation probably came from one of three sources: (1) lack of an intimate relationship with God, (2) lack of an intimate relationship with your mate, or (3) lack of an intimate understanding and acceptance of yourself. The first and last of these can be corrected without the help of your spouse. The second, of course, requires the cooperation of both husband and wife.

Radical change in all three areas is very possible. If you will begin working on your relationship with God and on developing a better understanding of yourself, you will be working on the reconciliation of your marriage—even if your spouse is not actively involved at this point.

Let a pastor, counselor, or Christian friend help you take a fresh look at God and yourself. Move toward God and seek his help in understanding your role in restoring your relationship with your spouse. Change yourself, and you open the door to the possibility of reconciliation. The apostle Paul tells us in Ephesians 3 that God can do more than we can ask or even think. He can restore your marriage.

> *Father, thank you for reminding me of the steps I can take toward reconciliation, even if my spouse isn't walking in that direction right now. I want to know you more, and I want to know myself better. Please guide me as I try to figure these things out.*

(If you are not separated, pray for a friend who is.)

SHOWING LOVE THROUGH SERVICE

Whenever we have the opportunity, we should do good to everyone—especially to those in the family of faith. GALATIANS 6:10

FOR SOME PEOPLE, actions speak louder than words. Acts of service is probably the primary love language of these people. It's what makes them feel loved. The words "I love you" may seem shallow to these folks if they are not accompanied by acts of service.

Mowing the grass, cooking a meal, washing dishes, vacuuming the floor, getting hairs out of the sink, removing the white spots from the mirror, getting bugs off the windshield, taking out the garbage, changing the baby's diaper, painting the bedroom, dusting the bookcase, washing the car, trimming the shrubs, raking the leaves, dusting the blinds, walking the dog—these types of things communicate love to the person whose primary love language is acts of service. In Galatians, Paul encourages us to take opportunities to do good and kind things for other believers. How much more should we do this for the one we love most?

Do these things, and your spouse will feel loved. Fail to do these things, and you can say, "I love you" all day long without making him or her feel loved. If you want your spouse to feel loved, you must discover and speak his or her primary love language.

Father, there are so many ways to show my love through acts of service. Please help me to notice the opportunities throughout the day.

JESUS MODELED SERVICE

[Jesus said,] "Whoever wants to be a leader among you must be your servant, and whoever wants to be first among you must become your slave. For even the Son of Man came not to be served but to serve others and to give his life as a ransom for many." MATTHEW 20:26-28

JESUS DEMONSTRATED the love language of acts of service when he washed the feet of his disciples. This was a task usually relegated to a servant, so it was shocking for a respected teacher to do—so shocking that at first Peter didn't want Jesus to serve him that way. But for Jesus this was not one random act; it was a way of life. The sentence that best describes his life is this: "He went about doing good" (Acts 10:38, ESV). He himself said that he "came not to be served but to serve others." Service was the central theme of his life. His ultimate act of service was to give his life for us so that we could be forgiven by God.

If your spouse's love language is acts of service, then let Jesus be your model. Read the Gospels again, and look for the ways in which he served others. Ask God to give you the attitude of Christ toward your spouse so that you can serve him or her in love.

Lord Jesus, your attitude of service is the ultimate model for me. Help me as I strive to imitate the generous ways you showed love to others. Please show me how to serve freely.

COMMUNICATING ABOUT SEX

Let everything you say be good and helpful, so that your words will be an encouragement to those who hear them. EPHESIANS 4:29

IF THERE IS ONE SKILL that is more important than any other in gaining sexual oneness, it is *communication*. Why are we so ready to discuss everything else and so reticent to communicate openly about this area of marriage? When talking about sexuality, we should endeavor to follow the apostle Paul's advice and share helpful, encouraging words with each other. Your communication can make a dramatic difference to the level of mutual sexual satisfaction in your marriage.

Your wife will never know your feelings, needs, and desires if you do not express them. Your husband will never know what pleases you if you do not communicate. I have never known a couple who gained mutual sexual satisfaction without open communication about sexual matters. You cannot work on a problem of which you are unaware.

Let me share a practical idea to help you get started. At the top of a sheet of paper, write these words: "These are things I wish my spouse would do or not do to make the sexual part of our marriage better for me." Write down some ideas, and then share your lists with each other. Information opens the road to growth. Remember, your goal is making sex a mutual joy.

Lord God, you know that talking about sex is sometimes hard for me. Help me to remember that you want my relationship with my spouse to be strong in every area—including sex. Please give us grace to speak helpfully to each other as we talk about what we like and don't like in our sexual relationship.

THE IMPORTANCE OF SEX

Let me see your face; let me hear your voice. For your voice is pleasant, and your face is lovely. SONG OF SOLOMON 2:14

WHY IS SEX such an important part of marriage? We are sexual creatures by God's design. The most obvious purpose of sexuality is reproduction, but that is not the only one.

A second purpose is companionship. God said of Adam, "It is not good for the man to be alone" (Genesis 2:18). God's answer was the creation of Eve and the institution of marriage, about which Scripture says, "The two are united into one" (Genesis 2:24). That's true literally and metaphorically. In sexual intercourse, we bond with each other. It is the opposite of being alone. It is deep intimacy, deep companionship.

A third purpose of sex is pleasure. The Song of Solomon is replete with illustrations of the pleasure of relating to each other sexually within marriage. The descriptive phrases may be foreign to our culture (an American man wouldn't typically compare his wife's teeth to sheep, for example), but the intent is clear: Maleness and femaleness are meant to be enjoyed by marriage partners.

Sex was not designed to be placed on the shelf after the first few years of marriage. God's desire is that we find and enjoy mutual sexual love throughout our married life.

 Father, thank you for creating sex as a means for procreation, companionship, and pleasure. May all of those purposes be fulfilled in our marriage.

POSITIVE ATTITUDE

Why am I discouraged? Why is my heart so sad? I will put my hope in God!
I will praise him again—my Savior and my God! PSALM 42:5-6

IN THE NEXT FEW DAYS, I want to share five realities that can change your marriage. The first one is this: *I am responsible for my own attitude.* Trouble is inevitable, but misery is optional. Attitude has to do with the way I choose to think about things.

Two wives have husbands who have lost their jobs. Wendy says, "My husband hasn't had a full-time job in three years. The good part is not being able to afford cable TV. We've done a lot more talking on Monday nights. We've learned a lot. Our philosophy is 'We don't need what everybody else thinks they have to have.' It's amazing how many things you can do without." On the other hand, Leslie says, "My husband hasn't had a job for ten months. We are down to one car, no phone, and we're getting food from the food bank. Life is miserable at our house."

The difference in these two wives—and the atmosphere in their homes—is basically a matter of attitude. We can choose to think negatively and curse the darkness, or we can choose to look for the silver lining behind the clouds.

The writer of Psalm 42 certainly knew the power of a good decision. Faced with discouragement, he made the choice to turn his attention to the hope that comes from God. When we remember the good things about our lives—including the salvation and love God gives us—we are choosing to change our attitude.

Lord, I know I tend to blame circumstances for my frustration. But the truth is, I need to be responsible for my own attitude. Help me to choose hope and optimism, and may that transform the way I view my marriage relationship.

CHANGING ATTITUDE TO CHANGE ACTIONS

[Elijah] sat down under a solitary broom tree and prayed that he might die. "I have had enough, LORD," he said. "Take my life, for I am no better than my ancestors who have already died." 1 KINGS 19:4

YESTERDAY WE LOOKED at the first reality that can change your marriage: I am responsible for my own attitude. Today, we'll see reality number two: *Attitude affects actions.* Attitudes are so important because they affect my behavior and words. I may not be able to control my environment or the issues I face—sickness, an alcoholic spouse, a teenager on drugs, a job loss, aging parents, and so forth—but I am responsible for what I *do* within my environment. My attitude will greatly influence my behavior.

The prophet Elijah gives us a vivid example of this. Fresh from defeating the false prophets of Baal in a showdown at Mount Carmel and proving that the Lord is God, Elijah fell into despair when his life was threatened by Queen Jezebel. His attitude of defeat led him to go into hiding by himself and essentially ask God to take his life. God refreshed Elijah, who then returned to his work as a prophet, but certainly at this point in his life, his attitude greatly affected his actions.

It's the same with us. If I focus on the negative, I'm more likely to give my spouse critical, condemning words. My behavior will fall into one of two categories: I'll do things to hurt my spouse, or I'll withdraw and consider leaving my spouse.

On the other hand, if I look for the positive in my marriage, then I'm more likely to talk positively, to speak affirming words to my spouse, and to do something that has the potential to enhance life for both of us.

Father, sometimes I tend to wallow in my despair and disappointment, much like Elijah did. That negative attitude seeps its way into my heart and affects my actions as well. Help me to keep my attitude under control before it negatively affects my behavior and my spouse.

POSITIVE INFLUENCE

Imitate God, therefore, in everything you do, because you are his dear children. Live a life filled with love, following the example of Christ. EPHESIANS 5:1-2

HAVE YOU EVER HEARD, "You can't change someone else"? It's true that *you cannot change the person you love, but you can and do influence him or her every day.* That's the third reality of marriage. If you are still trying to change your spouse, then you may be a manipulator. You reason, *If I do this, then my spouse will do that* or *If I can make him miserable enough or happy enough, then I'll get what I want.* I hate to discourage you, but you're on a dead-end road. Even if you manage to get your spouse to change, your manipulation will foster resentment.

A better approach is to be a positive influence on your spouse. You influence by your words and actions. If you look for something your spouse is doing that you like and give verbal compliments, you are having a positive influence. If you do something that you know your spouse will like, your actions have a wholesome influence. If you treat your spouse with respect and kindness, your example begins to rub off.

In Ephesians 5, Paul instructs us to follow the example of Christ and live with love. Just as a small boy imitates his father, so we should imitate our heavenly Father. When we follow that perfect model, we can't help but positively influence the ones we love. The reality of the power of positive influence holds tremendous potential for troubled marriages.

Lord, I know you are the perfect model of love, and I want to imitate you. As I do that, I pray that I would be a positive influence on my spouse.

NOT DRIVEN BY EMOTIONS

A person without self-control is like a city with broken-down walls.

PROVERBS 25:28

IN THE LAST FEW DAYS, I've been sharing realities that can change your relationship. Today, we come to reality number four: *My actions need not be controlled by my emotions.*

For the past thirty years or more, our culture has put undue emphasis on emotions. When applied to a troubled relationship, this philosophy advises, "If you don't have loving feelings, admit it and get out" or even, "If you feel hurt and angry, you would be hypocritical to say or do something kind to your mate." This philosophy might sound good, but it fails to reckon with the reality that people are more than their emotions.

We have feelings, yes, but we also have attitudes, values, and actions. If we jump directly from emotions to actions and ignore attitudes and values, we will destroy our marriages. Actions that are guided by values and positive attitudes are more likely to be productive.

The proverb above compares a person without self-control to a city with broken walls. In ancient times, a city's walls were its first and primary defense against enemies. Without strong walls, a city was vulnerable to attack. Similarly, when we let our emotions control us, we lose our perspective and are vulnerable to all kinds of temptations and hurtful behavior.

Don't let your emotions control you. Instead, stop, think, look for the positive, affirm it, and then do something that has positive potential.

Father, I want to be like a well-protected city, not one with broken-down walls. But I struggle with self-control. Too often my emotions drive my actions toward my spouse. Please help me as I strive to change that.

ADMITTING YOUR WRONGS

If we claim we have no sin, we are only fooling ourselves and not living in the truth. But if we confess our sins to him, he is faithful and just to forgive us our sins and to cleanse us from all wickedness. 1 JOHN 1:8-9

A FIFTH REALITY that can change your marriage is this: *Admitting my own imperfections does not mean that I am a failure.*

In most troubled marriages, there is a stone wall between husband and wife that has been built over the years. Each stone represents an event in the past where one of them failed the other. These are things people talk about when they sit in the counseling office. The husband complains, "She has always been critical of everything I do. I've never been able to please her." The wife complains, "He's married to his job. He has no time for me or the children. I feel like a widow." This wall of hurt and disappointment stands as a barrier to marital unity.

Demolishing this emotional wall is essential for rebuilding a troubled marriage. Admitting your part in building this wall does not make you a failure. It means that you are human and are willing to admit your humanity. In fact, the apostle John wrote that people who claim they have never made mistakes are just fooling themselves. Confessing sin is the first step toward being reconciled with God. Confessing past failures to your spouse is the first step toward a growing marriage.

Father, so often I deny that I've done anything wrong because I don't want to feel like a failure. But I know that only compounds the problem. Help me to admit my wrongs to my spouse so that we can break down the wall of hurt between us.

DISCOVERING LOVE LANGUAGES THROUGH HURTS

Search me, O God, and know my heart; try me and know my anxious thoughts; and see if there be any hurtful way in me, and lead me in the everlasting way. PSALM 139:23-24 (NASB)

WHAT DOES YOUR SPOUSE DO or say that hurts you most deeply? That is probably a clue to your primary love language. The hurt may not come from what he does or says, but rather what he fails to do or say. One wife said, "He never lifts a hand to help me around the house. He watches television while I do all the work. I don't understand how he could do that if he really loved me." Her love language is *acts of service*. In her mind, if you love someone, you do things to help. For her, actions speak louder than words.

For others, words may speak louder than actions. One husband told me, "All my wife ever does is criticize me. I don't know why she married me. It's obvious she doesn't love me." For him, if you love someone, you speak kindly. His love language is *words of affirmation*, which is why her critical words hurt him so deeply.

If you want to discover your spouse's love language, you might ask, "What is it that I do or say, or fail to do or say, that hurts you most deeply?" It may be a scary question, but the answer will likely reveal his or her love language. Also, Psalm 139 tells us that if we ask God, he will reveal things in our lives that are hurtful to others. Ask him to give you insight as you broach the subject with your spouse.

Father, you know everything about me, including what I do that most hurts my spouse. Please reveal that to me. As I talk to my spouse, help me to have a heart that's willing to listen, learn, and improve so I can love my spouse more effectively.

CREATING AN ATMOSPHERE OF RESPECT

In the same way, you husbands must give honor to your wives. Treat your wife with understanding as you live together. 1 PETER 3:7

WHEN THE WORD *intimacy* is mentioned, many husbands immediately think of sex. But sex cannot be separated from intellectual and emotional intimacy. The failure to recognize this reality leads to marital frustration.

If a woman does not feel free to express her ideas, or if she feels that her husband does not respect her ideas and will tell her they're foolish if she shares them, then she may have little interest in being sexually intimate with him. Her feelings of condemnation and rejection make it difficult for her to be sexually responsive.

If a wife does not feel loved by her husband, again the emotional distance stands as a barrier to sexual intimacy. A husband who ignores these realities will be frustrated at his wife's lack of interest in sex. The problem is not her lack of interest. Rather, it is the emotional barriers that exist between the two of them.

The apostle Peter encouraged men to honor their wives and treat them with understanding and consideration. Men should do this first and foremost because God commanded it, but the truth is that it benefits them as well. The wise husband will seek to create a climate where his wife feels accepted and loved as a person. In doing so, he opens the door to sexual intimacy.

Lord, I know that you always want us to treat each other with honor, respect, and love. When we do this, our relationship runs more smoothly—and it honors you. Help me to grow in this.

LISTEN FIRST, THEN RESPOND

If only someone would listen to me! Look, I will sign my name to my defense.

JOB 31:35

MOST OF US SHARE our ideas much too soon. We talk before we have really listened. In fact, one research project found that the average person will listen only seventeen seconds before interrupting.

The book of Job gives many illustrations of poor listening. As Job suffered with physical illness, grief, and loss of material things, he steadfastly maintained his good standing before God. But his "friends" brushed him off and stated insistently that he must have committed some great sin for God to allow him to suffer so much. Finally, after pages of speeches, Job gets fed up. We can hear his frustration in his words: "If only someone would listen to me!"

A good listener will never share his ideas until he is sure that he understands what the other person is saying. In marriage, this is extremely important. Ask questions, repeat what you think your spouse is saying, and ask, "Am I understanding you?" When your spouse says, "Yes, I think you understand what I'm saying and how I feel," then and only then are you ready to move on. You might say, "I really appreciate your being open with me. Now that I understand where you're coming from, may I share what I was thinking when I did that? I realize now that what I said was hurtful, but I want you to understand that I was not trying to hurt you." At this point, your spouse will hear your perspective, because you have first taken the time to really hear what he or she was saying.

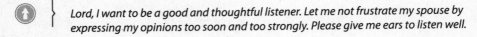

Lord, I want to be a good and thoughtful listener. Let me not frustrate my spouse by expressing my opinions too soon and too strongly. Please give me ears to listen well.

FINDING TIME FOR THE *OUGHTS*

Teach us to realize the brevity of life, so that we may grow in wisdom.

PSALM 90:12

AS CHRISTIANS, we know that life's ultimate meaning is to be found in relationships: first, in a relationship with God, and second, in our relationships with people. On the human level, the marriage relationship is designed by God to be the most intimate, with the parent-child relationship a close second. Yet some of us pursue activities that have little to do with building relationships. How do we stop the merry-go-round and get off?

Have you heard people say, "I know that I ought to, but I just don't have time"? Is it true that we don't have time to do what we ought to do? The word *ought* means to be bound by moral law, conscience, or a sense of duty. If we are not accomplishing our *oughts*, then we need to examine our use of time. Time is a resource the Lord has given us, and like any other resource, we need to be good stewards of it. The verse above, and many other places in the Bible, underscores the bottom-line reason for using our time well—because our time on earth is limited. Time is a precious commodity we shouldn't waste.

Ultimately, we can control how we use our time. We can accomplish our goals for our closest relationships. Making time for what's important means that we must say no to things of lesser importance. Do you need to sit down and take a fresh look at how you are using your time? Then do it today.

Lord, you know best how quickly our days on earth pass by. I want to use my time in the best way possible, and that means investing it in my relationship with you and my relationship with my spouse. Help me to make wise decisions as I evaluate my priorities.

MAKING TIME FOR THE IMPORTANT

Look carefully then how you walk, not as unwise but as wise, making the best use of the time. EPHESIANS 5:15-16 (ESV)

IF YOU AGREE that your marriage relationship is important, then what would you like to do to enhance it? Would a "daily sharing time" be helpful? Would a weekly date night be good? How about attending a marriage-enrichment weekend? Decide what would be profitable, and make time to do the important.

I say "make time" because if you don't put it into your schedule, it won't happen. Saying yes to the important may mean saying no to the less important. For example, setting aside a daily time for the two of you to talk uninterrupted may require that you give up a thirty-minute television program each night. A weekly date night may require that you eliminate something from your budget to have money for a babysitter. If it's important, you can make it happen.

The passage above from Ephesians 5 encourages us to be wise in how we use our limited time, and to make the best use of it. Time and money are your assets. You must manage them well in order to accomplish the important. No one else will do it for you. Only you can take control of your life and see that you actually do what you believe you ought to do.

Lord God, it's so easy for me to get stuck in the way I usually do things and to forget about the really important things. Please help me to make a priority of spending time with my spouse—and help us to set a plan in place so that it will happen.

RETURNING TO EMOTIONAL LOVE

Dear children, let's not merely say that we love each other; let us show the truth by our actions. 1 JOHN 3:18

FALLING IN LOVE is a temporary experience. It is not premeditated; it simply happens in the normal context of male-female relationships. What many people do not know is that it is always temporary. The average life span for being "in love" is two years.

The "in love" experience temporarily meets one's emotional need for love. It gives us the feeling that someone cares, that someone admires and appreciates us. Our emotions soar with the thought that another person sees us as number one. For a brief time our emotional need for love is met. However, when we come down off the emotional high, we may feel empty. That's sometimes accompanied by feelings of hurt, disappointment, or anger.

If emotional love is to return to your relationship, it will require each of you to discover and speak each other's primary love language. As we've discussed, there are only five basic languages: words of affirmation, acts of service, gifts, quality time, and physical touch.

The apostle John recounted an important truth when he wrote his first epistle: Love can be expressed in words, but it is shown to be true through our actions. Learn the language of your spouse, speak it regularly, and emotional love will return to your marriage.

Lord God, I want us to feel strong, emotional love as a couple again. Please help us reach that point by committing to loving each other by our actions, not just our words. Help us to learn each other's love language and speak it well.

LEARNING TO LOVE LIKE GOD DOES

May the Lord lead your hearts into a full understanding and expression of the love of God and the patient endurance that comes from Christ.

2 THESSALONIANS 3:5

ONE HUSBAND SAID to his wife, "You know I love you. Why do I have to keep saying it?" Another said, "I gave you a gift for your birthday. That was only two months ago. What do you mean I don't ever give you anything?"

Both of these husbands failed to realize that expressions of love must become a normal way of life, not occasional acts.

Emotional love must be nurtured. Speaking the primary love language of your spouse is the best way to keep love alive. So if *acts of service* is your spouse's love language, then cook a meal, clean the house, or mow the grass, and watch his or her love tank fill. If it's *words of affirmation*, give her a compliment, and she will feel loved. If it's *quality time*, sit on the couch and give him your undivided attention. If it's *physical touch*, put your hand on her shoulder. If it's *gifts*, give him a book, card, or special treat.

Love is a choice you make daily. As you make that choice, as the passage above says, the Lord will lead you into a greater understanding and expression of his love. He will teach you to love like he does.

Father, I want to love like you do. Please teach me how. Help me to begin by nurturing the love between me and my spouse, and by communicating through his or her love language.

SEEKING CHANGE

Don't copy the behavior and customs of this world, but let God transform you into a new person by changing the way you think. Then you will learn to know God's will for you, which is good and pleasing and perfect. ROMANS 12:2

UNFORTUNATELY, MANY PEOPLE are at a point of desperation in their marriage. A husband recently said to me, "I don't know what else to do. I find my love feelings for my wife dying and being replaced by pity and anger. I want to respect her. I want to love her. I want to help her, but I don't know how." Thousands can identify with the constant frustration of living with a difficult or irresponsible spouse.

Is there hope? Yes, and it begins with you. You must first of all adopt a positive attitude. This husband is doing what most of us do by nature: He is focusing on the problem rather than on the solution. There are scores of steps he can take, but they require a positive attitude.

First, he must agree that God is still in the business of changing lives. Romans 12:2 reminds us that God can transform us from the inside out. If we turn to God, he can change our thinking, which in turn will change our patterns of acting. There is hope. This husband must pray, "Father, I know there is an answer to our problems. Please show me the next step." This focus on seeking solutions will lead him to answers.

Lord, I believe that you can transform lives. I trust that you want my relationship with my spouse to be restored. Please show me what to do next.

REDEEMING STRUGGLES

We know that God causes everything to work together for the good of those who love God and are called according to his purpose for them. ROMANS 8:28

AUGUST 12 IS KAROLYN'S and my wedding anniversary. As I think back over the years, I have to admit they have not all been happy years. Early on we had significant struggles. I know the pain of feeling rejected. I was often plagued with the thought, *I've married the wrong woman.* In those days, no one ever offered us a book on marriage or recommended a marriage counselor.

We struggled, but by God's grace we eventually found answers. God taught us how to forgive and how to love again. For many years now, we have enjoyed the fruit of unconditional love. I would not want to relive the years of pain, but I know that God used them to give us a ministry to other struggling couples.

Think about the difficulties in your own relationship, whether past or present. In what ways can God use them to help you or others? Romans 8 tells us that in even the worst situation, God can work things for our good and for his own purposes. The most significant struggle may be the one that, years later, you look back on as a turning point in your relationship. The Lord can redeem any circumstance for his glory. In that I rejoice on this anniversary.

> *Lord God, thank you for this word of hope. No matter what struggles we face in our relationship, we know that the problems are not beyond you. You can bring good out of them. Please use our difficulties to fulfill your purposes.*

PRAYING FOR CHANGE

The earnest prayer of a righteous person has great power and produces wonderful results. JAMES 5:16

TRUE OR FALSE? When you are in a bad marriage, there are only two options: resign yourself to a life of misery, or get out.

Many couples live in deep pain. They have tried to improve things and have failed. Thus, they accept the commonly held dichotomy: I need to get out and start over, or else I must accept the fact that I'm going to live in misery the rest of my life. I want to suggest that there is a third option: Let God use you as a positive change agent in your marriage. It is true that you cannot make your spouse change. However, you can positively influence your spouse to change. Most of us underestimate the power of influence.

We also underestimate the power of prayer. The Scriptures include many examples of people pleading with God—and his answering them. James 5:16 tells us that our earnest prayer can bring remarkable results. And the apostle Paul reminded believers to devote themselves to prayer (see Colossians 4:2) and to pray constantly (see 1 Thessalonians 5:17). So pray for your relationship. Ask God to give you a clear picture of how you got to where you are in your marriage. What needs to change for you to have a growing relationship? Ask God to show you how you might be an instrument in his hand to influence your spouse. It's a prayer he will answer. And he will give you the power to do it.

Father, I come to you needing your help so much. Please show me how we got to this point as a couple and what needs to change. Use me as a change agent. May I have a positive effect on my spouse.

CONFESSION AND FORGIVENESS

Against you, and you alone, have I sinned; I have done what is evil in your sight. You will be proved right in what you say, and your judgment against me is just. . . . Purify me from my sins, and I will be clean; wash me, and I will be whiter than snow. PSALM 51:4, 7

I WISH THAT I WERE a perfect husband: always kind, thoughtful, understanding, considerate, and loving. Unfortunately, I am not. None of us are. I am sometimes selfish, thoughtless, and cold. In short, I fail to live up to the biblical ideal for a Christian husband. Does that mean that my marriage is destined for failure? Not if I am willing to admit my failures and if my wife is willing to forgive.

Forgiveness does not mean simply overlooking or ignoring the other person's failures. God's forgiveness should be our model. God forgives us based on what Christ did for us on the cross. God does not overlook sin, and God does not forgive everyone indiscriminately. God forgives *when* we confess our sin and express our need for forgiveness. Psalm 51, written by King David after his sin with Bathsheba, is a helpful model of true remorse for wrongdoing. David admitted his guilt, acknowledged God's justice, and asked for God's purifying forgiveness. And God gave it to him.

Genuine confession always precedes true forgiveness. So in order to have a growing marriage, I must confess my failures to my wife, and she must forgive me.

> *Father, it is often hard to confess my sins to my spouse. And it can be just as hard to forgive my spouse after I've been wronged. Please soften our hearts toward each other. Help us to forgive each other as you forgive us.*

FORGIVING AS GOD FORGIVES

Give us today the food we need, and forgive us our sins, as we have forgiven those who sin against us. And don't let us yield to temptation, but rescue us from the evil one. MATTHEW 6:11-13

THERE IS A DIFFERENCE between acceptance and forgiveness. You may *accept* many things about your spouse that you do not particularly like, such as a habit that you find annoying. In fact, such acceptance is necessary in healthy marriages. But wrong, unfair, or unjust treatment—which the Bible calls sin—cannot be accepted. Sin needs to be *forgiven*.

When a spouse continues to persist in sinning, the relationship will be strained. Ideally the wrongdoer will confess his or her failures and request forgiveness. That's the biblical model. When we choose to forgive someone, we are saying, "I will no longer hold this sin against you. I will respond to you as though it had not happened. I will continue working with you on our relationship. I love you."

But what are we to do when our spouse does not confess wrongdoing and, in fact, persists in sinful behavior? We are to release the person to God, along with our anger. Then we are free to return good for evil and thus have a positive influence on our spouse.

The challenge of Scripture is to forgive one another as God forgives us. Jesus stated this plainly when he taught his disciples what we know as the Lord's Prayer. The concept is echoed other times, including in Ephesians 4, where Paul tells his listeners to "be kind to each other, tenderhearted, forgiving one another, just as God through Christ has forgiven you" (4:32). Our goal is clear, but we may need to learn how to get there.

Father, I can't thank you enough for your glorious forgiveness through Christ. It's an amazing gift. Since you have done this wonderful thing for me, I know that I, too, need to forgive those who sin against me. Please help me as I strive to be better at forgiving my spouse when I need to. Thank you.

THOROUGH FORGIVENESS

Oh, what joy for those whose disobedience is forgiven, whose sin is put out of sight! PSALM 32:1

A HEALTHY MARRIAGE requires confession when we do wrong and forgiveness from the one whom we have wronged. The word *confess* means to tell or make known, to acknowledge a wrongdoing. When we confess, God forgives. The Bible describes God's forgiveness as thorough. The above verse from Psalm 32 refers to our sin as "out of sight," while Psalm 103 uses a wonderful image of distance: "He has removed our sins as far from us as the east is from the west" (Psalm 103:12). In the book of Hebrews, we hear God's promise to forget our sins: "I will never again remember their sins and lawless deeds" (Hebrews 10:17).

When your spouse sins against you, it stimulates hurt and perhaps anger. You may feel like lashing out, but the biblical response is loving confrontation. If he or she admits the wrong, the right response is to lovingly forgive. Perhaps you are saying, "But how can I forgive when it hurts so deeply?" Remember, forgiveness is not a feeling. It is rather a promise to lift judgment. "I'm deeply hurt and angry, but I choose to forgive you," is a realistic statement. You are honest about your feelings, but you are choosing to forgive. You will no longer hold the wrong against your loved one.

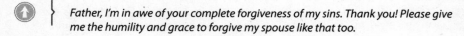

Father, I'm in awe of your complete forgiveness of my sins. Thank you! Please give me the humility and grace to forgive my spouse like that too.

DOES FORGIVING EQUAL FORGETTING?

Give all your worries and cares to God, for he cares about you. 1 PETER 5:7

THERE IS A DIFFERENCE between forgiving and forgetting. One wife said, "I've forgiven him, but I have trouble with my feelings when I remember what he did." Forgiveness does not destroy our memory. Our brains record every event we have ever experienced, good and bad. Memory may bring back the event and the feelings of hurt and pain. But keep in mind that forgiveness is not a feeling. Rather, it is a promise to no longer hold the sin against the other person.

So what do we do when the memory comes back and we feel the pain? We take it to God and say, "Father, you know what I'm remembering, and you know the pain I'm feeling, but I thank you that it is forgiven. Now help me to do something loving for my spouse today." We don't allow the memory to control our behavior. In time, the pain will diminish as we build new positive memories together as a couple. Don't be troubled by memories. As 1 Peter 5:7 reminds us, we can bring all our worries to God. He cares about us and will help us forgive.

Lord, I know that you command us to forgive others when they are repentant and ask for forgiveness. It's not optional. I want to follow your ways, but sometimes my feelings get in the way. Please help me to deal with those. Thank you for helping me to forgive my spouse.

LONG-TERM ANGER

Laughter can conceal a heavy heart, but when the laughter ends, the grief remains. PROVERBS 14:13

IF YOU SEEM to have lost the spark in your marriage, if your enthusiasm for life is waning, or if you find yourself irritable and often snap at your spouse or children, you may be suffering from long-term anger.

When we overreact to little irritations, it is a sign that we have anger stored inside. Stored anger can eventually lead to huge explosions. That's when people wonder, *What happened to him?* because the explosion seems out of character. But what people have not seen is the buildup of anger that has been going on inside the person, perhaps for years.

When we hold anger inside instead of getting rid of it, the pressure mounts. In Proverbs 14:13, King Solomon wisely observes that hidden emotions don't just go away. That's why the Bible says, "Don't let the sun go down while you are still angry" (Ephesians 4:26). Get rid of anger quickly. If you don't, you can become a chronically angry person, ready to explode at any time. That's never good for your marriage.

Father, forgive me for letting things build up inside me for so long. I don't want to hurt my spouse by such misplaced, explosive anger. Please help me to deal with my strong emotions when they come.

ACKNOWLEDGING PAST HURTS

Fools make fun of guilt, but the godly acknowledge it and seek reconciliation.

PROVERBS 14:9

LONG-TERM ANGER, held inside, can be detrimental to your relationship. Why? Because internal anger will eventually become external. You can't hold it in forever. Perhaps you've noticed that you are already like a pressure cooker—periodically blowing off steam. Your outbursts cause pain to your spouse, and he or she may lash back at you. Now you have more anger. Would you like to get rid of all of that and live a peaceful life?

Ask God to bring to your mind all the hurts of your past, and the people who hurt you. I suggest you write them down. Then lay the list before God and ask, "Have I also wronged these people? I know they hurt me, but have I been unkind to them?" If the answer is yes, then ask God to give you the courage to ask those people to forgive you for treating them unkindly. As the passage above from Proverbs says, wise and godly people admit when they have done wrong—because it's the right thing to do, and also because it's the path to reconciliation. Your apology may stimulate an apology from them. If both of you choose to forgive, your anger will disappear.

When this kind of reconciliation happens between you and your spouse, your relationship will improve.

Father, it's easy to focus on how others have wronged me. But please help me also to be honest about when I have hurt others. I need the strength of character to admit that and make it right so that reconciliation can result.

LOVE AS THE CORNERSTONE

We know how much God loves us, and we have put our trust in his love. God is love, and all who live in love live in God, and God lives in them.

1 JOHN 4:16

I REALLY DO BELIEVE that "love makes the world go round." Why would I say that? Because God is love. It is his love for us that makes all of life meaningful. First John 4 reminds us that when we realize how much God loves us, it is so magnificent that we put our trust in that love. Even those who do not believe in God are the recipients of his love. He gives them life and the opportunity to respond to his love. He wants to forgive and enrich their lives. His plans for them are good.

What does all of this have to do with marriage? God instituted marriage because he loved us. His intention was certainly not to make us miserable; he made us for each other. Husband and wife are designed to work together as a mutually supportive team to discover and fulfill God's plans for their lives. It's beautiful when it works.

What is the key to having that kind of marriage? In a word, *love*. It is the choice to look out for each other in the same way that God looks out for us. It is allowing God to express his love through us. It doesn't require warm feelings, but it does require an open heart.

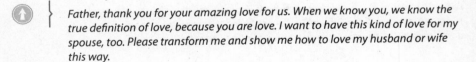

Father, thank you for your amazing love for us. When we know you, we know the true definition of love, because you are love. I want to have this kind of love for my spouse, too. Please transform me and show me how to love my husband or wife this way.

NO FEAR

Such love has no fear, because perfect love expels all fear. 1 JOHN 4:18

LOVE IS NOT our only emotional need, but it interfaces with all our other needs. We also need to feel secure, to have a healthy sense of self-worth, and to feel that our lives are significant. When two people choose to love each other, they also meet these needs. For example, if I know that my wife loves me, I feel secure in her presence.

The apostle John, who is known as "the disciple Jesus loved," writes a lot about love in his letters to believers. He wrote, "Perfect love casts out fear" (1 John 4:18, NKJV). In our relationship with God, this means that when we know the Lord loves us and has saved us, we are no longer afraid of judgment. In a sense, we can face anything. Genuine love in a human relationship has some of the same effects. Why should I be afraid if I am loved?

If I feel loved by my wife, then I also feel good about myself. After all, if she loves me, I must be worth loving. Ultimately, it is discovering that God loves me that gives me my greatest sense of worth. But my wife is an agent of God's love.

If my spouse loves me, I'm also more likely to feel that my life has significance. We want our lives to count for something; we want to make a difference in the world. When we give love to and receive love from our spouse, we *are* making a difference. We are enriching his or her life. This is what God called us to do—express his love in the world. Why not start at home?

Father, I want to make a difference—and I know I can start at home by loving my spouse. May my love be so strong and genuine that it changes the way he or she feels about life. May I always understand that my true worth comes because of your love.

ENCOURAGING EXCELLENCE

Let us think of ways to motivate one another to acts of love and good works.

HEBREWS 10:24

MARRIAGE GIVES a husband and wife an opportunity to minister to each other. They accept each other as they are, but they can also encourage each other to excellence. God has plans for each life. Spouses can help each other succeed in accomplishing these plans, and often this is done by expressing love.

Not everyone feels significant. Some people grew up in homes where they were given negative messages: *You are not smart enough. You're not athletic or talented. You'll never amount to anything.* All of these messages are false, but if they are all you have ever heard, you are likely to believe them.

When you learn your spouse's primary love language and speak it regularly, you are filling his love tank. You are also impacting her concept of herself. *If he loves me,* she thinks, *I must be significant.* You become God's agent for helping your spouse feel loved. Few things are more important in encouraging your spouse to accomplish God's plans. As the author of Hebrews wrote, as believers, we should consider how we can encourage each other to greater love and service. That's even more true within a marriage.

Marriage is designed to help us accomplish more for God. Two are better than one in his Kingdom.

Father, thank you for the plans you have for our lives. We are significant to you, and we can make a difference. Please help me to encourage my spouse in his or her walk with you.

ARGUING OVER MONEY

The body is a unit, though it is made up of many parts; and though all its parts are many, they form one body. So it is with Christ.

1 CORINTHIANS 12:12 (NIV)

DO YOU FIND YOURSELF fighting about money? A national survey indicated that 64 percent of American couples frequently argue about finances. "Where did the money go?" "Did you buy something without telling me?" "Don't tell me you forgot to record the check again." Sound familiar? How do we find financial harmony in a marriage?

It begins with identifying *why* we do what we do. Why does one person fail to record checks after writing them? Is it a deliberate attempt to frustrate the spouse? Is it an effort to hide the cost of an item? Most likely, it's a matter of personality. The person who fails to record the check is probably the person who also spends hours looking for car keys. When the organization genes were given out, he didn't get one, and those details aren't important to him. The solution is to make sure the organized person is the one balancing the checkbook. If that's you, stop arguing, and do your job.

Remember, 1 Corinthians 12 underscores that God has created us all with different gifts. Husbands and wives generally have different strengths. Your spouse will compensate for you in other areas as you work together. That's what marriage is all about—teamwork.

Father, thank you for the reminder that some problems have simple solutions. Sometimes we argue about the same thing over and over when it would be much easier just to change responsibilities so whichever of us is better suited to a certain area can take care of it. Please show us the best way to handle our differences about money.

FINANCIAL HARMONY

Each of you should look not only to your own interests, but also to the interests of others. PHILIPPIANS 2:4 (NIV)

HOW DO WE FIND financial harmony in marriage? There is no quick route to financial unity, but each couple can and must find a way to achieve it. The process requires talking, listening, understanding, and seeking a new way—not *my* way or *your* way, but *our* way. We must try to understand the reasons behind our partner's feelings and thoughts.

For example, say a wife wants to build up five thousand dollars in a savings account. Why is that so important to her? Possibly because it gives her emotional security. With that money safe and readily available, she knows that her children will not go hungry, no matter what emergency may arise.

Now imagine that her husband is an investor who wants to make his money work for him. He feels it's a waste of resources to keep any more than one hundred dollars in a savings account. Perhaps he feels that he is not being a good steward if he does not make wise investments. That's a worthy perspective.

Until this couple understands each other's feelings and thoughts on this issue, they will find themselves arguing over what to do. But once the husband understands the emotional impact on his wife when they only have one hundred dollars in savings, then he can stop arguing and accept her need for security.

The solution? He can use whatever is available beyond the five thousand dollars for investments. Now the argument is over, and both are having their needs met. Learning to work as a team and consider others' needs and interests, as Paul challenges us to do in Philippians 2, leads to financial harmony.

Lord God, I pray for grace to understand my spouse better when it comes to financial decisions. Please help me to see the need behind the request. Remind me to consider my spouse's interests, not just my own, and to be selfless enough to accommodate them.

MAINTAINING COMMUNICATION

An open rebuke is better than hidden love! Wounds from a sincere friend are better than many kisses from an enemy. PROVERBS 27:5-6

IF YOU'RE LIKE most couples, you will arrive at a point in your relationship (likely multiple points) where, instead of sharing your feelings and trying to resolve differences, you will be tempted to ask yourself, *Why bother?* Don't make that mistake. Once communication lines are down between you and your spouse, it may be difficult to restore them.

Maintaining communication with your spouse will take a boatload of patience and persistence. At times, you may feel like you're beating your head against a wall. Take some aspirin, and keep pounding. Eventually, your work will pay off.

Never assume that silence or indifference is preferable to conflict. It's not. As the above passage from Proverbs makes clear, sincerity is always better than buried feelings. Truthful responses can be painful, but they can also bring healing and genuine communication. As long as you and your spouse are interacting and actively trying to resolve your differences, there's hope. When you stop talking, hope dies. Keep your relationship on the front burner. Neglect your relationship, and you will poison your intimacy. Talking and listening are the ways we learn to work together as a team, and that's what a growing marriage is all about.

Father, thank you for the reminder that we should not avoid conflict at all costs. Please help me to remember that communicating is always worth it, even when it feels frustrating. Help me to take the hard path through the conflict, not the easier but ultimately dangerous path around the conflict.

SHOWING LOVE TO CHILDREN

Children are a gift from the Lord; they are a reward from him. PSALM 127:3

HUSBANDS, if you'd like to have a happy wife, I can tell you how: If you have children, love them. This means engaging your children in conversation. "What happened at school today?" is a start. But don't stop with the reciting of events. Ask questions that evoke more information, such as, "How did you feel about your art class?" The child's answer may reveal a great deal about his or her inner thoughts and feelings.

Children talk best if you ask open-ended questions. Try, "What did you like about your trip to the zoo?" rather than "Did you have a good time at the zoo?" The second question can be answered by a yes or no and tells you little about what the child is thinking. Once you've asked some questions, you might share your memories about going to the zoo.

Informal conversation is a child asking questions and receiving answers. Conversation is one of the essential tools of successful parenting. When your wife sees you talking and listening to your child, her respect for you rises. Few things please her more than knowing that you care enough to spend time conversing with your children. After all, the Bible is clear that children are a blessing and gift from the Lord. Make sure you treat them that way.

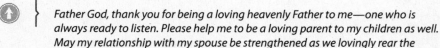

Father God, thank you for being a loving heavenly Father to me—one who is always ready to listen. Please help me to be a loving parent to my children as well. May my relationship with my spouse be strengthened as we lovingly rear the children you have given us.

INSIGHT INTO UNDERLYING MOTIVES

Always be humble and gentle. Be patient with each other, making allowance for each other's faults because of your love. EPHESIANS 4:2

WHAT YOU SEE is not always what you get; life is much more complex than that. Human behavior is almost always motivated by unseen needs that propel us to action. That means that you can see my behavior, but you don't know my underlying motives. After all, even I may not be conscious of my motives. All of us are moved along by these strong inner forces. If we are going to understand each other, we'll have to go beneath the surface.

What are these inner needs that affect our behavior so strongly? They fall into two categories: physical and emotional. Physical needs are easy to understand—for example, thirst, hunger, or sleep. Much of our behavior is motivated by physical needs such as these.

Emotional needs are much more difficult to identify, but they are just as powerful. For example, the need to feel loved and appreciated motivates much of our behavior. If someone gives me affirming words, if I sense that they genuinely care about me, then I am motivated to spend time with that person. That's why learning to meet your spouse's need for love is so important if you want to have a growing marriage.

When you don't understand your spouse's actions, respond patiently and humbly, as the apostle Paul reminds us to do in Ephesians 4. Take a minute to consider the needs that might be behind the behavior. That may give you new insight into what's going on and how to respond.

Father, you know the depths of the human heart. Only you understand all the different things that motivate our behavior. I ask for wisdom and insight into my spouse's actions. Please grant me the grace to respond patiently and thoughtfully, considering what needs may be behind what I see.

HIDDEN MOTIVES

The LORD's light penetrates the human spirit, exposing every hidden motive.

PROVERBS 20:27

WHEN WE TRY to understand the "hidden self," we realize that emotional and spiritual needs motivate much of our behavior. If you can understand the motives behind your spouse's behavior, it should help you relate to him or her in a more positive way. Here are some questions to help you in the process.

- What motivates my spouse's behavior? What needs is he or she consciously or subconsciously trying to meet?

- What motivates my own behavior? What needs am I trying to meet?

Human behavior is not a mystery, but it does require examination. We must look beyond the behavior to what motivates it. If I understand that my spouse's motive for joining a hunting club is to meet the need for belonging, then maybe I can affirm his behavior even though I would rather he join a volunteer group.

Understanding motives gives us guidance on how to help each other. Only God knows the depths of our hearts and everything that motivates us, as the psalmist makes clear in the passage above. God can guide us as we seek to understand our spouse's actions. If we don't look for motives, we may end up condemning each other's behavior and destroying intimacy. Understanding motivation enables us to be companions rather than competitors.

Lord God, I pray for insight into my spouse's actions that only you can give me. Help me to be patient and understanding. I want our relationship to be strengthened as I gain insight into his or her needs. When I'm hurt or confused, please show me how to meet those needs.

COMBATING DEFENSIVENESS

Make up your mind not to worry beforehand how you will defend yourselves.

LUKE 21:14 (NIV)

DEFENSIVENESS STOPS THE FLOW of communication in a marriage. Imagine that your wife says, "It's about time you took the garbage out. The flies were about to take it out for you." That cutting comment makes something inside you get huffy, and your response is to avoid your wife. So the rest of the evening, no matter what she says, all you do is grunt. If she keeps talking, you leave the room. Or perhaps your response is to say something equally cutting back to her so that she will feel hurt too.

What's going on? What your wife said blasted your self-esteem. Perhaps her message was the same one you used to hear from your mother: "You're irresponsible." No one wants to be an irresponsible person. So when your wife implied you were one, you got defensive and went after her. But remember, your wife is not your enemy. Rather, the message she spoke is the enemy.

Jesus told his disciples that they would face many obstacles and false charges. People would persecute them, but they didn't need to worry about how to defend themselves. Why? First, because the charges weren't valid, and second, because the Holy Spirit would give them the words they needed to say. We're not talking about being persecuted for our faith, of course, but we can still trust God to help us respond appropriately.

Defensiveness indicates that your self-esteem has been attacked. Focus on the right enemy, and you can turn your negative feelings into positive actions.

Lord God, when I feel defensive, please help me to consider the message objectively. If it is true, let me be willing to take steps to make a positive change. If it's not true, help me not to respond angrily but to trust that you will give me the right words to say. Thank you, Lord.

IDENTIFYING YOUR TRIGGERS

Since God chose you to be the holy people he loves, you must clothe yourselves with tenderhearted mercy, kindness, humility, gentleness, and patience. Make allowances for each other's faults, and forgive anyone who offends you.

COLOSSIANS 3:12-13

DEFENSIVENESS CAN MAKE or break a marriage. We can learn a lot about ourselves and our spouse if we analyze our defensive moments. All of us have emotional hot spots. When our spouse says or does certain things that touch on those hot spots, we get defensive—typically because our self-worth has been threatened. Initially, we may not know what these emotional hot spots are. But if we take time to analyze each event, we can get to know them quite well.

Perhaps you find that when your spouse criticizes your driving, you go ballistic. Or when he or she says something about your appearance, you snap. You have discovered hot spots. Don't ignore them, but let yourself calm down. Then later that week, ask yourself, *Why did I get so defensive?* Your reaction will almost always be tied to your childhood and your self-esteem. Identify the source, and then share it with your spouse.

A loving partner will choose not to exploit these triggers. As Paul writes in Colossians, we should be kind and compassionate with each other, bearing with each other's weaknesses. That includes never using your knowledge of your spouse to make him or her miserable. Instead, together you can explore ways of addressing these areas in the future. How can your spouse communicate with you in a way that will not come across as an attack on your self-worth? This kind of thoughtful, compassionate discussion is the road to a growing marriage.

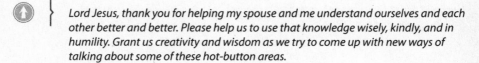

Lord Jesus, thank you for helping my spouse and me understand ourselves and each other better and better. Please help us to use that knowledge wisely, kindly, and in humility. Grant us creativity and wisdom as we try to come up with new ways of talking about some of these hot-button areas.

HELPING YOUR LOVED ONE SUCCEED

Oh, the joys of those who ... delight in the law of the LORD, meditating on it day and night. They are like trees planted along the riverbank, bearing fruit each season. Their leaves never wither, and they prosper in all they do.

PSALM 1:1-3

WHAT IS SUCCESS? Ask a dozen people, and you may get a dozen different answers. A friend of mine said, "Success is making the most of who you are with what you've got." I like that definition. Every person has the potential to make a positive impact on the world.

Psalm 1 compares a successful person to a tree—planted by the riverbank, stable and with deep roots, healthy, flourishing, and fruitful. When we are deeply rooted in God, he can use us and we can make a significant difference in the world. It all depends on what we do with what we have. Success is not measured by the amount of money we possess or the position we attain, but by how we use our resources and our opportunities. Position and money can be used to help others, or they can be squandered or abused. The truly successful people are those who help others succeed.

The same is true in marriage. A successful wife is one who expends her time and energy helping her husband reach his potential for God and for doing good in the world. Likewise, a successful husband is one who helps his wife do the same. If you help your spouse succeed, you end up living with a winner—and someone who feels fulfilled and purposeful. Not a bad life.

Heavenly Father, I want to be well-rooted in you and able to have a positive impact on those around me. I want that for my spouse, too. Please help me to make it my goal to help him or her succeed in making the most of his or her abilities.

DEALING WITH PARENTS AND IN-LAWS

Honor your father and mother. Then you will live a long, full life in the land the LORD your God is giving you. EXODUS 20:12

A WIFE RECENTLY SAID to me, "When we first got married, my mother-in-law really irritated me. I complained to my husband, who to his credit supported me. As my mother-in-law grew older, I began to think about what it means to 'honor' your parents and in-laws. That's a command, not an option, so I do it . . . even though sometimes she still gets under my skin." This woman is right that God commands us to honor parents; in fact, that verse comes directly from the Ten Commandments. But it's not always easy.

For better or for worse, our parents and parents-in-law are a part of our lives. But whether we're newlyweds or an "old married couple," how should we relate to in-laws? Actually, we need them. That is, we need the warmth and the wisdom of parents and in-laws. But we *don't* need to be controlled by them. Mutual freedom and mutual respect should be the guiding principle for parents and their married children.

What guidelines does the Bible give for in-law relationships? Two principles must be kept in balance: *leaving parents* and *honoring parents*. We'll talk more about these in the next few days.

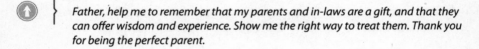

Father, help me to remember that my parents and in-laws are a gift, and that they can offer wisdom and experience. Show me the right way to treat them. Thank you for being the perfect parent.

MAKING YOUR OWN DECISIONS

"Haven't you read," [Jesus] replied, "that at the beginning the Creator 'made them male and female,' and said, 'For this reason a man will leave his father and mother and be united to his wife, and the two will become one flesh'? So they are no longer two, but one. Therefore what God has joined together, let man not separate." MATTHEW 19:4-6 (NIV)

IN GENESIS 2, we read that a man will leave his parents and be united to his wife. Jesus quoted this and expanded on it when he answered the Pharisees' questions on marriage and divorce, as we read in Matthew 19. Marriage involves a change of allegiance. Before marriage, our primary family allegiance is to our parents, but after marriage it is to our spouse. We must cut the proverbial apron strings. If there is a conflict of interest between a man's wife and his mother, the husband is to stand with his wife. No couple will reach their full potential in marriage without this psychological break from parents.

This "leaving of parents" is especially important in decision making. When you're considering a significant decision, your parents or in-laws may have good suggestions. Each suggestion should be taken seriously, but in the end, you and your spouse must make your own choices. There is a time to say to parents, "I love you very much. I really appreciate your ideas, but in this case we have decided to do it this way. I hope you understand, because I want to continue the relationship we have enjoyed through the years." Kindness but firmness is the key.

Father, please forgive me for the times when I have gotten my priorities mixed up and have been more loyal to my parents than to my spouse. Help me to understand that we are united as a couple, and that's your plan for our marriage.

HONORING PARENTS

Listen to your father, who gave you life, and don't despise your mother when she is old. PROVERBS 23:22

HOW DO YOU HONOR your parents after you are married, without allowing them to control you? The Lord has never rescinded his command to honor your parents (see Exodus 20:12). As long as they live, it is right to honor them. Some people find this easy because their parents are honorable and don't seek to control their lives. For others, this command is difficult.

One wife said, "How can I honor my mother when she made such a mess of her life and now seeks to make life miserable for me and my family?" The word *honor* means "to show respect." Sometimes we do not respect the lifestyle of our parents or in-laws, but we must respect their position. In the providence of God, they gave us life. For that we respect them. They are our parents, so we treat them kindly. We do what we can to help them, but we do not allow them to control our lives by intimidation or fear. Proverbs 23:22 suggests two more applications of *honoring* parents—first, listening to them; and second, caring for them, not despising them, when they are old. These go along with basic respect.

Honor does not mean that you must do everything that your parents request. Honor is seeking to do what is best for them.

Father, please help me to show appropriate honor to my parents. Guide me as I seek to treat them as you want me to—with love, kindness, and respect. I know that approach will help strengthen my marriage.

AVOIDING EGOCENTRISM IN COMMUNICATION

Fools have no interest in understanding; they only want to air their own opinions. PROVERBS 18:2

EMPATHETIC LISTENERS approach every conversation with this attitude: *I want to know what is going on in my spouse's mind and heart.* This is not the attitude most people hold. Psychologist Paul Tournier expressed it well when he said, "Each one speaks primarily in order to set forth his own ideas. . . . Exceedingly few exchanges of viewpoints manifest a real desire to understand the other person."*

By nature, we are all egocentric. In other words, we unconsciously think, *The world revolves around me. The way I think and feel is the most important issue.* It is a giant step in maturity when we choose to develop an attitude of empathy—honestly seeking to understand the thoughts and feelings of our loved ones. The above verse from Proverbs states bluntly that those who are concerned only about their own opinions are foolish. Why? Because they will never learn more—about either the topic being discussed or about the people discussing it.

The apostle Peter instructs husbands to "be considerate as you live with your wives, and treat them with respect" (1 Peter 3:7, NIV). This challenge goes for wives as well. When we respect the ideas and feelings of our spouse, we are listening empathetically.

Lord Jesus, selfishness so often pervades our communication as a couple. Please give me the self-control and the wisdom to respect my spouse's ideas and try to understand him or her as we talk.

---

* Paul Tournier, *To Understand Each Other*, trans. John S. Gilmour (Atlanta: John Knox, 1967), 4.

WAITING FOR THE FACTS

Spouting off before listening to the facts is both shameful and foolish.

PROVERBS 18:13

IF I LISTEN to my wife with a view to "setting her straight," I will never understand her, and most of our conversations will end in arguments. It is the propensity to pass judgment that sabotages the conversations of thousands of couples. Consider a woman who says, "I think I am going to have to quit my job." Suppose her husband responds, "You can't quit your job. We can't make it without your salary. And remember, you're the one who wanted this house with the big mortgage payment." They are either on the road to an intense argument or else they will withdraw and suffer in silence, each blaming the other.

Once again, in the proverb above, King Solomon is blunt in his appraisal of those who answer before they have all the information. He calls their behavior shameful and foolish. Not only does it lead to arguments, but it stops the process of exchanging information, and no further wisdom can be attained.

How very different things will be if the husband withholds judgment and instead responds to his wife by saying, "It sounds like you had a hard day at work, honey. Do you want to talk about it?" He has now opened up the possibility of understanding his wife. And when she feels heard and understood, together they can make a wise decision regarding her job. Withholding judgment, waiting for the facts, allows the conversation to proceed.

Father, in situations like these, help me to hold my tongue. Let me not offer my spouse the first response that comes to my mind, which is often full of my strong opinions. Please give me the wisdom to ask questions and invite a deeper conversation.

SERVING EACH OTHER

After washing their feet, [Jesus] put on his robe again and sat down and asked,
"Do you understand what I was doing? . . . Since I, your Lord and Teacher,
have washed your feet, you ought to wash each other's feet. I have given you
an example to follow. Do as I have done to you." JOHN 13:12, 14-15

PERHAPS JESUS' GREATEST ACT of service—apart from his sacrificial
death—was taking a basin of water and performing the lowly task of washing
his disciples' feet. What a simple yet profound act of service. By doing what
needed to be done, but what no one else wanted to do, Jesus demonstrated
humility, love, and true leadership.

Husbands, are you willing to humble yourself and serve your wife? Wives,
are you willing to humble yourself and serve your husband? I'm not talking
pious theology; I'm talking about truly following Jesus. In John 13, he told
the disciples that he had given them an example to follow. That goes for us,
too. Similarly, in Mark 10:45, he said, "For even the Son of Man came not to
be served but to serve others." It's a great paradox: The way up is down. True
greatness is expressed through serving. Why can't we start this at home?

It took me several years to discover the joy of serving my wife, but when
I did, our marriage went from winter to spring in a few short weeks. A good
question to start with is, "What can I do to help you?"

Lord Jesus, thank you for your example of service. If you humbled yourself to serve
your disciples, how can I complain about serving others? Please work in me and
give me a servant's heart toward my spouse.

TAKING THE FIRST STEP TOWARD SERVICE

When we were utterly helpless, Christ came at just the right time and died for us sinners. Now, most people would not be willing to die for an upright person, though someone might perhaps be willing to die for a person who is especially good. But God showed his great love for us by sending Christ to die for us while we were still sinners. ROMANS 5:6-8

IS YOUR RELATIONSHIP cold and harsh? Have you lost hope? If you want to breathe new life into your marriage, change your attitude. If you think negatively about your relationship and your spouse, you'll probably stay in a winter marriage—one that's negative, cold, and uncaring.

It took me a long time to figure out that life's greatest meaning is found in giving, not in getting. I remember the day I prayed a simple prayer: "Lord, give me the attitude of Christ. I want to serve my wife as Jesus served his followers." As I look back over the years since our wedding, I'm convinced that was the most important prayer I ever prayed regarding my marriage. When I began to look for ways to serve my wife, her attitude toward me also began to change.

It's natural to treat your spouse the way he or she treats you. But remember, God loved us while we were still sinners. He didn't wait for us to get our act together; he approached us first with immense love and grace. With his help, we, too, can love and serve even when we have lost hope. Nothing is more powerful than unconditional love.

Father, I am so grateful that you loved me even before I turned to you. Please help us to follow that example even in a small way as a couple. I want to serve my spouse, regardless of how I am being treated in return. I need your help, Lord.

PURSUING RECONCILIATION

If you are presenting a sacrifice at the altar in the Temple and you suddenly remember that someone has something against you, leave your sacrifice there at the altar. Go and be reconciled to that person. Then come and offer your sacrifice to God. MATTHEW 5:23-24

IN A PERFECT WORLD, there would be no need for apologies. But in our imperfect world, we cannot survive without them. We are moral creatures; we have a strong sense of right and wrong. When we are wronged, we experience hurt and anger. The wrong becomes a barrier between the two people involved. In marriage, this creates tension, and our unity is threatened. Things are not the same in the relationship until someone apologizes and someone forgives.

When wrongdoing has fractured a relationship, something within us cries out for reconciliation. The desire for reconciliation is often more potent than the desire for justice. The more intimate the relationship, the deeper the desire for reconciliation. Reconciliation is so important to God that Jesus instructed his hearers to settle any offenses before offering a sacrifice to the Lord. Before we can humble ourselves before God, we need to humble ourselves and confess our wrong to those we have offended.

When a husband treats his wife unfairly, she often has two reactions. On the one hand, she wants him to pay for his wrongdoing; but at the same time, she wishes for reconciliation. It is his sincere apology that makes genuine reconciliation possible. If there is no apology, her sense of morality will push her to demand justice. Apologies are necessary for good relationships.

Father, I see how important reconciliation is to you. Thank you for reminding me that apologizing and forgiving are integral parts of a marriage. Help me to be willing to reconcile with my spouse so that our relationship will remain strong.

CONFESSION BEFORE FORGIVENESS

If my people who are called by my name will humble themselves and pray and seek my face and turn from their wicked ways, I will hear from heaven and will forgive their sins and restore their land. 2 CHRONICLES 7:14

CAN YOU FORGIVE without an apology? If your definition of forgiveness is to release the person, your hurt, and your anger to God, then you can forgive without an apology. But if by forgiveness you mean reconciliation, then an apology is a necessary ingredient. Christians are instructed to forgive others in the same manner that God forgives us. How does God forgive us? The Scriptures say that if we confess our sins, God will forgive us (see 1 John 1:9). In 2 Chronicles 7, the Lord tells Solomon that he will forgive the people if they pray humbly and repent. Nothing in the Scriptures indicates that God forgives the sins of people who do not confess and repent.

We often want our spouse just to forget about what happened. We don't want to talk about it, and we don't want to apologize. We just want it to go away. But things don't just "go away." God has provided a pattern for human forgiveness, and that pattern requires apologizing for our wrongs. The apology is a way of accepting responsibility for our behavior and expressing regret. We recognize that what we did to our spouse has put a barrier between us, and we show that we want it removed. When we apologize, we are likely to receive forgiveness.

Father, thank you for your promises of forgiveness for those who confess their sins and turn away from them. Please help me to be willing to confess my wrongs to my spouse, so that he or she can forgive me freely. Too often I try to pretend that nothing happened, but I know that's not the way to a stronger relationship. Change my heart, Lord.

GOD'S PLAN FOR SEX

Kiss me and kiss me again, for your love is sweeter than wine.

SONG OF SOLOMON 1:2

MANY CHRISTIANS HAVE GROWN UP with the idea that sex is sinful and worldly—and that good Christians don't talk about sex. Nothing could be further from the truth. Dr. Ruth did not invent sex; sex was invented by God. And let me remind you that when God finished the creative act whereby he made us male and female, he saw that it was "very good" (Genesis 1:31).

As with most of his creatures, God made us sexual. But the purpose of human sexuality is far more than reproduction. The Scriptures indicate that in sexual intercourse, the husband and wife become "one flesh." In this act, our lives become bonded together. It is not simply the joining of two bodies. Something happens emotionally, spiritually, intellectually, and socially. It involves the total person. It is God's way of uniting us in a deep, lifelong, intimate relationship.

As we think about God's gift of sex, we can appreciate the guidelines he gave us for how to use it. Within marriage, sex is bonding, pleasurable, and planned for our enjoyment.

Lord Jesus, thank you for the gift of sex and the amazing role it can play in a marriage. Forgive me for sometimes being ashamed to talk about sex, or even for thinking that it's ungodly. Help my spouse and me to celebrate our sexual relationship as a gift from you that can strengthen our bond as a couple.

MEETING SEXUAL NEEDS

The husband should fulfill his wife's sexual needs, and the wife should fulfill her husband's needs. The wife gives authority over her body to her husband, and the husband gives authority over his body to his wife. Do not deprive each other of sexual relations. 1 CORINTHIANS 7:3-5

HOW ARE YOU DOING in meeting your spouse's sexual needs? In 1 Corinthians 7, husbands and wives are challenged to meet each other's sexual needs. "Do not deprive each other," the Scriptures say. Our bodies are to be a gift to each other; we are to be available to give sexual pleasure to each other. This is God's design.

Why do we often struggle so much to experience this mutual pleasure? Perhaps we have forgotten the key ingredient of love. Love means looking out for the other person's interests. The question is, how may I bring you pleasure? Love doesn't demand its own way. Love is not pushy or irritable, but thinks first of how to please the other person.

It's sad that "Let's make love" has often been reduced to "Let's have sex." Sex without genuine loving care for each other will be empty indeed. God's idea is that sex will be an expression of our deep love and lifelong commitment to each other. Anything short of this misses God's intention.

Lord, it's true that selfishness can cause problems in our sexual relationship. When I only think of myself and my own pleasure, sex becomes empty—and I know that's not the way you want it. Please guide me as I seek to think first of my spouse. Renew our love as a couple, and help us to express that love through sex.

MAKING ROOM FOR QUALITY TIME

O God, you are my God; I earnestly search for you. My soul thirsts for you; my whole body longs for you in this parched and weary land where there is no water. PSALM 63:1-2

HOW MUCH TIME do you spend with your spouse each day? Chances are, you are apart more than you are together, if you don't count the time you are asleep. That's pretty normal. One or both of you are likely working, and normally we don't work at the same place.

When you are together, how much time do you spend actually talking with each other? One hour a day? Probably not. Most couples spend less than thirty minutes each day in conversation. Much of this is spent on logistics, like, "What time am I supposed to pick up Jordan from soccer practice?" When do you have quality conversation, where you talk about issues, desires, frustrations, and joys?

Why not start with fifteen minutes a day? Call it couple time, talk time, or couch time. What you call it is not important. What is important is that the two of you spend quality time each day talking and listening to each other. Not only do you exchange information, but you communicate that you care about each other.

As believers, we may make time with God a priority but not time with our spouse. When King David wrote Psalm 63, he vividly expressed his longing for time and communication with the Lord, comparing it to water in a dry and weary place. Time with God refreshes us spiritually, and quality time with our spouse refreshes us emotionally and relationally. Quality time sends a strong emotional message: "I think you're important. I enjoy being with you. Let's do this again tomorrow."

Father, you know how much I need you—and how much I need my spouse. Time with him or her refreshes me, connects us, and shows that I care. Please help us to make this a priority as a couple.

COMMUNICATING LOVE THROUGH QUALITY TIME

Love each other with genuine affection, and take delight in honoring each other. ROMANS 12:10

QUALITY TIME is one of the five basic languages of love. It is some people's primary love language, and nothing else makes them feel more loved. What is quality time? It's giving your spouse your undivided attention. More than simply being in the same room, it's making eye contact, talking and listening sympathetically, or doing something together. *What* you do is not so important. Your focus is on being with each other, not on the activity.

How long has it been since you planned a weekend getaway? If that seems overwhelming, maybe you should start with a night out. Or how about just twenty minutes on the couch talking to each other? Better yet, ask your spouse what he or she would like to do.

If quality time is your spouse's primary love language and you haven't been speaking that language, chances are he or she has been complaining. You might hear, "We don't ever spend any time together. We used to take walks, but we haven't taken a walk together in two years." Some might even say, "I feel like you don't love me." Rather than getting defensive, why not recognize the problem and respond positively? Remember, the Bible tells us to love each other genuinely and to "take delight" in pleasing and honoring each other. Say, "You're right, honey. Why don't we take a walk tonight?"

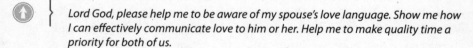

> *Lord God, please help me to be aware of my spouse's love language. Show me how I can effectively communicate love to him or her. Help me to make quality time a priority for both of us.*

WHEN THE CHILDREN LEAVE HOME

Live happily with the woman you love through all the . . . days of life that God has given you under the sun. ECCLESIASTES 9:9

A QUESTION I OFTEN HEAR from middle-aged couples is this: "The children are gone. Now what?" How do we relate to each other after the children leave the home? During the transition to the empty nest, the focus of the past twenty years becomes apparent. If you have focused solely on the children, you may have to start back at ground zero and rebuild your marriage. If you have focused on each other while raising the children, then you will climb to new heights of marital satisfaction with the extra time you now have together. In the book of Ecclesiastes, Solomon encourages couples to live contentedly with each other through all stages of life. Marriage is a gift in the early years before children, in the often hectic child-rearing years, and in the years after the children leave, which can be filled with newness and promise.

Whatever your situation, now is the time to assess the state of your marriage and take steps of growth. I suggest that you attend a weekend marriage-enrichment event, which will expose you to ideas on how to stimulate growth in your marriage. Also, try sharing a book on marriage by reading a chapter each week and discussing the content. One recommendation is *The Second Half of Marriage* by David and Claudia Arp. Focus on your marriage. Don't just rock along; be intentional.

Father, help me to look at this new stage of marriage as an adventure rather than as a loss. Show us how best to focus on one another, and strengthen our relationship even more as we make this transition to being empty nesters.

COMMUNICATION WITH GOD

Jesus replied, "The most important commandment is this: 'Listen, O Israel! The LORD our God is the one and only LORD. And you must love the LORD your God with all your heart, all your soul, all your mind, and all your strength.' The second is equally important: 'Love your neighbor as yourself.'"

MARK 12:29-31

THE FUNDAMENTAL BUILDING BLOCK in any relationship is conversation—two-way communication. I share my ideas and you listen; you share your ideas and I listen. The results? We understand each other. If we continue conversation over a period of time, we get to know each other. Why, then, is communication so difficult? Why do 86 percent of those who divorce say, "The main problem was, we got to a place where we just couldn't talk"?

I want to suggest that one problem is that we stop talking to God long before we stop talking to each other. If I'm talking with God daily, he will be influencing my thoughts and attitudes toward my spouse. God has clearly said that he wants to make me more and more like Jesus (see Romans 8:29). When I cooperate with the process, my communication with my wife flows pretty smoothly. When I get my wires crossed with God, then my attitudes toward my wife begin to deteriorate.

I don't think it's a coincidence that in Mark 12, Jesus said the most important commandments were (1) loving God wholeheartedly, and (2) loving others as ourselves. When we love God and are in tune with what he wants, loving others will come naturally.

I'm convinced that many of the communication problems in marriage would fade away if we spent more time talking and listening to God.

Father, help me to remember that the best thing I can do—both for my relationship with you and for my marriage—is to spend time communicating with you. As I read your Word, pray, and listen, please conform me more and more to the image of Christ. I know that will spill over into the way I treat my spouse.

SEEKING THE GREATEST GOOD

Our earthly fathers disciplined us for a few years, doing the best they knew how. But God's discipline is always good for us, so that we might share in his holiness. HEBREWS 12:10

"I DID IT BECAUSE I LOVE HER." We often use the word *love* to explain our behavior. Who doesn't remember a parent saying, "I'm punishing you because I love you"? As children we had a hard time figuring that out, but it was likely true. Parents discipline children because they love them. God does the same to his children, as the above verse from Hebrews makes clear. His ultimate goal is for us to become more like him, and his discipline molds and shapes us to that end. But in a marriage, there is no parent—only two partners. We don't discipline each other, but we do love each other and want our partner to fulfill his or her God-given potential.

The question is, how do we know when our action is loving? Love is doing what is best for the other person, but at times this can be difficult to figure out. For example, the wife of an alcoholic picks up the pieces after her husband's latest episode. She calls it love, but the psychologist calls it codependency. Did her action help him? Perhaps in the short term, but not in the long term.

We must learn to love effectively by doing what will best serve the emotional, spiritual, and physical health of our spouse. At times that means love must be tough. If this is a situation you face, ask God to give you the wisdom to make the right choices about how best to love your spouse.

Father, sometimes it's difficult for me to discern what approach to my spouse is really the loving one. I need your wisdom. Please help me to keep the end goal in mind—that my husband or wife would be healthy emotionally, spiritually, and physically. Thank you that your ultimate goal for both of us is to be more like you.

DEALING WITH A DIFFICULT SPOUSE

Love never gives up, never loses faith, is always hopeful, and endures through every circumstance. 1 CORINTHIANS 13:7

FOR SOME PEOPLE, marriage is an extreme challenge. One woman came to my office and told me this: "My husband has been fired from four jobs in the past six years. He doesn't seem to have any desire to build a stable career or provide steady income for us. I figured that since he's not working, the least he could do is take care of some repair jobs around the house. No way. He's too busy surfing the Internet or playing softball with his friends. We're talking about having kids, but I sometimes feel like I'm already living with one."

What would you suggest to this wife? Some people would say, "Leave the bum." I can understand that, but that counsel doesn't take into account the apostle Paul's teaching in 1 Corinthians that love never gives up but is always hopeful. Nothing is impossible with God! With that in mind, my advice to her was twofold: first show tender love, and then show tough love.

The natural tendency is to jump to tough love and offer ultimatums. But if you're going to take a new approach, always start with tender love. I suggest three months of speaking your spouse's primary love language at least once a week. Try hard to connect with him or her on an emotional level. If this fails to effect change, then move to tough love and start setting some boundaries. At that point, your spouse will miss the tender love and realize that he or she is about to lose something. Tender or tough, love is the best road.

Father, marriage can be challenging when my spouse is acting irresponsibly. Please help me to remember that nothing is impossible with you. Show me how to communicate my love to my spouse. And if tender love isn't working, give me wisdom as I seek to navigate tough love, for the good of my spouse and the good of our relationship. Only you have the wisdom I need, Lord.

DEALING WITH VERBAL ABUSE

I am determined not to sin in what I say. PSALM 17:3

ARE YOU MARRIED to a verbally abusive spouse? One husband said, "My wife called me a 'pathetic excuse for a husband' and said that she would have been better off staying single—all because I didn't take out the trash in time for the garbage truck to pick it up. It's been like this since we got married. I don't know what to do."

First, understand the source: Low self-esteem lies at the heart of most verbal abuse. Most verbal abusers were themselves verbally abused. Therefore, if you want to help, you must affirm your spouse's need but reject his or her behavior. You should never accept verbal abuse as normal, but neither should you lash back in self-defense. Make sure *your* words are God-honoring; like the psalmist, be determined not to sin in what you say. You might say something like: "I know you must be extremely frustrated to say things like that to me. I would like to help you, but I'm feeling hurt by your words. Perhaps we can talk about this after both of us calm down."

Affirming your spouse's need for self-worth, love, and acceptance is healthy, but you must also be honest about your own hurt. Seek a solution, not a victory.

Father, you know that we are all capable of saying horrible things to each other. Please forgive me for the times when I have done that. When my spouse is verbally abusive to me, show me the right way to respond. Help me to commit to keeping my words above reproach.

BIBLICAL INTIMACY

[Eve] took some of the fruit and ate it. Then she gave some to her husband, who was with her, and he ate it, too. At that moment their eyes were opened, and they suddenly felt shame at their nakedness. So they sewed fig leaves together to cover themselves. GENESIS 3:6-7

WHAT IS THE BIBLICAL PICTURE of intimacy in marriage? It's found in Genesis 2:25: "The man and his wife were both naked, but they felt no shame." This is a vivid image of marital intimacy: two distinct persons, equal in value, totally transparent, and without fear of being known. It is that kind of openness, acceptance, trust, and excitement to which we refer when we use the word *intimacy*.

But this was before sin entered the picture. It's interesting that Adam and Eve's immediate response to eating the forbidden fruit was to feel shame at their nakedness and cover themselves. In other words, after sin there were clothes. Something came between Adam and Eve, and they were no longer transparent. They were no longer willing to be freely known; now they had to work at intimacy.

The same is true for us. Because we are fallen creatures, we sometimes fear being known. Why? Because with intimacy comes the possibility of condemnation and rejection. To overcome that fear, we must develop a relationship of trust with our spouse.

Father God, our struggles with intimacy go all the way back to Adam and Eve and the first sin. I confess to you my fear of being fully known to another person, even my spouse. Please help us as a couple to work to overcome these fears and become as one.

OVERCOMING THE SEPARATION THAT COMES FROM SIN

Peter came to him and asked, "Lord, how often should I forgive someone who sins against me? Seven times?" "No, not seven times," Jesus replied, "but seventy times seven!" MATTHEW 18:21-22

IS THERE ANYTHING in contemporary experience that parallels the excitement of Adam and Eve before the Fall? I believe there is. It is the experience we commonly call "falling in love." It is an emotional experience fully as spontaneous as that moment when Adam first saw Eve. The experience of falling in love has the same elements as that initial meeting:

- ✎ feeling amazement

- ✎ feeling that we belong to each other

- ✎ knowing that we were meant for each other

- ✎ feeling something within each of us that cries out for something deep within the other

- ✎ sensing that God arranged our meeting

- ✎ experiencing a willingness to be open with each other, to share our deepest secrets, and to know in our hearts that we will love each other no matter what

- ✎ being willing to give ourselves totally to each other

What happens to all of those emotions after marriage? The same thing that happened to Adam and Eve. We sin, and sin separates us. We come to distrust each other, and as a result, we keep our distance to protect ourselves. What's the answer? Confession, repentance, and forgiveness.

Confession means I admit that what I did or said was wrong. Repentance means I am willing to turn away from that sin and walk in a new direction. And forgiveness means I am willing to accept your confession and repentance and let you back into my life.

Jesus told Peter we must be willing to forgive a repentant person over and over again—because that's the way God forgives us! It's not always easy, but you can have an intimate marriage if you are willing to deal with your failures.

Father, I thank you for your remarkable forgiveness. Thank you for forgiving me when I am repentant, even when I do the same thing over and over. Please give me this same attitude toward my spouse. I pray for a growing atmosphere of intimacy in our marriage as we learn to confess, repent, and forgive each other.

SETTING A STRONG EXAMPLE OF FAITH

I could have no greater joy than to hear that my children are following the truth. 3 JOHN 1:4

FOR THE CHRISTIAN COUPLE, the greatest joy is to see our children walking in truth. This sentiment is echoed by the apostle John in his last epistle. He considered the believers his "children" since he had been a father figure to them as their faith grew, and their faithfulness to Christ brought him much joy. Conversely, the greatest sorrow is seeing our children turn away from God.

The greatest influence we have on our children's religious beliefs happens in the first eighteen years of their lives. Children listen to what we say, and they observe our actions. The closer our practice is to our preaching, the more our children respect our faith. However, the greater the distance between what we proclaim and what we practice, the less likely they are to follow our religious beliefs.

What if our children are already grown, and we failed to do this when they were young? It is never too late to say, "I realize that when you were growing up, my lifestyle did not demonstrate very well what I claimed to believe. I wish I could go back and live parts of my life again. Of course, that's impossible, but I want you to know that I regret the way I failed you." This, coupled with a changed life, opens the door for further influence on your adult child. None of us are perfect. Dealing with past failures is the first step to renewed relationships.

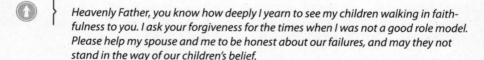

Heavenly Father, you know how deeply I yearn to see my children walking in faithfulness to you. I ask your forgiveness for the times when I was not a good role model. Please help my spouse and me to be honest about our failures, and may they not stand in the way of our children's belief.

PRAYING FOR YOUR SPOUSE

We ask God to give you complete knowledge of his will and to give you spiritual wisdom and understanding. COLOSSIANS 1:9

PRAYING FOR YOUR SPOUSE may be your greatest ministry. What could be more important? Through word and example, the Bible shows us that prayer is powerful. James 5:16 says, "The earnest prayer of a righteous person has great power and produces wonderful results." Think of all the amazing examples of intercession in the Bible. Abraham pleaded with God to spare Sodom. Moses interceded for Israel after they had built the golden calf. Daniel fasted and prayed in great humility, confessing his sins and the sins of Israel. Paul prayed that the Christians at Colosse would be filled with the knowledge of God's will. Jesus prayed that Peter's faith would not fail after he denied Christ.

How are you praying for your spouse? Perhaps you could use Colossians 1:9-14 as a place to begin. As you pray for your spouse what Paul prayed for these believers—that their faith would be strengthened and that God would equip them with endurance and patience—you will be ministering to him or her. You may also find your heart growing more tender toward your spouse.

Intercessory prayer is a service to the person you are praying for. Prayer is one of God's ordained means of accomplishing his will on earth. As he allows us to preach and teach, so he allows us to pray—and so we cooperate with him in his work. Pray for your spouse today, and watch how it affects your marriage.

Lord God, thank you for the privilege of bringing requests to you. Thank you, too, for the example of Paul's prayer, which goes beyond the logistical details of our lives to the things that really matter—my spouse's relationship with you. Help me to be faithful as I pray for my mate.

PRAYING TOGETHER

[Jesus said,] "For where two or three gather together as my followers, I am there among them." MATTHEW 18:20

MANY COUPLES find it difficult to pray together. Why? One reason may be that they are not treating each other with love and respect, and that stands as a barrier between them. The answer to this problem is confession and repentance. First John 1:9 says, "If we confess our sins to him, he is faithful and just to forgive us our sins." It is a sin to fail to love your spouse, or to fail to treat him or her with kindness and respect. Such sin needs to be confessed and forgiven; then you will be able to pray together.

A second reason couples are unable to pray together may be that one or both of them have never learned to pray with another person. To many people, prayer is private. While you should pray in private *for* your spouse, you should also pray *with* your spouse. After all, Jesus told his disciples that if even two or three of them were gathered together, he would be present among them. That's a powerful statement and a great testimony to praying together as a couple.

An easy way to get started is with silent prayer. It works like this: You hold hands, close your eyes, then pray silently. When you have finished praying, you say, "Amen," and then wait until your spouse says, "Amen." Praying silently while holding hands is one way of praying together, and it will enhance your marriage.

Father, I'm grateful for your promise to be present with us when we pray together. Sometimes that feels awkward or difficult, but please help us to commit to praying together as a couple. I know it's important for us spiritually and emotionally.

CONVERSATIONAL PRAYER

Devote yourselves to prayer with an alert mind and a thankful heart.

COLOSSIANS 4:2

THE BIBLE MAKES CLEAR that prayer is important. In Colossians 4, the apostle Paul encourages believers to "devote" themselves to prayer; in another epistle, he tells believers to pray continually (see 1 Thessalonians 5:17). We often take prayer for granted, but it's really an amazing concept. We can talk directly to the Creator of the universe! Why wouldn't we want to make that a habit with our spouse?

Yesterday I talked about praying silently together with your spouse. It's the easiest way to get started. Today I want to encourage you to try *conversational prayer*. In this approach, the two of you take turns talking to God. You may each pray one or more times about the same subject. Then one of you changes the subject, and you repeat the process. It's talking to God like you would talk to a friend.

For example, the husband might pray, "Father, thank you for protecting me on the way home from work today." The wife might then pray, "Yes, Father, I know that there are many accidents each day, and I sometimes take your protection for granted. I also want to thank you for protecting the children today." The husband prays, "I agree, and I pray especially that you will protect our kids from those who would pull them away from their faith." The wife prays, "Oh, Father, give us wisdom in how to teach our children to know and love you." And so the conversation with God continues. It is an exciting way to pray with your spouse. Not only will it draw you closer to your heavenly Father, but it will draw you and your spouse closer together as you hear and pray about each other's concerns.

Father God, I am amazed that I can talk to you at any time, and you hear me! What an incredible gift. Please help us to use this gift as a couple. I know that praying together will help us grow in our love for you and our love for each other. Give us the courage to get started and the discipline to continue.

RESPECTFULLY REQUESTING CHANGE

Respect everyone, and love your Christian brothers and sisters. 1 PETER 2:17

IF YOU'RE NEWLY MARRIED, you may have discovered some things about your loved one that you're not crazy about. He snores like a lumberjack. She squeezes the toothpaste in the middle. He thinks Burger King and laser tag are the ingredients for a romantic evening. She sings the wrong lyrics to every song on the radio. He clips his toenails in front of the TV and leaves the evidence on the coffee table. She serves Hamburger Helper twice a week for dinner.

The key to working through such irritations is to keep them in their proper perspective. Don't let small things become big problems. Remind yourself that these are not life-threatening issues. If you can find solutions, fine. If not, you can live with them.

Here's a plan for requesting change: Tell your spouse three things you like about him or her, and then make one request. For example, "Could you please rinse the hairs out of the sink when you finish getting ready in the morning?" Since commendation preceded your request, your spouse is more likely to accept the request for change.

One guideline: Never request change more than once every two weeks. Perhaps you could agree that this week your spouse may make a request of you, and next week you can request a change. The bottom line is respect. The apostle Peter encourages us to treat each other with love and respect, and that certainly applies to our spouse. When you are polite, loving, and respectful, you will see changes happen.

Father, it's easy for me to assume that my way is right. I tend to focus on some of my spouse's flaws that seem so big to me. Please help me to see them in the right perspective. Help me to treat my spouse with love and respect as we address these small issues, and help me to be willing to listen and change myself as well.

AFTER THE WEDDING

Let's not get tired of doing what is good. At just the right time we will reap a harvest of blessing if we don't give up. GALATIANS 6:9

TOO MANY COUPLES view the wedding as the finish line of their relationship. They work and work to make it to their wedding day, and then they sit back and wait for "happily ever after" to begin.

That's not how marriage works. If doing nothing is your strategy for keeping love alive in your relationship, you're in trouble. It's similar to the Christian who sees salvation as the final step in the journey. Once that's done, he thinks he can coast spiritually for the rest of his life. But that's hardly biblical. In the verse above, the apostle Paul encourages us to persist in service and good deeds. We need to keep working on our relationship with God, and we also need to keep working on our marriage relationship. Remember, the wedding is the first step, not the final one. To make your relationship work over the long haul, you need to invest the same kind of time, energy, and effort after the wedding as you invested when you were dating.

What were some of the things you did when you were dating? Did you give gifts? Did you make an effort to arrive on time? Did you go to nice restaurants? Did you speak to each other kindly? Did you reach over and touch his neck when you were waiting at a traffic light? Did you open the car door for her? Did you wash her car? Maybe it's time to ask your spouse, "Of all the things that I did when we were dating, which would you most like for me to do now?" Let his or her answer lead you to a growing marriage.

Lord Jesus, I know that I shouldn't "coast" spiritually. But too often I do that in my marriage relationship. I just get by and expect our love to stay alive. Please help me to treat my spouse the right way and put in the energy my relationship needs to grow.

ENCOURAGING SERVICE

Let us think of ways to motivate one another to acts of love and good works.

HEBREWS 10:24

IN MARRIAGE, we have a unique opportunity to encourage each other in our efforts to serve God by serving others. Under the lordship of Christ, we derive satisfaction and self-esteem from being a part of his larger purpose. It makes us feel valuable and energized, and that's good for a marriage.

If your wife plays the piano at church or tutors a disadvantaged student, you should be her greatest fan. If your husband teaches a Bible class or volunteers at the homeless shelter, he needs your encouraging words. Look for positive ways in which your spouse is seeking to use his or her abilities to help others, and encourage that. The Bible makes clear that we should "spur one another on" to express our love through action and to do good to others.

Encourage your spouse, and sit back and see what God will do!

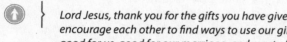

Lord Jesus, thank you for the gifts you have given to my spouse. Please help us to encourage each other to find ways to use our gifts for your glory. I know that is good for us, good for our marriage, and most of all, good for your Kingdom.

EXPRESSING LOVE TO THE UNLOVELY

We know how dearly God loves us, because he has given us the Holy Spirit to fill our hearts with his love. ROMANS 5:5

HOW CAN WE LOVE an unlovely spouse? Through almost thirty years of counseling, I have met with many individuals who live in unbelievably difficult marriages. Without exception, the root problem of marital difficulties is selfishness, and the root cure is love. Love and selfishness are opposites. By nature we are all self-centered, but when we become Christians, the Holy Spirit brings the love of God into our hearts, as Romans 5:5 indicates. Galatians 5 lists the character qualities the Holy Spirit will produce in our lives if we allow him, and these include love. We now can become God's agents for expressing his love. Sharing this divine love flowing through us is the most powerful thing we can do for our spouse.

I want to give you the challenge I have given many people through the years. Try a six-month experiment of loving your spouse unconditionally. Discover your spouse's primary love language, and speak it at least once a week for six months, no matter how you are treated in return. I have seen hard, harsh, cruel people melt long before the six months are over. When you let God express his love through you, you can become the agent of healing for your spouse and your marriage.

Heavenly Father, thank you for filling my heart with your love. No matter how frustrated I am with my marriage, I want to commit to loving my spouse unconditionally for the next six months and speaking his or her love language. Please give me the determination to do this. I know you can transform my marriage.

DECISION MAKING AS A TEAM

The heart of the discerning acquires knowledge; the ears of the wise seek it out.

PROVERBS 18:15 (NIV)

IF DECISION MAKING in marriage is a team effort—and it should be—then how do we find agreement? As individuals, we have personal thoughts and feelings on every subject, and those do not always agree with our spouse's. If we are to reach agreement, we must listen, understand, and compromise.

First, *listen* so you can learn what your spouse is thinking. As we see in Proverbs 18:15, wise people seek out new knowledge. That involves listening and discernment. Trying to see the world through your spouse's eyes enables you to *understand* his or her thoughts and feelings. Once you've done that, you can move on to *compromise*. This is not a negative word. Webster's dictionary says a compromise is "a settlement by consent reached by mutual concessions." We each share our perspective, and then we look for that on which we can agree. Each partner must be willing to give and to change.

The motivation for this is love. We are to be thinking about the benefit of the other person. Love says, "I want what is best for you. Therefore, I am willing to change my plans in order to meet your needs." In Colossians 1:8, Paul writes about the love for others that the Holy Spirit has given us as believers. Without that spirit of love, we may never reach agreement.

> *Lord Jesus, you know that making decisions can be difficult at times for my spouse and me. Please help me to remember that it's not ultimately about winning or doing what I want to do, but rather about coming to a decision that is workable for both of us. Please help me to be willing to listen, understand, and compromise for the sake of our marriage.*

FINDING COMPROMISE

Wise words bring many benefits, and hard work brings rewards. Fools think their own way is right, but the wise listen to others. PROVERBS 12:14-15

IN MAKING DECISIONS, husbands and wives often disagree. If we don't learn how to come together, we may spend a lifetime fighting. In yesterday's devotion, I said that agreement requires listening, understanding, and compromise. Compromise expresses a willingness to move. It is the opposite of being rigid. King Solomon said it bluntly in Proverbs 12: "Fools think their own way is right, but the wise listen to others." If we respect our spouse as our partner, we should also respect his or her viewpoint. It's neither wise nor loving to cling to our own viewpoint to the exclusion of our mate.

There are three possible ways to resolve a disagreement. One is what I call "Meet you on your side." In other words, you might say, "Now that I see how important this is to you, I'm willing to do what you want." You agree to do it your spouse's way for his or her benefit.

A second possibility is "Meet you in the middle." This means you might say, "I'd be willing to give a little if you could give a little, and we'll meet in the middle." For example, "I'll go with you to your mother's for the Friday night dinner if you will return with me Saturday morning in time for the big game."

The third possibility is "Meet you later." A couple in this position might say, "We don't seem to be making any progress. Why don't we just agree to disagree and discuss it again next week?" In the meantime, call a truce and treat each other kindly.

Father, thank you for these ideas on how to compromise. Please help me to let go of my need to do things my way. You know that I love my spouse and want to respect his or her ideas. I want to commit to loving compromise as we make decisions.

ASKING FORGIVENESS

If we claim we have no sin, we are only fooling ourselves and not living in the truth. But if we confess our sins to him, he is faithful and just to forgive us our sins and to cleanse us from all wickedness. 1 JOHN 1:8-9

WHY IS IT SO HARD for some people to say, "Will you please forgive me?" Often it is fear of losing control. To ask others to forgive us means that we put the future of the relationship in their hands. It might also be fear of rejection. When we ask for forgiveness, the other person may say no, and that rejection can be supremely hurtful. Another significant barrier is fear of not doing things right. Admitting we were wrong can seem equivalent to saying, "I'm a failure."

Understanding the Scriptures can remove all of these fears. Romans 3:23 tells us, "For everyone has sinned; we all fall short of God's glorious standard." And the verses above from 1 John tell us openly that if we claim we've never done anything wrong, we're fooling ourselves. But the next verse offers a wonderful promise: If we confess our sin to God, he will forgive us and cleanse us. To admit that we have done wrong is simply to admit that we are human. In our relationship with God as well as in our closest human relationships, requesting forgiveness is the first step toward healing.

Lord, why is it so hard for me to admit I was wrong? Thank you for your promise of forgiveness when I confess my sin to you. Help me to be willing to ask forgiveness from my spouse as well, and in doing so heal the hurt that I caused.

REQUESTING FORGIVENESS

I am boldly asking a favor of you. I could demand it in the name of Christ because it is the right thing for you to do. But because of our love, I prefer simply to ask you. Consider this as a request from me—Paul, an old man and now also a prisoner for the sake of Christ Jesus. PHILEMON 1:8-9

IT IS ALWAYS RIGHT to request forgiveness. It is never right to demand forgiveness. The husband who says, "I told you I'm sorry. What more can I say?" is demanding forgiveness. He is not likely to receive it, because none of us respond well to demands.

When the apostle Paul wrote to a fellow brother in Christ named Philemon to ask a favor, he could have demanded that Philemon respond the way Paul wanted him to. After all, Paul was an apostle and had likely had a significant impact on Philemon's faith. Even more, the favor was something morally right. But even with all that, Paul chose to *ask* Philemon—to make a request and allow Philemon the chance to process it and decide for himself. That's wise with many things, and particularly when asking for forgiveness.

Forgiveness is a choice to lift the barrier and let the other person back into our lives. There is always the risk that he or she will hurt us again. Some people have been hurt so many times that they are reluctant to forgive. However, without forgiveness, the relationship cannot grow. If you are in a stalemate as a couple, I urge you to apologize and request forgiveness. Then give your spouse time to process his or her pain before responding. In the meantime, pray and love.

Father, keep me from demanding my own way. When I wrong my spouse, let me admit my wrong and ask for forgiveness. Then help me to allow her the space to decide when she's ready. Thanks for always forgiving.

OUT-OF-PROPORTION ANGER

The LORD replied, "Is it right for you to be angry about this?" JONAH 4:4

MUCH OF OUR ANGER is distorted. It grows out of our own self-centeredness, our controlling personality, or sometimes just our lack of sleep.

It always helps to get the facts. Suppose your spouse promised to be home at 6:00, but he or she walks in at 6:30. Is that sinful? You really don't know until you ask some questions. If he willfully said to himself, *I know what I promised, but I choose not to keep my promise,* then he has sinned and your anger is legitimate. But if he left the office in plenty of time to arrive at 6:00 and got caught in a traffic jam, that is not sinful, and your anger is distorted. It's out of proportion to the offense.

One biblical example of distorted anger comes from the prophet Jonah. You may remember him primarily because of his exploits in the belly of a whale. But after that, he finally preached his message of judgment to the city of Nineveh. The people repented—and God chose to have mercy on the city. Jonah was angry about this. Why? Because he had prophesied God's wrath, and it had not come to pass. He thought this made him look bad! Jonah's anger was tied up in his pride, and clearly it was not justified. God himself asked him, rhetorically, "Is it right for you to be angry about this?"

In our earlier example, you may be all fired up when your spouse walks in late. However, when you find out that the traffic jam is the culprit, you need to release your anger—and not on your spouse. Try this prayer: "Father, you know that I'm upset. Help me not to take it out on my loved one. I give my anger to you and ask that you fill me with love." Your anger will subside, and the evening is now yours to enjoy.

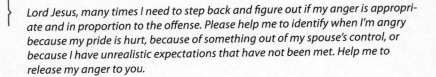

Lord Jesus, many times I need to step back and figure out if my anger is appropriate and in proportion to the offense. Please help me to identify when I'm angry because my pride is hurt, because of something out of my spouse's control, or because I have unrealistic expectations that have not been met. Help me to release my anger to you.

DEALING WITH DISTORTED ANGER

A gentle answer deflects anger, but harsh words make tempers flare.

PROVERBS 15:1

DISTORTED ANGER can destroy your marriage. Distorted anger is the emotion you feel when you don't get your way. It is sometimes called selfish anger, because its root is in you rather than in any external circumstance. Legitimate anger is your emotional response when your spouse sins against you, but distorted anger can be sparked by almost anything. Maybe your spouse is watching television instead of helping you in the kitchen, or she forgot to pick up the milk on her way home from the office.

How you handle distorted anger can make or break your marriage. To lash out at your spouse with critical words, or to withdraw in silence, will destroy your marriage. As Proverbs 15:1 says, "Harsh words make tempers flare." One person's distorted anger can flame the other's, with very negative results. On the other hand, requesting a time to share your feelings in a non-condemning way will lead to understanding. Feelings need to be shared, but spouses don't need to be condemned for being forgetful or thoughtless.

Consider this approach: "I want to share this with you, not to condemn you, but so that you will know me better." These are the words of a wise spouse. Such open sharing releases distorted anger and leads to a growing marriage.

Father, forgive me for those times when I let my anger take control of me. Please show me how to share my feelings without condemning or snapping at the one I love. I want our relationship to grow.

LETTING ANGER GO

"Don't sin by letting anger control you." Don't let the sun go down while you are still angry, for anger gives a foothold to the devil. EPHESIANS 4:26-27

IT HAPPENS TO ALL OF US. We get bent out of shape by some little comment or action of our spouse. She let the dog out without a leash, and now the neighbor is calling to complain. He left his socks on the floor instead of moving six inches to put them into the laundry hamper. It's the little things that stimulate distorted anger.

How do we handle our emotions? First, we admit them. "I'm feeling angry." Second, we refuse to let the anger control us. "So I'm going to take a walk." Third, we ask ourselves some key questions. *Did my spouse do this on purpose? Was he trying to hurt me? Or is this simply the result of being married to a human? Have I done similar things in the past? Is this big enough to talk with my spouse about, or shall I let it go?*

Either let it go or talk with your spouse about it. Don't hold anger inside. The Bible warns that we should get rid of anger before dark. When we hold on to anger, it has a tendency to start controlling us—and, as Paul writes, that gives a "foothold to the devil." In other words, holding on to anger makes us likely to sin more and more. Our anger becomes increasingly distorted, and that paves the way for all sorts of ugly interactions in a marriage. Anger should be treated as a visitor, never a resident.

Heavenly Father, you know that I sometimes hold on to a grudge against my spouse. Please help me to stop! Remind me to stop my response, figure out why I'm angry, and then decide whether to bring it up with my spouse or to let it go. I need wisdom, Lord, so I don't let anger take control of me.

CELEBRATING DIFFERENCES

If the whole body were an eye, how would you hear? Or if your whole body were an ear, how would you smell anything? But our bodies have many parts, and God has put each part just where he wants it. 1 CORINTHIANS 12:17-18

DIFFERENCES CAN BE DELIGHTFUL. An old adage says, "Some people read history; others make it." Usually, these two types of people are married to each other. Now I ask you, isn't that the way God designed it?

Our differences are meant to be complementary. How tragic it would be if your spouse were just like you. God tends to place an aggressive person with a more passive person, a neatnik with a slob, an organized person with a spontaneous person. Why? Because we need each other. It's sad when we allow our differences to become divisive. Why do we do this? Because we are egocentric. *Life revolves around me,* we think. *My way is the best way. Be like me, and we'll be happy!*

But is that really what we want? I don't think so. In 1 Corinthians 12, the apostle Paul compares the church to a body. It has many parts, and every part is needed. Paul takes this illustration almost to absurdity, asking his readers to imagine how the body would function if it were just one great big ear. It wouldn't! How limited life would be.

The same holds true in marriage. We are different, and we need each other. Your aggressiveness pushes me to attempt things I would never try on my own. My passiveness keeps you from jumping off the cliff. The Bible is right: Two are better than one.

Father, thank you for the differences between me and my spouse. Please show me how to look at them positively rather than negatively. Help us to work effectively together as a team.

AFFIRMING WORDS

Worry weighs a person down; an encouraging word cheers a person up.

PROVERBS 12:25

MANY COUPLES HAVE never learned the tremendous power of verbally affirming each other. Verbal compliments, or words of affirmation, are powerful communicators of love. King Solomon, author of the ancient Hebrew "wisdom literature" we find in the Bible, wrote several proverbs about words. The passage above, Proverbs 12:25, highlights the importance of encouraging words. Proverbs 18:21 is even more dramatic, saying, "The tongue can bring death or life." Cutting, critical comments can kill a person's spirit, but affirming words bring renewal and hope.

Read the following statements and ask yourself, *Have I said anything similar to my spouse within the last week?*

- "You look sharp in that outfit."

- "Wow! Do you ever look nice in that dress!"

- "You have got to be the best potato cook in the world. I love these potatoes."

- "Thanks for getting the babysitter lined up tonight. I want you to know I don't take that for granted."

- "I really appreciate your washing the dishes."

- "I'm proud of you for getting that positive job review. You're a hard worker, and it shows."

Want to improve your marriage? Say something positive to your spouse today.

Lord Jesus, why is it so much easier for me to criticize than to affirm? Please help me to train myself to notice the good things about my spouse—and to say something about them. I want my words to bring life, not discouragement. I need your help to develop new patterns, Lord.

CHANGE THROUGH AFFIRMATION

Encourage one another daily, as long as it is called Today, so that none of you may be hardened by sin's deceitfulness. HEBREWS 3:13 (NIV)

WHAT WOULD LIFE be like if your spouse gave you encouraging words every day? "Like heaven," one husband said. One woman responded, "I'd think my husband was drunk." How tragic that we typically give each other so few words of affirmation. We allow the emotions of hurt, disappointment, and anger to keep us from speaking positive words to each other, or maybe we simply get stuck in a pattern of negative comments. As a result, distance and dissatisfaction grow.

All of us long to hear affirming words, and those whose primary love language is affirming words long for them even more. We like to sense that our efforts are appreciated, and that our spouse sees something good in us. When we are affirmed, we aspire to be better. When we are ignored or condemned, we either become discouraged and withdraw, or become angry and hostile. Positive words can change the emotional atmosphere in a marriage. We need to look for something good in our spouse and affirm it.

The apostle Paul challenged his readers to "encourage each another and build each other up" (1 Thessalonians 5:11). The author of Hebrews suggested that believers give each other daily encouragement as a safeguard against hardened hearts and sin. Encouragement is important. Our words are like medication to a sick relationship. There is healing, and it often begins with words of affirmation.

Father, I don't want my spouse's heart to be hardened by my negativity. Please help me to encourage through my loving, encouraging words. I see so much in my loved one that is good, and I need to say so. Thank you for affirming me through the loving words I read in the Bible.

ENCOURAGING SUCCESS

I commend to you our sister Phoebe, who is a deacon in the church in Cenchrea. Welcome her in the Lord as one who is worthy of honor among God's people. Help her in whatever she needs, for she has been helpful to many, and especially to me. ROMANS 16:1-2

ENCOURAGING WORDS often make the difference between success and failure. For example, imagine that your spouse expresses the desire to lose weight. How you respond can be either encouraging or discouraging. If you say, "Well, I hope you don't try one of those expensive weight-loss programs or join a pricey gym. We can't afford that," then you have discouraged your spouse. Chances are, he or she will drop the idea and make no effort to lose weight.

On the other hand, consider this response: "Well, one thing I know. If you decide to lose weight, you will, because you have the discipline to do it. That's one of the things I admire about you." Wow! Your spouse is encouraged and will likely take action immediately.

At the end of the book of Romans, Paul writes a number of personal greetings, many of them including affirmations. In the verses above, he mentions a woman named Phoebe, who is "worthy of honor" and "helpful." Later in the chapter, he mentions several others by name and lists their contribution to his work. Imagine being praised in Paul's letter! The specifics he included give impact to his encouraging words.

When you have a chance to respond to your spouse, think before you speak. Ask yourself, *What can I say that would affirm and encourage my spouse to reach his or her goals?* Most of us are motivated when we hear encouraging words.

Lord Jesus, I pray that you would help me to think before I respond to my spouse. Show me how best to be an encouragement. I don't want to stand in the way of my loved one's goals, so please help me develop a pattern of encouragement and specific affirmation. I know that will strengthen our relationship.

DEALING WITH INFIDELITY

LORD, you know the hopes of the helpless. Surely you will hear their cries and comfort them. PSALM 10:17

WHAT DO YOU DO when you discover that your spouse has been sexually unfaithful? Hurt and anger are healthy emotions in that situation. They reveal that you are human and that you care about your marriage. They indicate that you see yourself as a valuable person who has been wronged. They reveal your concern for rightness and fairness. These emotions are entirely appropriate; they just need to be processed in a positive way.

Initially crying, weeping, and sobbing are healthy responses to intense hurt and anger. However, the body is limited in how long it can sustain such agony; thus, sessions of weeping must be interspersed with periods of calm. Verbally expressing your hurt to your spouse is also a healthy way to process anger. I would encourage you to start your statements with *I* rather than *you*. For example: "I feel betrayed. . . . I feel hurt. . . . I feel used. . . . I feel that you don't love me. . . . I feel like I don't ever want to touch you again." All of these statements reveal your thoughts and feelings to your spouse. Any recovery requires that your spouse hear and understand the depth of your hurt and anger.

Remember, too, that you can express all of your emotions to God, who loves you wholeheartedly and weeps with you. He hears your cries, as Psalm 10 reminds us. Psalm 147:3 says that he "heals the brokenhearted and bandages their wounds." Allow him to comfort you in your distress.

Father, I can't imagine many things more painful than discovering that my spouse has been unfaithful. I pray that neither my spouse nor I will ever have to undergo this hurt. But if we do, please lead us through. I thank you for your tenderness and compassion for those who are suffering.

FORGIVING INFIDELITY

Have mercy on me, O God, because of your unfailing love. Because of your great compassion, blot out the stain of my sins.... Create in me a clean heart, O God. Renew a loyal spirit within me. PSALM 51:1, 10

IS THERE LIFE after an affair? Can the marriage be healed? Yes, if there is genuine repentance and genuine forgiveness. Repentance means "to turn around." In the case of an affair, it means that the adulterous relationship must be broken off.

If you are the one who had the affair, tell the other person involved that you know you have done wrong, that you have asked God to forgive you, and that you are going to work on restoring your marriage. Ask the person to forgive you for doing what you knew was wrong and involving him or her in your infidelity. Then stop the extramarital relationship. In most cases, this will require breaking off all contact.

Now you are ready to ask your spouse to forgive you. Tell your mate that your sincere desire is to restore the marriage. Don't press for a quick and easy forgiveness. It will take time for your spouse to process the hurt and anger, so allow time to think and pray. Express your willingness to go for counseling. Don't expect an immediate healing. Allow time for talking, praying, and reading together. If you are sincere and your spouse is willing to forgive, then you can have a growing marriage.

Psalm 51 reveals King David's remorse after his adulterous affair with Bathsheba and his conspiring to have her husband killed. Read through this passage for a model of heartfelt repentance, and put David's model into practice as you seek to pick up the pieces of your marriage.

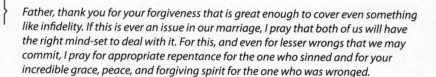

Father, thank you for your forgiveness that is great enough to cover even something like infidelity. If this is ever an issue in our marriage, I pray that both of us will have the right mind-set to deal with it. For this, and even for lesser wrongs that we may commit, I pray for appropriate repentance for the one who sinned and for your incredible grace, peace, and forgiving spirit for the one who was wronged.

TRUST AFTER AN AFFAIR

The godly walk with integrity; blessed are their children who follow them.

PROVERBS 20:7

HOW DO YOU REBUILD TRUST after an affair? One wife told me, "I'm willing to forgive my husband, but I don't know if I can ever trust him again." She was being honest. Forgiveness does not restore trust. Forgiveness is the decision to lift the penalty, restore the offender, and let him or her back into your life, but it does not immediately restore trust. If you had an affair, you broke the marriage covenant of fidelity. You destroyed trust in the heart of your spouse, and now only you can restore that trust.

Trust grows when you are trustworthy, so don't lie to your spouse. When you say you are going to do something, do it. If you promise to break off all contact with your former lover, do it—right down to the briefest e-mail or phone call. When you say you are going to see a friend, be sure that is where you go. Encourage your spouse to call and check up on you. Every time you prove that you are trustworthy, your spouse's trust grows. But if you continue to be deceptive, trust will never recover.

Ask God to make you a person of character and integrity, as Proverbs 20:7 mentions. Keep yourself completely above reproach; avoid even the appearance of wrongdoing (see 1 Thessalonians 5:22, KJV). That is the fastest way to restore trust in the heart of your spouse.

Father, only you can restore trust in a broken relationship. I pray for your healing, your grace, and your restoration in our marriage for both large and small violations of each other's trust. Make us both willing to take the necessary steps.

DIFFERENCES IN PARENTING

If you need wisdom, ask our generous God, and he will give it to you. He will not rebuke you for asking. JAMES 1:5

ONE OF THE ISSUES that often disrupts marital unity is differences of opinion on how to rear children. One wife said, "We didn't have any problems in our marriage until the baby came. Since then, we haven't had anything *but* problems. Our styles of parenting are so different."

Actually, this is a very common problem, and how you handle the problem will make or break your marriage. You may never agree on all the details of parenting, but you must find some common ground.

Let me suggest that the starting place is prayer. Pray that God will bring the two of you together on the basics of child rearing. Also, pray that he will help you understand the best way to rear your child. God is concerned about your children, and he also knows them perfectly. Therefore, when you ask for wisdom, God is fully qualified to help. James 1:5 reassures us that if we ask for wisdom, God will give it to us. He wants to guide us, and he can.

No one is a perfect parent, but you can avoid some pitfalls. Your parenting will improve when you avoid the pitfalls of overprotection, permissiveness, or excessive distance from your children. Remember that your ultimate goal is for your children to grow up secure in your love, strong in their faith, and with sound character. As you and your spouse talk together and pray together, the Lord will help you accomplish these goals together.

Father, raising children can be difficult. Thank you for promising wisdom to us when we ask for it. I pray that you will bring my spouse and me together as we discuss parenting styles and approaches. You know us and our children perfectly, and I pray that you will show us the best way to rear our kids to know and love you.

A FUTURE AND A HOPE

"For I know the plans I have for you," says the LORD. "They are plans for good and not for disaster, to give you a future and a hope." JEREMIAH 29:11

HAVE YOU EVER FELT as if your marriage was hopeless? Contrary to your present feelings, your future can be bright. God's plans for you are good, as the above passage reminds us. God gave these words to the prophet Jeremiah when the Israelites were in captivity in Babylon. They didn't think their present circumstances could be much worse! Many of them had been sent away to a foreign country, where the culture was antagonistic toward Jews. Those who were left at home faced conditions that were often desolate. They must have wondered if God had abandoned them, but his words to Jeremiah reassured them that he still had good plans for them. The same is true for you.

Past failures need not destroy your hope for the future. If you start making the right choices today, the prospects of a growing marriage are good. Your communication and understanding of each other can be much more intimate than you have ever known. As you forgive the past, share feelings, find understanding, and learn to love each other, you and your spouse can find fulfillment in your marriage.

This is not wishful thinking. It has become reality for hundreds of couples who have committed themselves to walk the road of reconciliation. It begins when you decide to make the most of what you have, one day at a time.

Father, thank you for this hopeful word from the book of Jeremiah. You never abandon your people, and you always have good plans for us. I am grateful for that reassurance for my marriage. Please help me to forgive things in the past, to make good choices in the present, and to look ahead to a fulfilled future.

LIVING IN THE PRESENT

Be thankful in all circumstances, for this is God's will for you who belong to Christ Jesus. 1 THESSALONIANS 5:18

IF YOU'RE IN A BAD MARRIAGE, you may be tempted to run, but you know there must be a better way. There is, and it comes from making the most of what you have, one day at a time. Don't spoil your future by allowing bitterness to consume your spirit. Don't destroy yourself with self-pity. Don't drive your friends away by constantly refusing their comfort.

You can make your life miserable by focusing on your problems. Or you can say with the psalmist, "This is the day the LORD has made. We will rejoice and be glad in it" (Psalm 118:24). You may not be able to rejoice over the past or over your present situation, but you can rejoice that God has given you the ability to use this day for good. You can also follow the apostle Paul's challenge from 1 Thessalonians 5 to be thankful in all circumstances. This doesn't mean you must be thankful *for* all circumstances, but that in every situation, you can choose to see something for which to thank God. He is present in your circumstances, and the more you look for him, the more you will find him.

Don't try to live all of your future today. Jesus emphasized the importance of living one day at a time (see Matthew 6:34). Some good questions to ask yourself are *What can I do today that may improve my situation? What do I need to pray about today? With whom do I need to talk today? What action do I need to take today?* God has entrusted to you only the present, and wise use of today is all that he expects.

Father God, you have made today, and I will choose to rejoice in it regardless of my circumstances. I know you have good plans for me, and I am thankful that I can choose to use this day for good. Please help me to turn away from the negativity that only makes me miserable. I want to learn to see you in my circumstances.

MAKING THE MOST OF TODAY

Come, let us worship and bow down. Let us kneel before the LORD our maker, for he is our God. We are the people he watches over, the flock under his care. If only you would listen to his voice today! PSALM 95:6-7

IN DIFFICULT MARRIAGES, we are tempted to wallow in our pain. Each day becomes a rerun of the past. But in God's economy, each day is an opportunity for change. Do a search for *today* in the Bible, and you'll find a long list of occasions when people were presented with a choice. That very day they could choose between following God or turning away, between listening to his voice or ignoring it. (See Psalm 95 and Deuteronomy 11:26-27 for just a few examples.) What they did "today" would set the tone for the days to follow. It's the same for you. All of your life cannot be straightened out today, but if you make the most of it, you can work on cleaning up one corner of your life. Choose a corner that you think is most important right now.

As you clean up the corners of your life day by day, all of life begins to look brighter. You cannot change your spouse? Then change your attitude about your spouse's behavior. Change your own behavior by confessing past failures. Ask God to help you do one kind deed for your spouse today. You cannot *change* your spouse, but you can *influence* your spouse. One act of kindness each day is likely to change the climate in your relationship, and eventually it may influence your spouse to reciprocate.

Never give up. There is always something good that can be done today. Making the most of today is the most powerful thing you can do for a better tomorrow.

Lord Jesus, I know that each day presents a choice. I can concentrate on my past struggles and remain in the same place, or I can choose to make a positive change. Please give me the courage and determination to make the right choices today. May my small steps forward bring our marriage to a stronger, more loving place.

WHAT IS AN APOLOGY?

He has removed our sins as far from us as the east is from the west.

PSALM 103:12

HAVE YOU EVER NOTICED that what one person considers an apology is not what another person considers an apology? Consider this exchange between a couple in my office. The wife says, "I'd forgive him if he would apologize." The husband responds, "I did apologize." "You did not apologize," she says. "I told you that I was sorry," the husband replies. "That is not an apology," she declares. So, what is an apology?

The truth is, it's different things to different people. After three years of research, Dr. Jennifer Thomas and I have concluded that there are five basic elements to an apology. We call them the five languages of apology. Just like love languages, each person has a primary apology language; one of the five speaks more deeply to him or her than the other four. If you don't speak the right language, the person you have wronged may consider your apology insincere. For the wife in my office, "I'm sorry" was not her apology language. The husband may have been sincere, but it did not come across that way to her.

Fortunately for us, God always hears and responds when we ask for forgiveness, as we see from the passage above. He who is able to know our hearts is more concerned with our sincerity than which words we choose to express it. But as mere humans, we often get stuck on the words. In the next few days, we'll talk about the five languages of apology.

Father, I want to communicate well with my spouse, especially when I am apologizing for something. Please help me to understand the best way to communicate. Thank you for always hearing me when I confess my sin to you.

COMMUNICATING SINCERITY

You were cleansed from your sins when you obeyed the truth, so now you must show sincere love to each other as brothers and sisters. Love each other deeply with all your heart. 1 PETER 1:22

HAVE YOU EVER QUESTIONED the sincerity of someone's apology? It's probably because the person did not speak your "apology language." Perhaps he said, "I'm sorry," but you wanted to hear, "I was wrong." Maybe she said, "Will you forgive me?" but what you wanted to hear was, "What can I do to make this right?" He said, "I was wrong. I really feel badly about it," but it was the same thing he apologized for last week. What you want is evidence of repentance and some assurance that this will not keep happening.

Many of our apologies come across as insincere because we are not speaking the apology language of the offended person. If couples can learn each other's primary apology language and speak it when they offend each other, forgiveness will be much easier. You can choose to forgive someone even if you question his or her sincerity, but it's much easier if in your heart you believe the person is sincere. First Peter 1:22 makes clear that we are to show sincere love to each other as believers—love that comes from our whole heart. Let's make sure we are communicating that love as well.

Father, you know how deeply I love my spouse. Please help me to communicate that even in apologizing so that he or she can see how sincere I am.

LANGUAGES OF APOLOGY

"O Lord," I prayed, *"have mercy on me. Heal me, for I have sinned against you."* PSALM 41:4

DO YOU KNOW the five languages of apology? What I'm going to share could greatly improve your ability to apologize effectively.

- ❧ Apology language #1 is *expressing regret.* Examples are "I'm sorry" or "I feel badly about what I did."

- ❧ Apology language #2 is *accepting responsibility.* "I was wrong" or "It was my fault."

- ❧ Apology language #3 is *making restitution.* "What can I do to make it right?"

- ❧ Apology language #4 is *genuinely repenting.* "I don't want to continue hurting you. I know that it is wrong, and I don't want it to happen again."

- ❧ Apology language #5 is *requesting forgiveness.* "Will you please forgive me?" or "I value our relationship, and I hope you will forgive me."

Out of these five, your spouse likely has a primary apology language. One of these is more important to him or her than the other four. To give a successful apology, you must learn to speak the apology language of your spouse.

You may discover your primary apology language by the way you confess your sin to God. Listen for the words you typically use as you confess and ask forgiveness; they will give you clues. Fortunately, the Lord knows our hearts and doesn't depend on our words to decide whether we're sincere!

Father, thank you for making people so different. Please help me to understand my spouse and figure out what is most important to him or her in an apology. Thank you for your constant forgiveness.

CHANGE BEGINS WITH ME

Don't just listen to God's word. You must do what it says. Otherwise, you are only fooling yourselves. . . . If you look carefully into the perfect law that sets you free, and if you do what it says and don't forget what you heard, then God will bless you for doing it. JAMES 1:22, 25

IMPROVING A MARRIAGE is not easy, but I can tell you a surefire way to do it: Begin by changing your own attitude. Instead of cursing the darkness, light a candle in your own heart. Say to God, "If you will give me a vision of what a godly spouse would look like, then I'm willing to make changes." Then read the Bible and look for those passages that tell you what a Christian husband or wife should be.

Let this be your dream, and meditate on it throughout the day. Ask God to help you live up to his model. Every day do something that will make you a better spouse. For example, look for things you can give a genuine compliment about. Think about how you could serve your mate. Think about a gift that would enrich his or her life. Think about how you could spend more time together. But don't just think about it—do it!

In the passage above, we see that James challenged his readers to do more than just hear God's Word. If we hear and don't change our behavior, we're essentially fooling ourselves. It's when we put God's guidance into practice that transforming change can take place.

When your attitude and behavior change, you will have a positive influence on your spouse. This influence will be far more powerful than your former criticisms. Certainly your marriage can change, and the change begins with you.

Father, I often complain about my marriage, but I'm not willing to do anything about it. Please forgive me for my arrogance in assuming that my spouse is to blame. I want to commit to changing myself. Please show me how I can be a godly spouse. Transform my words and my thinking; conform me to your image. May I be a positive influence in my marriage.

GOD'S FAITHFULNESS FOR A DIFFICULT MARRIAGE

Yet I still dare to hope when I remember this: The faithful love of the LORD never ends! His mercies never cease. Great is his faithfulness; his mercies begin afresh each morning. LAMENTATIONS 3:21-23

I AM OFTEN ASKED a variation on this question: "We got married because I was pregnant, and now I feel like I have made a big mistake. Can I get a divorce, or do I have to stick it out? If so, where do I begin?"

This question assumes that there are only two alternatives: stay in the marriage and be miserable the rest of your life, or get a divorce and be happy. I suggest that there is a third alternative that offers far more hope: Work to build a successful marriage. Many people get married in less-than-ideal circumstances. For some, it was pregnancy. For others, it was emotional dependency, desire to get out of a bad home situation, misguided romantic feelings, and any number of other factors. Getting off to a rocky start, or getting married for the wrong reasons, does not mean that you cannot have a good marriage.

Any couple can build a successful marriage if they will seek God's help. Through prayer, reading the Scriptures and Christian books on marriage, and getting wise counsel, you can have a growing marriage. The prophet Jeremiah penned some beautiful, inspirational words in the book of Lamentations. No matter what the circumstances—and Israel's were pretty dire at the time of this prophecy—the Lord is faithful. He gives new mercies every day! There is always hope with him. God can bring healing to past failures and supply hope for the future.

Father, I am so grateful for your faithful love that never fails. In the midst of my marriage struggles, I thank you for giving me hope. Nothing is too hard for you! Please help me to commit to doing whatever I can to improve my marriage, knowing that you desire us to have a strong, godly relationship. Work in me, Lord, I pray.

DEALING WITH EXPECTATIONS

Get rid of all bitterness, rage, anger, harsh words, and slander, as well as all types of evil behavior. EPHESIANS 4:31

OUR SOCIETY HAS UNDERGONE a great deal of change in the basic role expectations of the husband-wife team. Traditionally, the husband was the provider and the wife the homemaker. Currently, however, more wives work outside the home than follow the traditional role of domestic engineer. This is not without benefits, but it has spawned fresh areas of conflict in marriage.

If the wife is going to work outside the home and play an equal role with the husband in financial provision, then will he take an equal degree of responsibility for household tasks? Probably not, according to the latest research. As a result, the wife often feels put upon, feeling that she has two full-time jobs. These negative feelings, if not dealt with, may develop into bitterness. We know that's not what God wants for us. In fact, the apostle Paul makes clear that we need to eradicate bitterness and harsh words from our hearts. So how do we deal with these negative emotions?

The best way is to share the feelings and seek to negotiate a change. Stating requests positively will likely elicit a better response. For example, a wife might say, "I love you and I really want to be a good wife, but I'm about to go under. I need your help." Then she can go on to describe the pressure she feels from having so much to do. It's all part of an ongoing conversation every couple needs to have about who will do what tasks in a marriage.

Father, sometimes I feel overwhelmed with everything I am trying to do—at work, at home, with my family, and in my other commitments. I want to be a good husband or wife, but often I don't think I can keep up, and that makes me resentful. Please help me to deal with these emotions in a healthy way, by discussing them with my spouse. Give us patience and understanding as we sort out who should do what in our marriage.

WORKING AS A TEAM

Two people are better off than one, for they can help each other succeed. If one person falls, the other can reach out and help. But someone who falls alone is in real trouble. ECCLESIASTES 4:9-10

MANY COUPLES ENTER MARRIAGE with the assumption that their household will be run the way Mom and Dad did it. The problem is, there are two moms and dads, and they probably didn't do things the same way. His parents and her parents didn't have the same game plan, so husband and wife have very different expectations. What's the answer? We must construct our own game plan.

Make a list of all the household responsibilities that come to your mind. Washing dishes, cooking meals, buying groceries, vacuuming the carpet, washing the car, mowing the grass, paying the bills—everything. Ask your spouse to do the same. Then put your two lists together and come up with a "master list" of responsibilities. Next, each of you should take the list and put your initials by the things you think should be your responsibilities. Finally, get together and see where you agree. The differences will need to be negotiated, with someone being willing to take responsibility.

Try it for six months and then evaluate how things are going. Do you feel the responsibilities are divided fairly? Is one person struggling with a certain task that perhaps the other could do more easily? What changes need to be made?

As you talk through these issues, remember that you're on the same team. As Ecclesiastes 4 says, two people working together can help each other succeed. Isn't that what you want for your marriage? Use your strengths to help each other.

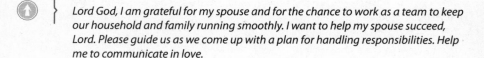

Lord God, I am grateful for my spouse and for the chance to work as a team to keep our household and family running smoothly. I want to help my spouse succeed, Lord. Please guide us as we come up with a plan for handling responsibilities. Help me to communicate in love.

AVOIDING STANDOFFS

Work willingly at whatever you do, as though you were working for the Lord rather than for people. COLOSSIANS 3:23

I ONCE HAD A COUPLE in my office who were at a standoff over who would clean the toilet. He insisted it was a woman's job. She maintained that it was a manly task. Mold was growing in the commode because neither would budge.

"What about hiring someone to come in each week and clean the commode?" I asked.

"We can't afford that," the husband said.

"Well, do you know of someone who might come in and clean it without charging?"

"My mother," he answered, "but I'm not going to ask her to do that. That would be stupid."

"Then what's the most logical thing to do?" I inquired.

"The logical thing is for her to clean it," he said.

"No, the logical thing is for him to clean it," his wife replied.

"Then you have just solved your problem," I said. "You clean the commode this week, and she will clean it next week."

"But that's giving in," he objected.

"Yes," I said, "and that is what marriage is all about."

This couple didn't have a commode problem but an attitude problem. When both husband and wife choose an attitude of love, standoffs like this won't happen, and tasks will get accomplished. Remember, as Colossians 3:23 tells us, we should do our work willingly, as if we were serving the Lord rather than people. As you negotiate responsibilities with your spouse, the bottom line should not be about individual rights, but about serving God and expressing love for each other.

Father, it's easy for me to get caught up in what is fair and thinking only about my own side of the discussion. Please help me to remember that by serving my spouse, I am also serving you. Forgive me for the times when I am stubborn and unloving. Show me how to talk through these questions of household responsibilities with an attitude of love.

GIFTS AS SYMBOLS OF LOVE

So the people of Israel—every man and woman who was eager to help in the work the LORD had given them through Moses—brought their gifts and gave them freely to the LORD. EXODUS 35:29

MOST WEDDING CEREMONIES include the giving and receiving of rings. The pastor says, "These rings are outward and visible signs of an inward and spiritual bond that unites your two hearts in love that has no end." That is not mere rhetoric. It is verbalizing a significant truth—symbols have emotional value.

Visual symbols of love are more important to some people than to others. That's why individuals have different attitudes toward wedding rings. Some never take the ring off. Others seldom wear their wedding band. This often correlates to love language. If receiving gifts is my primary love language, I will place great value on my wedding ring, and I may be hurt if my spouse doesn't seem to feel the same way. Also, I will be emotionally moved by the other gifts my spouse gives me through the years, because I will see them as expressions of love. Without gifts as visual symbols, I may come to question my spouse's love.

Throughout the centuries, people have shown their love for their Creator by giving him gifts. Exodus 35 talks about the Israelites freely giving gold, silver, bronze, linen, and other fine gifts that could be used in the Tabernacle. The Lord certainly didn't need their offerings, but the act of giving those things showed their love and sincerity. A similar dynamic occurs in many marriage relationships.

If you hear, "You didn't bring me anything?" when you come home from a trip, or if your loved one seems deeply hurt when you forget to give a birthday gift, then you can know that his or her love language is receiving gifts. Speak that language, and keep your spouse's love tank full.

Father, I know that when I give something to my spouse, it is a reassurance of my love. I want to show that our relationship is a priority to me. Help me to communicate well through the gifts that I give.

LEARNING TO BE A GIFT GIVER

Since you excel in so many ways—in your faith, your gifted speakers, your knowledge, your enthusiasm, and your love from us—I want you to excel also in this gracious act of giving. 2 CORINTHIANS 8:7

A WIFE COMPLAINS, "My husband never gives me gifts."

His reply? "I'm not a gift giver. I didn't receive many gifts growing up, and I never learned how to select gifts. It just doesn't come naturally for me."

Congratulations! You have just made the first discovery in becoming a great lover: You and your spouse speak different love languages. Now that you have made that discovery, get on with the business of learning your second language.

Where do you begin? Make a list of all the gifts your spouse has expressed excitement about receiving through the years. The list will give you an idea of the kind of gifts he or she likes. Also, listen to those casual comments, such as "I'd like to have one of those," as the two of you are shopping, or as your loved one looks through a magazine. Write it down so you don't forget. Another approach is to recruit family members to help you. Your sister may be the perfect person to help you select a gift for your wife, or your brother-in-law may know exactly what to give your husband.

The apostle Paul wrote to the church in Corinth, encouraging them to contribute to a financial gift for the believers in Jerusalem, who were suffering. As the Corinthians grew in their faith, he wanted them to excel in the "gracious act of giving." Of course, he was referring to monetary gifts. But the inherent principles are similar. The believers expressed their love for Christ and for their fellow Christians through giving, and we can express our love for our spouse through the same selfless and thoughtful acts. As you do this, you're on the road to learning the art of gift giving.

Lord Jesus, I want to be a generous giver, because I know that gifts communicate my love to my spouse. Please show me how to be thoughtful and loving as I select gifts. May my loved one's pleasure be my motivation and my goal. Thank you for your example of giving so generously to us.

EXPRESSING LOVE THROUGH GIFTS

A person who promises a gift but doesn't give it is like clouds and wind that bring no rain. PROVERBS 25:14

I'VE HEARD IT, and you've heard it: "It's the thought that counts." But I remind you, it is not the thought left in your head that counts. Rather, what counts is the gift that came out of the thought in your head! Good intentions are not enough. The proverb above gives a somewhat humorous description of someone who promises a gift but doesn't deliver—he is like "clouds and wind that bring no rain." If gifts are important to your spouse, make sure you follow through.

Gifts come in all sizes, colors, and shapes. Some are expensive, and some are free. To the person whose primary love language is receiving gifts, the cost of the gift will matter little, unless it is greatly out of line with what you can afford.

Gifts may be purchased, found, or made. The husband who picks a wildflower has found himself an expression of love (unless his wife is allergic to flowers!). For three dollars you can buy a nice card, or you can make a simple one for free. Fold paper in the middle; take scissors and cut out a heart; write, "I love you" and sign your name. Gifts need not be expensive. Even a candy bar or a drugstore trinket can bring a smile to your spouse's face. It truly is the thought that counts.

Father, I don't want to disappoint my spouse with good intentions that don't lead anywhere. Please help me to follow through with giving gifts that will be meaningful. May my efforts reassure my husband or wife of my love.

LOVING HONESTY

Righteousness and justice are the foundation of your throne. Unfailing love and truth walk before you as attendants. PSALM 89:14

A HUSBAND SAID TO ME, "My wife is so fragile emotionally, and I don't want to hurt her, so I keep all my feelings inside. But sometimes I feel like I'm going to explode." Do you think this husband is doing his wife a favor? His intentions may be good, but I think he's destroying his marriage.

Psalm 89 mentions "unfailing love and truth" as two of God's most prominent characteristics. When truth is ignored, love is compromised. The Bible also says that we are to speak the truth in love—and that doing so helps us grow more and more like Christ (see Ephesians 4:15). Both of those points are important: (1) speak the truth and (2) do it in a loving way.

Remember, love edifies. Love builds up. Love seeks to do what is best for the other person. Holding your frustrations, hurts, and pain inside is not good for your mate or your marriage. In fact, it is extremely unfair because it shuts him or her out. Your spouse cannot respond to your pain if he or she is not aware of it.

If you're in this situation, you might say, "Honey, I love you very much, and I realize that I have wronged you by not sharing this with you sooner. I didn't want to hurt you, but that's no excuse. Please hear me. I'm not trying to put you down; I'm trying to let you know how I feel." Then tell the truth about your emotions. Now your spouse has a chance to help. You might be surprised at the response.

Father, thank you for showing us through your Word that truth and love are both inherent in your nature—and should be inherent in ours. When I hold back the truth because I don't want to hurt my spouse, I'm usually fooling myself about my motives. Please help me to speak honestly but kindly as I try to love my spouse enough to communicate clearly.

COUNTERING MARRIAGE MYTHS

You will know the truth, and the truth will set you free. JOHN 8:32

I WANT TO SHARE four myths that often destroy our motivation for working on our marriages. If I believe these myths, I will be in bondage, but the walls of my prison will really be made of paper. They can only hold me if I think they're too strong for me to break through. Jesus told his hearers that when we know the truth, it will set us free. We can be free from these myths when we counter them with truth.

Myth #1: My state of mind and the quality of my marriage are determined by my environment.

The Truth: God can give peace of mind even in the worst of situations (see John 14:27). I can be God's instrument for improving my marriage.

Myth #2: People cannot change.

The Truth: People do change every day, often dramatically. God is in the business of changing lives (see 2 Corinthians 5:17).

Myth #3: When you are in a bad marriage, you have only two options: be miserable or get out.

The Truth: You can be a positive change agent in your marriage (see Romans 12:2).

Myth #4: Some situations are hopeless.

The Truth: With God, no situation is hopeless (see Romans 15:13). He is the God of miracles. Focus your eyes on him rather than on your situation.

Lord God, thank you for the truth of your Word, which counters the lies we often believe. Please help me to cling to your truths—that change can happen, that nothing is hopeless, that you desire good for my marriage. Transform me, Lord, and give me a transforming love for my spouse.

REMOVING THE PLANK

Do not judge, or you too will be judged. For in the same way you judge others, you will be judged, and with the measure you use, it will be measured to you. Why do you look at the speck of sawdust in your brother's eye and pay no attention to the plank in your own eye? . . . First take the plank out of your own eye, and then you will see clearly to remove the speck from your brother's eye. MATTHEW 7:1-3, 5 (NIV)

IT IS EASY FOR US to identify the failures of our mates, but more difficult to admit our own. When couples come to me for counseling, I often give each individual a sheet of paper and ask them to list their spouse's faults. They will write profusely for ten or fifteen minutes. Some even ask for more paper.

Then I ask them to make a list of their own faults. Most people can think of *one*. But I have seen them sit there and sit there trying to think of a second. Seldom has anyone come back to my office with more than four things on that list. We see twenty-seven things wrong with our spouse, but we only have four on our own list.

We tend to see ourselves through rose-colored glasses. Our faults do not look very big to us because we are used to them. We have lived with them for years. Naturally, then, we attribute the real problem to our mate's behavior. But Jesus warned us not to judge each other, because the level of criticism we use against others will be used against us—likely by our spouse! He told us to first get the plank out of our own eye. Once we've done that, we can see more clearly to help our mate deal with his or her faults.

When it comes to seeking genuine reconciliation with our mate, admitting our own failure is the first step.

Lord Jesus, I am ashamed at how often I criticize my spouse harshly yet don't give my failings a second thought. Please forgive my judgmental spirit. Help me to deal with my own issues before I cast blame on my spouse. And please help me to express love, patience, and kindness to my husband or wife, rather than criticism.

ANGER AT GOD

The Lord is close to the brokenhearted; he rescues those whose spirits are crushed. PSALM 34:18

WE MAY NOT TALK about it much, but the fact is that Christians sometimes get angry with God when we feel that God has treated us unfairly. This often comes after a difficult event, such as a child being diagnosed with a serious disease or being born with a physical or mental abnormality. If this anger is not dealt with properly, it will cause marital discord. Why? We don't feel comfortable expressing our anger to God, so we may express it to our spouse. Our spouse will feel trampled on when the situation was not his or her fault. As a result, our spouse will also become angry. Two angry people do not make for a good marriage.

If you feel that God has been unfair to you, let me encourage you to take your anger directly to him. You need not feel ashamed of your emotions; you can freely express your heart to God. You will not upset him, and your anger will not catch him by surprise.

When Job was going through a time of intense suffering, he desperately wanted to know why. He brought his questions to God, and God listened—and eventually responded. God did not explain everything; in fact, he responded with more questions than answers. However, Job was reassured that God was present, had heard him, and was fully in control. He responded in wonder, "I had only heard about you before, but now I have seen you with my own eyes" (Job 42:5). Often when we express our anger to God, he comforts us by renewing our perspective.

The Lord knows your heart and wants to walk with you through your pain. As Psalm 34 reminds us, he is close to the brokenhearted. The first step in finding healing is admitting to him that you are feeling anger.

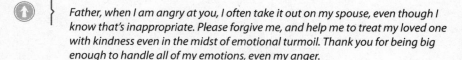

Father, when I am angry at you, I often take it out on my spouse, even though I know that's inappropriate. Please forgive me, and help me to treat my loved one with kindness even in the midst of emotional turmoil. Thank you for being big enough to handle all of my emotions, even my anger.

MOTIVATED BY NEED

A new command I give you: Love one another. As I have loved you, so you must love one another. JOHN 13:34 (NIV)

WE WILL NEVER be able to address the real problems in a relationship until we understand what motivates the other person's behavior. All of our behavior is motivated by inner needs, including the need for love.

Barb complains that her husband doesn't have time for her. She often raises her voice and delivers angry lectures to him, accusing him of not caring for her. Sometimes these lectures work, and her husband, Bob, will sit down and talk with her—but he is typically resentful. How much better their interactions would be if Bob understood that Barb's primary love language is quality time and made an effort to talk with her regularly. Addressing her need for love might well eliminate her negative behavior.

As believers, we're called to love each other as Christ loves us. That was the "new command" Jesus gave his disciples in John 13, and it's a tall order. But one way we can go about that is to make sure we're responding patiently, even when provoked. Loving our spouse with Christlike love means looking at his or her heart. Learning to identify the emotional need that is behind your spouse's behavior—rather than just arguing about the symptoms—is a major step in being a positive influence in an otherwise difficult relationship. Don't curse the behavior. Address the need.

Father, when I'm tempted to roll my eyes or lash out, help me to be patient enough to look beyond the way my loved one is acting. I pray for wisdom to see the needs that are behind the actions and for grace to meet those needs.

ALLOWING FREEDOM

You have been called to live in freedom, my brothers and sisters. But don't use your freedom to satisfy your sinful nature. Instead, use your freedom to serve one another in love. GALATIANS 5:13

YESTERDAY WE TALKED about the emotional need for love. Another of our deepest emotional needs is the need for freedom. In a marriage, we want to be free to express our feelings, thoughts, and desires. We want the freedom to make choices. We often do things for each other, but we don't want to be manipulated or forced into it. If we feel like we are being controlled, we get defensive and angry.

Freedom is never to be absolute. Freedom without boundaries is not a life of love. In Galatians 5, the apostle Paul underscored that believers are free in Christ. Free from the law, free from sin, free to be the people God created us to be. Yet he encourages us to use that freedom to serve each other in love. We don't do it out of guilt or manipulation, but by choice. Love chooses to look out for the beloved's best interests.

When we realize that everyone has this need for freedom, we will allow our spouse freedom to make choices. We will make requests but not demands. We will express our opinions, but also extend the freedom to disagree. Love and freedom are two key elements in a healthy marriage.

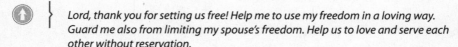

Lord, thank you for setting us free! Help me to use my freedom in a loving way. Guard me also from limiting my spouse's freedom. Help us to love and serve each other without reservation.

DEALING WITH WORKAHOLISM

The LORD has declared today that you are his people, his own special treasure, just as he promised. DEUTERONOMY 26:18

IS YOUR SPOUSE a workaholic? If so, you need to understand that the desire for significance is one of the primary emotional needs that push some people. Many workaholics do not realize that our real significance comes from being children of God and living out his plans for us. After all, Deuteronomy 26 talks about God's children as his own "special treasure." Our heavenly Father loves us not because of anything we are or do, but because he created us. We can't do anything to increase or decrease our value in his sight.

Workaholics tend to forget this. As a result, they put all their effort into excelling in the marketplace and often neglect even their closest relationships. Perhaps a man's father said, "You will never amount to anything"—so he spends a lifetime trying to prove his father wrong. It's a bitter, never-ending cycle.

If you are married to a workaholic, don't curse your spouse's work. Instead, offer praise, admiration, and encouragement. Say how proud you are. The more praise you give, and the more you value your spouse for who he is rather than for what he does, the more likely your workaholic partner will be to spend more time away from work and with you.

Father, thank you for loving us and valuing us unconditionally. Help me to remember that my ultimate significance comes only from you, not from anything I can accomplish. Please help me to communicate that to my spouse as well.

QUALITY TIME FOR KIDS

The LORD is like a father to his children, tender and compassionate to those who fear him. PSALM 103:13

WE'VE HEARD A GREAT DEAL of talk about quality time in recent years. With busy schedules, more and more two-income families, and so many single parents, we are all pressured for time. But while adults are talking about quality time, children are starving for it. Indeed, if you have children, you may observe that much of their misbehavior is a cry for quality time. To the child, even negative attention seems better than no attention.

We're fortunate that we never have to revert to negative behavior to get attention from God. Psalm 103 compares him to the best kind of father, full of tenderness and compassion for his children. When we speak, he hears. When we call, he is there. That's a great example of giving quality time.

Quality time means giving a child your undivided attention. We have to do this when they are infants, but as they get older we often let other responsibilities pull us away from them. I challenge you to make time to look your children in the eyes, to listen as they talk, to ask questions, and to communicate to them, "You are important to me." It's time well invested. A closer relationship with your children will benefit your marriage as well.

Father God, thank you for always being available for me. Help me to fill that need for my children as well. Please give me the patience and wisdom to stop what I'm doing and give my child my undivided attention. Help me to communicate how much my children mean to me—and to you, too.

TELLING STORIES

Fix these words of mine in your hearts and minds. . . . Teach them to your children, talking about them when you sit at home and when you walk along the road, when you lie down and when you get up.

DEUTERONOMY 11:18-19 (NIV)

ALL CHILDREN LOVE STORIES. When they are small, we read to them, and the story often leads to exciting conversations. Stories stimulate emotions. Asking children, "How does that make you feel?" is a way of helping them learn to express emotions. Children also like to hear about your childhood. Parents and grandparents give the child a sense of belonging and family history when they share such stories.

If you have children, remember that reading and telling stories is one way to give a child quality time. For those brief moments, the child has your undivided attention. If this is the child's primary love language, then nothing is more important in making him or her feel loved. When you meet a child's need for love, you are laying the foundation for a bright future.

The Bible is also clear that telling stories of the faith is an important way to teach our children about God. Whether we're retelling events from the Bible or sharing about how God worked in our lives today, we can set a strong foundation of faith—even as we spend important minutes with our kids. Your whole family will benefit.

Lord God, there is so much I want to communicate to my children. Help me to take the time to talk, to connect, to tell stories, and especially to teach about you. Please help my spouse and me to be good partners in parenting as well.

COVENANT RELATIONSHIP

God showed his great love for us by sending Christ to die for us while we were still sinners. ROMANS 5:8

WHEN YOU GOT MARRIED, did you sign a contract or make a covenant? When you sign a mortgage contract, the bank loans you the money *if* you agree to make the monthly payments. Stop making payments, and the bank will foreclose on your house to get their money back.

Many couples have the same attitude about marriage. They might say, "I will love you and be faithful to you *if* you will love me and be faithful to me." That is not the biblical view of marriage. Biblically, marriage is a covenant, not a contract. Covenant marriage is based on unconditional love—love no matter what.

God is the author of unconditional love. Romans 5 reminds us that God loved us and sacrificed for us even when we were sinful, undeserving, and ungrateful. The prophet Isaiah even compared our best efforts to "filthy rags" (64:6). We have nothing to offer God, but he loves us nonetheless. Loving the unlovely is the hallmark of God. It is also the key to a successful marriage.

Lord Jesus, thank you for loving me when I can offer nothing in return. Help me to love my spouse the same way—freely and fully, no matter what.

THE POWER OF APOLOGY

When I refused to confess my sin, my body wasted away, and I groaned all day long. . . . Finally, I confessed all my sins to you and stopped trying to hide my guilt. I said to myself, "I will confess my rebellion to the LORD." And you forgave me! All my guilt is gone. PSALM 32:3, 5

THE CLASSIC SEVENTIES MOVIE *Love Story* advised us that true love means never having to say, "I'm sorry." I don't think they got it right, for one simple reason: We are all human, and humans are not perfect. All of us end up hurting the people we love most. Having a good marriage does not demand perfection, but it does require us to apologize when we fail.

When I say, "I'm sorry," I'm expressing regret that my words or behavior have brought you pain. It's a basic guideline for getting along with others. It also reflects the spiritual truth that to receive forgiveness, we first need to admit what we've done. Ignoring our sin doesn't make it go away, as King David experienced before he wrote the words of Psalm 32. In fact, ignoring it often makes us feel far worse. But when we express regret for our wrongdoing and the hurt it caused, we pave the way for forgiveness and reconciliation. That's true in our relationship with God as well as in our marriage.

When was the last time you said, "I'm sorry," to your husband or wife? If it's been a while, then you probably owe him or her an apology. Love means always being willing to say, "I'm sorry."

God, sometimes it's so hard to humble myself to say a simple, "I'm sorry." Help me not to take my spouse's forgiveness for granted, but to be willing to admit when I am wrong.

BEYOND "I'M SORRY"

The ear tests the words it hears just as the mouth distinguishes between foods.

JOB 12:11

PERHAPS YOU HAVE SAID, "I'm sorry," but your spouse is finding it hard to forgive you. You may feel frustrated and say to yourself, *I apologized. What else can I do?* If you're serious, I'll tell you. Ask your spouse this question: "What can I do to make this up to you?" You might also say, "I know I hurt you, and I feel badly about it, but I want to make it right. I want to do something to show you that I love you."

This is far more powerful than simply saying, "I'm sorry." Why? Because sometimes words don't mean much unless they're backed up with action. The Old Testament figure Job was overrun with words from his friends, who tried to make sense of his terrible suffering. But much of what they said was wrong, and in the passage above, Job says that he tested their words to determine what was true. We all do the same thing—test words to see if they are genuine and if they will likely be followed up with action.

To establish trust, you need to show that your words are genuine. When you ask your spouse how you can make the situation right, you are trying to make restitution. You are demonstrating that you really care about your relationship. After all, what your spouse wants to know is whether your apology is sincere. Make sure your answer is clear.

Lord, often I need to go the extra mile to make amends. Help me to show my spouse that I am sincere, and that I desire to do what is right. Help me to be willing to seek the reconciliation that our relationship needs.

BUILDING INTIMACY THROUGH LISTENING

Pay attention to how you hear. To those who listen to my teaching, more understanding will be given. But for those who are not listening, even what they think they understand will be taken away from them. LUKE 8:18

BUILDING INTIMACY is a process, not an event. We don't obtain intimacy and keep it on the shelf as a treasure for the rest of our lives. Intimacy is fluid, not static. And the way we maintain intimacy is communication.

Communication involves two simple elements: *self-revelation* and *listening*. One person tells the other his or her thoughts, feelings, and experiences (self-revelation) while the other *listens* with a view to understanding what the spouse is thinking and feeling. The process is then reversed, and the speaker becomes the listener. The simple act of talking and listening maintains intimacy.

If this is all it takes, what's the big problem? It's called selfishness. Too often, we stop listening and start preaching. When both partners are preaching, neither preacher has an audience. When we get tired of talking at each other, we withdraw in silent resentment. We will never be able to return to intimacy until we apologize and forgive each other for being selfish.

Jesus talked about listening, as we can see in Luke 8:18. When we listen intently, he said, we gain understanding. But when we aren't paying attention, we lose even the understanding we once had. That's how important genuine listening is in building intimacy.

Father, I need to be a better listener—to you as well as to my spouse. Help me to stop my mind and my mouth from moving when it's my loved one's turn to talk. Please give me greater understanding so that we can build greater intimacy.

FAMILY FAVORITISM

God does not show favoritism. ROMANS 2:11

HOW CAN WE *leave* parents after we're married and at the same time *honor* them? This can get sticky because, of course, two sets of parents are generally involved in a couple's life. Issues can particularly arise during the holidays. Perhaps the wife's mother wants the couple home for Christmas Eve, and the husband's mother wants them home for Christmas dinner. That may be possible if the two families live in the same town, but not if they live five hundred miles apart.

The guiding principle must be equality. Romans 2:11 says, "God does not show favoritism." In this particular passage, the apostle Paul is reminding his readers that God makes no distinction between Jewish and Gentile believers, but God's lack of favoritism certainly extends to other groups as well. He is our model. We must seek to treat both sets of in-laws with equality. This may mean Christmas here this year and Christmas there next year, or Christmas with one family and Thanksgiving with the other. The same principle applies to phone calls, e-mails, visits, dinners, and vacations.

You are not responsible for your parents' happiness; that will be determined by their own attitude. You are simply seeking to show equal honor and respect for them. Having done so, you have followed the biblical injunction: Honor your father and your mother.

Father, thank you for not showing favoritism. You welcome everyone who turns to you. Help me to treat my parents and my in-laws with equal honor and respect, and to make sure my spouse and I are fair in the way we spend our time. Please give us grace as we discuss these issues.

HANDLING ADVICE

Get all the advice and instruction you can, so you will be wise the rest of your life. PROVERBS 19:20

HERE'S A COMMON QUESTION I hear as a counselor: "We recently had our first child, and my mother insists on doing things that contradict our parenting choices. I don't want to hurt her feelings. What shall we do?" It always helps to begin by realizing that your mother's (or mother-in-law's) intentions are good. Give her credit for trying to help you. In fact, some of her ideas may be excellent, so don't write her off simply because she is your mother.

Remember, the book of Proverbs speaks highly of those who seek advice and instruction. When it comes to rearing children, others' knowledge and ideas—whether from a parent or from books—are often beneficial. On the other hand, you must not let your mother control your parenting choices. You and your spouse are responsible for rearing your child.

I suggest you listen to your mother's ideas and thank her for sharing them with you. Then you and your spouse do what you think is best for your child. If your mother is upset because you did not take her advice, say, "I can understand that, Mom, and I really appreciate your advice, but we must do what we think is best for our child. That's what you and Dad did, right? And I think you did a pretty good job with me."

Your mother may not be happy, but she will learn to back off and wait until you ask for her advice—which, incidentally, would be a wise move on your part.

Thank you, God, for the child you have given us to rear. Thank you, too, for loving, concerned parents. We pray for wisdom to sift through advice and make wise decisions as we rear our child.

PERSONAL GROWTH

You made all the delicate, inner parts of my body and knit me together in my mother's womb. Thank you for making me so wonderfully complex! Your workmanship is marvelous—how well I know it. PSALM 139:13-14

MARRIAGES FAIL for three primary reasons: (1) lack of an intimate relationship with God, (2) lack of an intimate relationship with our mate, or (3) lack of an intimate understanding and acceptance of ourselves. It is the last of these that I want to address in the next few days.

Most of us tend to either underestimate or overestimate our value. We perceive ourselves either as useless failures or as God's gift to the world. Both of these extremes are incorrect. In reality, every person on earth is a miracle of God's workmanship and is "wonderfully complex," as the psalmist says above. And at the same time, every person on earth has sinned and fallen short of God's glory (see Romans 3:23). None of us are worthy because of anything we have done, but rather because the Lord created us and saved us.

The truth is that your pattern of feeling, thinking, and behaving, which is your personality, has both strengths and weaknesses. The first step in making the most of who you are is identifying your strengths and seeking to channel them into productive actions. Next, identify your weaknesses and seek to grow. Personal growth will likely spill over into your marriage.

> *Lord Jesus, help me to see myself accurately. I know that you have created me in your image—yet I fail so often. I need to acknowledge my strengths and weaknesses and work to change in the way you want me to. I want to grow personally so that I can also become a better husband or wife.*

CHANGED BY THE HOLY SPIRIT

Let the Spirit renew your thoughts and attitudes. Put on your new nature, created to be like God—truly righteous and holy. EPHESIANS 4:23-24

IS YOUR PERSONALITY an asset or a liability to your marriage? Most personality traits are expressed by contrasting words. We speak of an individual being optimistic or pessimistic, critical or complimentary, extroverted or introverted, patient or impatient. While our personalities are developed in childhood, they are not set in concrete. We can change.

If I realize that my tendency to withdraw and remain silent is detrimental to my marriage, I can learn to share my feelings and thoughts. If I realize that my critical attitude is killing my mate's spirit, I can break the pattern and learn to give compliments. The message of the Bible is that God loves us as we are, but he loves us too much to leave us as we are. We all need to grow, and growth requires change. I am influenced by my personality, but I need not be controlled by it. Instead, I am to be controlled by the Holy Spirit. In Ephesians 4, Paul tells us to "let the Spirit renew [our] thoughts and attitudes." He will work in our lives, but we need to allow him to do it. When I yield to him, I will see significant changes in my approach to life and marriage.

Holy Spirit, through your power I know you can change me. I want to be renewed. I want to be more like Jesus. Please help me to yield to you. I want to reap the benefits in my life and in my marriage.

LOOKING AHEAD

Forgetting the past and looking forward to what lies ahead, I press on to reach the end of the race and receive the heavenly prize for which God, through Christ Jesus, is calling us. PHILIPPIANS 3:13-14

PERSONAL GROWTH leads to marital growth. Personal growth can come in many ways, including dealing with feelings of inferiority and superiority, or understanding our personality and how it affects our marriages. Today, I want to address the need to accept those things about yourself that cannot be changed.

Perhaps the most influential unchangeable factor in your life is your history. By definition, it cannot be changed. Your parents, for better or for worse, dead or alive, known or unknown, are your parents. Your childhood, pleasant or painful, is your childhood and stands as history. Your marriage or past relationships fall into the same category. No matter what the circumstances, it is futile to reason, "We should never have gotten married in the first place." The fact cannot be changed. You can divorce, often with great pain, but you can never erase your marriage. Your history is not to be changed, but accepted and dealt with.

The apostle Paul had a past he would have liked to erase. Once a self-righteous Pharisee, he zealously persecuted Christians, having some of them imprisoned. He turned around completely when he became a believer, eventually becoming the most well-known missionary in the early church. He accomplished much for the Kingdom of God—yet he always had to live with the memories of his past. It's clear from these verses in Philippians that Paul did that primarily by looking ahead, toward the future. The same goes for us. We must confess our own failures, accept God's forgiveness—and then move on. When you accept your past and focus on the future, you are moving toward a growing marriage.

Father, thank you for Paul's example of moving beyond his past. You know there are things I would like to change, both things I have done and things that were done to me. I bring all of those to you. Please help me to accept your forgiveness and comfort and then move on, looking to the future. May it include a strong marriage!

THE POWER OF LOVE

Imitate God, therefore, in everything you do, because you are his dear children. Live a life filled with love, following the example of Christ. He loved us and offered himself as a sacrifice for us, a pleasing aroma to God.

EPHESIANS 5:1-2

IN THE CONTEXT OF MARRIAGE, if we do not feel loved, our differences are magnified. We each come to view the other as a threat to our happiness. We fight for self-worth and significance, and marriage becomes a battlefield rather than a haven.

Love is not the answer to every problem, but it creates a climate of security in which we can seek answers to those issues that bother us. In the security of love, a couple can discuss differences without fear of condemnation. Conflicts can be resolved. Two people who are different can learn to live together in harmony and discover how to bring out the best in each other. Those are the rewards of love.

Love really is the most powerful force in the world. It was love that led Christ to give his life for us. We have eternal life because of his love, and we also have an opportunity to love each other as his representatives. In Ephesians 5, the apostle Paul encourages us to follow Christ's example and live a life of love. Marriages function best when both partners feel genuinely loved. The decision to love your spouse holds tremendous potential, and learning his or her primary love language makes that potential a reality.

Father, thank you for the transforming power of love. Your love for me gives me so many things—self-worth, purpose, and eternal life. May I learn to imitate you in the way I love my spouse, and may that love lead to greater unity.

DIALECT OF TOUCH

Husbands, live with your wives in an understanding way. 1 PETER 3:7 (ESV)

IN MARRIAGE, the love language of "physical touch" has many dialects. This does not mean that all touches are created equal. Some will bring more pleasure to your spouse than others. Your best instructor is your spouse. Your wife knows what she perceives as a loving touch; don't insist on touching her in your way and in your time. Respect her wishes. Learn to speak her dialect. Don't make the mistake of believing that the touch that brings pleasure to you will also bring the most pleasure to her.

First Peter 3:7 says that husbands are to dwell with our wives "according to knowledge" (KJV) or "in an understanding way." In other words, we need to know our spouse on a deep level. Men, the primary source of knowledge about what makes your wife feel loved is your wife. Some wives enjoy a back rub, others can take it or leave it, and others find it annoying. Women, of course the same goes for husbands.

God made your spouse unique. Physical touch is one of the five love languages, but you must discover what *kind* of touches your spouse enjoys. When you speak the right dialect of physical touch, your loved one will feel loved.

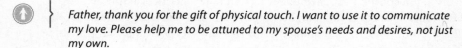

Father, thank you for the gift of physical touch. I want to use it to communicate my love. Please help me to be attuned to my spouse's needs and desires, not just my own.

CREATIVE TOUCH

Kiss me and kiss me again, for your love is sweeter than wine.

SONG OF SOLOMON 1:2

LOVE TOUCHES may be extended or brief. A back rub takes time, but putting your hand on your spouse's shoulder as you pour a cup of coffee takes only a moment. Sitting close to each other on the couch as you watch your favorite television program requires no additional time, but it may loudly communicate your love.

Touching your spouse as you walk through the room where he is sitting takes only a second. Touching each other as you leave the house and again when you return may involve only a brief kiss or hug, but it may speak volumes to your spouse.

If you discover that physical touch is your spouse's primary love language, coming up with new ways and places to touch can be an exciting challenge. You may find that you can fill your spouse's emotional love tank as you stroll across the parking lot, simply by holding hands. A kiss after you get in the car might make the drive home much shorter. The Song of Solomon is a description of a husband and wife taking joy in touching each other. It can be inspiring reading if you're trying to think of new ways to express love to your spouse through physical touch.

Dear Lord, help me to be generous with my time and touches. I want to express my love to my spouse in more and creative ways.

SPEAKING A LOVE LANGUAGE THAT'S NOT YOUR OWN

The husband should fulfill his wife's sexual needs, and the wife should fulfill her husband's needs. The wife gives authority over her body to her husband, and the husband gives authority over his body to his wife. Do not deprive each other of sexual relations. 1 CORINTHIANS 7:3-5

ONE WIFE TOLD ME, "I want to touch my husband, but when I try, he draws back. He acts like it irritates him, unless of course we are having sex." What is this man telling his wife by his behavior? That physical touch is not his primary love language. He will respond much better to words of affirmation or one of the other love languages. If physical touch is your spouse's primary love language, he or she will welcome tender touches any time you want to give them.

Often, people speak their own love language to others. So if your spouse is always wanting to hug or kiss, it may be because that is what he or she would like from you.

Some people will find it difficult to speak the language of physical touch. Perhaps they were not touched as children, and touching is uncomfortable for them. But anyone can learn to speak this language. The marriage advice in the verses above from the apostle Paul makes clear that we are not to deprive our spouse of sexual intercourse—or any other meaningful touch. When we marry, our bodies are no longer just our own. We can use touch as a gift to each other. Remember, love is about seeking to meet your spouse's need, not your own. You don't touch because it feels comfortable to you but because it communicates love to your beloved.

Father, you've made clear that touch is a gift not to be withheld from my spouse. Please help me to offer it freely and generously, as a gift of love.

LOVING MONEY

The love of money is the root of all kinds of evil. And some people, craving money, have wandered from the true faith and pierced themselves with many sorrows. 1 TIMOTHY 6:10

WHY HAS MONEY become such a problem in American marriages? Some of the poorest couples in America have abundance compared to the masses of the world's population. I am convinced that the problem lies not in the amount of money that a couple has, but in their attitude toward money and the way they handle it.

This is in keeping with Paul's words in 1 Timothy 6:10. When we love money above other things, we may be willing to do almost anything to get more. Paul refers to believers whose eagerness for money has caused them to leave the faith and experience "many sorrows." Such sorrows are not the result of having money or not having money, but of letting money be the central focus of our life. If money is more important than God and our marriage, then we will have problems on both fronts.

Check your attitude. Are you looking to money for happiness, or are you looking to God? Your answer will have a profound impact on your marriage.

Father, money can be so seductive. I don't want to love it and pursue it to the detriment of my faith or my relationships with others around me. Please guard my heart and keep our priorities right as a couple.

WHERE DO WE FIND SATISFACTION?

Pursue righteousness and a godly life, along with faith, love, perseverance, and gentleness. Fight the good fight for the true faith. Hold tightly to the eternal life to which God has called you, which you have confessed so well before many witnesses. 1 TIMOTHY 6:11-12

MANY COUPLES BELIEVE that if they only had a hundred dollars more each month, they could be financially at ease. They say, "If we can just make it over this hump, we'll be satisfied." But that's faulty reasoning. Meet them two years later, and they are still trying to get over the hump.

Real satisfaction is found not in money, but in "righteousness and a godly life, along with faith, love, perseverance, and gentleness"—in short, in living with God and according to his values. This is the way the apostle Paul encouraged his young friend Timothy to live. Doing right, expressing love, being patient with imperfection, and having a realistic appraisal of yourself are the things that bring true fulfillment to a life and a marriage.

"But I must have food, clothing, and shelter," you might say. True, and these are promised by God to those who will put him first in life. Jesus said, "Seek the Kingdom of God above all else, and live righteously, and he will give you everything you need" (Matthew 6:33). Our physical provisions are the by-products of right and godly living. When we focus on the Lord and on our marriage relationship, satisfaction will follow.

> *Lord Jesus, thank you for the promise that you will provide everything we need. Please help us as a couple to pursue godly living and put your values first—not our finances.*

WORKING TOGETHER FOR STEWARDSHIP

The master was full of praise. "Well done, my good and faithful servant. You have been faithful in handling this small amount, so now I will give you many more responsibilities. Let's celebrate together!" MATTHEW 25:21

A COMMON BIBLICAL WORD regarding money is *stewardship*. We are responsible for using wisely all that God gives us. The amount of our resources is relatively unimportant, but the faithful use of our resources is all-important. When Jesus told the parable of the talents, he finished by sharing the above words where the master congratulates the servant for his hard work and faithfulness. The Lord doesn't expect all of us to have the same amount of money or talent, but he does expect us to work hard with whatever we do have.

Financial resources have tremendous potential for good. As stewards, we are responsible to use all that God has entrusted to us. Sound planning, buying, saving, investing, and giving are all a part of our stewardship.

But in marriage, all of this must be done in cooperation with our spouse. We cannot be lone rangers financially and think that we can still have intimacy in marriage. Finances are an important part of marriage, and both spouses must be included in how they are handled. Succeeding with money and failing with marriage is an empty success.

Lord Jesus, I'm grateful for the parable of the talents and the reminder that you care about the details of what we do with our time and money. Please help us to work together as a couple. Remind us that all we have is yours, and help us to use those resources wisely.

SHARING OUR EMOTIONS

Long ago the LORD said to Israel: "I have loved you, my people, with an everlasting love. With unfailing love I have drawn you to myself."

JEREMIAH 31:3

HAVE YOU EVER FELT disappointed, sad, frustrated, fearful, or angry? Did you know the Bible teaches that emotions, both positive and negative, are gifts from God? How dull life would be if we had no feelings. Try to imagine watching a sunset, a ball game, or the ocean with no emotions. Imagine standing beside the open grave of a friend and feeling nothing.

We are made in the image of God, and a part of what that means is that we are emotional creatures. God feels anger, love, hate, and compassion. The above passage from the book of Jeremiah is just one of many places throughout the Bible where the Lord expresses strong emotions toward his people. Jesus, who was God in the flesh, felt depressed and sorrowful when he was approaching his death on the cross (see Matthew 26:36-46). He is not dispassionate, and that should not be our ideal either.

All humans experience emotions, but some couples do not share them. Perhaps they were taught as children to hide their feelings. "Big boys are not afraid," some parents may have said. Marriage is meant to be an intimate relationship. If we fail to share emotions, we inhibit intimacy, and as a result, we create a distance between us. Sharing positive emotions will enhance the joy. Sharing negative emotions will ease the pain. Letting your spouse into the inner world of your emotions will build intimacy in your marriage.

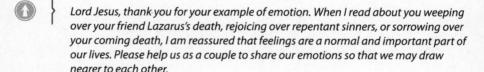

Lord Jesus, thank you for your example of emotion. When I read about you weeping over your friend Lazarus's death, rejoicing over repentant sinners, or sorrowing over your coming death, I am reassured that feelings are a normal and important part of our lives. Please help us as a couple to share our emotions so that we may draw nearer to each other.

USING EMOTIONS WISELY

You are a slave to whatever controls you. 2 PETER 2:19

WHY ARE WE SO FEARFUL of negative emotions? Perhaps because we have seen friends who followed similar emotions and made poor decisions. They did what they felt like doing, and everyone around them suffered.

We must distinguish between negative feelings and negative actions. For example, let's say you are feeling sad about the emotional distance between you and your spouse. You could share these feelings and seek to build your relationship—a wise approach. On the other hand, you could have an affair with someone else—an extremely foolish approach.

Emotions always stimulate us to take action. However, we must make responsible decisions. We don't choose our emotions, but we do choose our actions. Our emotions do not have to control us. In fact, if they do, we become slaves to them, according to 2 Peter 2:19. Emotions are not our masters, but they can be valuable tools.

Sharing your emotions with your spouse opens the possibility of additional insights. Failure to share emotions limits your thoughts and actions to your own wisdom. The Scriptures say two are better than one (see Ecclesiastes 4:9). Remember, at the heart of marriage is the idea of sharing life. Emotions are a part of life.

Father, thank you for giving me the opportunity to share joys and sorrows with my spouse. When I do that, the joys are magnified and the sorrows are lessened. That's a wonderful gift. Please help us to share our emotions with each other more freely.

AVOIDING BITTERNESS

Look after each other so that none of you fails to receive the grace of God.
Watch out that no poisonous root of bitterness grows up to trouble you,
corrupting many. HEBREWS 12:15

YOUR SPOUSE HURT YOU DEEPLY, and you are feeling angry. What are you going to do about it?

Anger is a natural emotion when we have been wronged. But if it is not handled properly, it can be extremely destructive. The book of Hebrews warns against letting the "poisonous root of bitterness" grow, because it can bring trouble, corruption, and hardened hearts. Given this truth, how should we react when we become angry?

One response is to repress the anger—holding it inside and letting it smolder. When we do this, the unexpressed anger grows into bitterness and becomes a malignant cancer that slowly destroys the fiber of life. Another response is an uncontrolled expression of anger. Like an explosion, it destroys everything in its range. Such an outburst is like an emotional heart attack and may produce permanent damage.

There is a better way. It begins by saying to yourself, *I'm extremely angry about what my spouse has done. But I will not allow his or her wrong to destroy me, and I will not attempt to destroy him or her. I will turn my spouse over to God, who is just, and I will release my anger to him.*

Lord Jesus, you know that there are times when my heart is bitter toward my spouse. Please help me to stop focusing on the wrong that I experienced and instead turn the situation over to you. I know you can heal me, Jesus.

CONFESSING BITTERNESS

Get rid of all bitterness, rage, anger, harsh words, and slander, as well as all types of evil behavior. EPHESIANS 4:31

YOU HAVE A RIGHT to feel angry, but not bitter! Yes, you are within your rights to feel angry, but you do not have the right to destroy one of God's creatures—yourself.

In the Bible, bitterness is always viewed as sin because it results from a choice. The feeling of anger cannot be avoided, but bitterness results from a daily choice to let anger live in your heart. Thus, in Ephesians 4, Paul directs believers to get rid of bitterness. The author of Hebrews warns us not to let bitterness take root, lest it corrupt us and turn us away from the faith (see 12:15). We must confess bitterness as sin and accept God's forgiveness.

Still, it's important to realize that a one-time confession of bitterness may not alleviate all hostile feelings. If you have been harboring the bitterness for a long time, the feelings that accompany the bitter attitude may be slow to die.

What do you do when thoughts and feelings of anger and bitterness return? You might pray, "Father, you know what I'm thinking and feeling, but I have given those emotions to you. Now help me to do something good with my life today." Regardless of the circumstances, let God love your spouse through you.

Father, sometimes I want to hold on to my anger and bitterness. It feels good momentarily, but over time it hardens my heart and changes the way I view my spouse. I confess my bitterness to you and ask for your forgiveness. Please help me to let it go—now and each time it comes back.

AVOIDING ARGUMENTS

Avoiding a fight is a mark of honor; only fools insist on quarreling.

PROVERBS 20:3

I'VE OFTEN HEARD this comment in counseling sessions: "I don't like to talk with my spouse because we always end up arguing!" Some people love to argue; others do not. The Bible says that it's honorable to avoid a fight and wise not to quarrel. That's a good rule of thumb for marriage, but that doesn't mean you should shut down communication altogether. Do you ever withdraw from conversation because you fear an argument? That may be a natural reaction, but where does it lead? To silence and isolation. That's not a growing marriage.

How can you learn to talk with an argumentative spouse without arguing? First of all, acknowledge that you have a problem: Fear of arguments is keeping you from effective communication. You need to share this with your spouse. You might say, "I really want us to have a good marriage with good communication. I think that is what you want, too, but I need to share something. Lately, I've drawn back from talking with you because I am afraid that we will get into an argument. Have you noticed that?" Wow! Now you have laid it on the table. Your spouse has a chance to respond. Whatever he or she says, I suggest you offer the following idea: "Could we agree to dedicate one night a week to arguing? The rest of the week we could talk about the good things in our lives."

Your spouse may well be open to this new format. After all, why argue all the time if you can limit it to one evening a week? If an issue comes up that you need to address, commit to discussing it calmly. If you can't do that, write it down and come back to it at your designated "conflict discussion" time. And if you are the argumentative spouse, perhaps you can be the one to suggest this new idea. You may see your communication blossom when the threat of constant argument is gone.

Lord God, sometimes our different levels of comfort with conflict and arguing cause our communication to shut down. Help me to be aware of when either my spouse or I am shutting down because of quarreling. Please give us the restraint to discuss things calmly and communicate well without constant arguing.

ASKING QUESTIONS

*May the words of my mouth and the meditation of my heart be pleasing
to you, O LORD, my rock and my redeemer.*   PSALM 19:14

TALKING IS THE MOST fundamental art of marriage—and often the most
ignored. How would you respond to this question: "Will you share with me
one experience you had today and how it affected you?" How do you think
your spouse would respond? Why not ask it and see! Sharing with each other
is not that difficult, and it is encouraged by questions.

Questions need to be specific and open ended. "Did you have a good
day?" is likely to elicit only a yes or a no. Instead, try, "What were the high and
low points in your day and why?" It will take a little reflection, but you and
your spouse can answer that question, and your answers may lead to more
involved conversations. Questions should not be asked for the purpose of
creating an argument, but so that you can understand what is going on in
your spouse's life.

Silence leads to isolation and separation. Sharing your thoughts leads to
understanding and closeness. Marriage should involve two people having fellowship with each other, not two people living in the same house alone. As we
talk, we can pray that our words and conversations would be pleasing to the
Lord. Ask a question today, and stimulate meaningful conversation.

*Father, I want the communication in our relationship to honor you. Please help us
to reach out to each other by asking questions. I want to be genuinely involved in
what's going on in my spouse's life. Show me how to encourage honest, meaningful
conversation by what I ask.*

ENHANCING COMMUNICATION

Don't use foul or abusive language. Let everything you say be good and helpful, so that your words will be an encouragement to those who hear them.

EPHESIANS 4:29

LEARNING TO SHARE your thoughts is the most foundational element of communication. In marriages that fail, almost all couples say, "Our communication just broke down." How do we keep this from happening? We do what we did when we were courting: Listen when the other person talks. Listen without condemnation.

If your spouse comes up with a new idea that surprises you, resist the urge to respond with criticism. Instead, ask questions. You might say, "That's an interesting idea. If we tried to apply that to our marriage, what would it look like? What need would this meet for you? If we did it, what would be the downside?" Questions like these can lead to meaningful dialogue.

Statements such as "That won't work for us" or "I don't want to do that" stop conversation cold. It's okay to have those thoughts and even okay to express them—if you do it in a positive way, *after* you have listened carefully to your spouse. You might say, "I'm afraid that might not work for us. I'm not sure that I really want to do it. Can we spend a few days thinking about it and then discuss it again?" That's being respectful and helpful, following the advice Paul gives in Ephesians 4. Our words to each other should be encouraging, not abusive or discouraging.

When you're keeping communication open and respectful, you're moving toward a growing marriage.

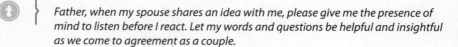

Father, when my spouse shares an idea with me, please give me the presence of mind to listen before I react. Let my words and questions be helpful and insightful as we come to agreement as a couple.

THE GIFT OF MARRIAGE

The man who finds a wife finds a treasure, and he receives favor from the LORD. PROVERBS 18:22

THE RESEARCH IS IN, and marriage is the winner. It's true. Married people are happier, healthier, and more satisfied with life than are singles. (And the people who are happiest of all are those who have been married to the same person over the long haul.) It seems that contemporary people are discovering by means of sociological research what the Bible declared to be true thousands of years ago.

It was God who said, "It is not good for the man to be alone" (Genesis 2:18). The first man, Adam, had a vocation. He had a place to live and plenty of animals to pet. He even had a relationship with God. But it was God's analysis that Adam needed a wife. God had created all the animals in pairs—male and female—but had initially created only one human. Eve's creation was not an afterthought. God didn't say, "Oh, I forgot to make a woman. I'd better take care of that." No! It was a matter of timing. God's intention all along was to create people both male and female, but he first wanted to give Adam time to survey the world and discover the need for companionship—a counterpart to himself. Then God created what he termed "a helper who is just right for him."

King Solomon tells us in Proverbs 18 that the man who finds a wife—or, we can extrapolate, the woman who finds a husband—finds a treasure. Marriage is a beautiful gift from the Lord.

Father, thank you for my spouse and for the gift of marriage. I am so grateful to have a mate who can be my companion through life. Let me never forget that my spouse is a treasure and a reward from you. Help me to treat him or her accordingly.

BENEFITS OF MARRIAGE

Since they are no longer two but one, let no one split apart what God has joined together. MATTHEW 19:6

AT THE VERY HEART of what marriage is all about is the concept of companionship. When God said of Adam, "It is not good for man to be alone," he was identifying something about human nature. We were not created to live in isolation, cut off from others. After he created Eve, God said, "The two shall become one flesh." This is the opposite of being alone.

Marriage is male and female relating to each other as counterparts. It is not competition, but cooperation as teammates. We are joined together by God for life, to accomplish his purposes for our lives. Jesus said that once a man and woman are joined in marriage, no one should divide them. We are joined as one in a covenant relationship.

Now I am fully aware that some people are called of God to live a life of singleness. But I believe that is the exception, not the rule. I'm also aware that all of us live a portion of our lives as singles, both before and after marriage. Before marriage, singleness helps us discover our need for companionship. After the death of a spouse, we adjust to being alone and we bask in the memories of our intimacy through the years. Marriage is God's idea, and it is designed for humans' good and God's glory.

Lord Jesus, I'm grateful that you have joined us together as a couple. May nothing come between us or split us apart. Instead, may we be a strong team, working in cooperation rather than competition. Thank you, Lord, for the gift of marriage.

WHEN ALCOHOLISM ENTERS THE MARRIAGE

Who has anguish? Who has sorrow? . . . It is the one who spends long hours in the taverns, trying out new drinks. . . . For in the end [wine] bites like a poisonous snake; it stings like a viper. PROVERBS 23:29-30, 32

FEW THINGS DAMAGE marital intimacy more than alcoholism. In fact, research has shown that a marriage in which one partner is a drug or alcohol abuser has only a one-in-ten chance of survival. With an estimated twelve million alcoholics in the United States, we are dealing with a problem of colossal magnitude.

Alcoholism is not a new problem; it's been around since Old Testament times. In fact, in Proverbs 23, King Solomon wrote a vivid description of the negative effects of chronically drinking too much. Alcoholism brings anguish and sorrow.

Why is alcoholism so destructive to marriage? The answer lies in the behavior that grows out of substance abuse. The alcoholic is extremely egocentric; life centers on meeting his or her own needs. In his effort to hide his addiction, the abuser becomes a master of deceit. Such deceit builds walls of separation between marital partners. The alcoholic is insensitive to the feelings of those who care for him, and his addiction often leads to verbal abuse and loss of jobs.

The partner who focuses on these symptoms rather than on the real problem will be greatly frustrated. Too often, the partner becomes an enabler, doing anything possible to keep the peace in the family. Ultimately, the only thing that will help an alcoholic is tough love.

Father, I pray for your guidance and help as we figure out how to deal with the addictions or habits in our lives that threaten our marital unity, including those that may not be as blatant as substance abuse. Please grant us wisdom.

LOVING AN ALCOHOLIC

Above all, clothe yourselves with love, which binds us all together in perfect harmony. COLOSSIANS 3:14

LIVING WITH AN ALCOHOLIC or any type of addict calls for tough love. Barbara realized this after ten years of living with an alcoholic husband. Alcoholics know how to manipulate, con, and lie in order to be successful addicts. Their stories and excuses sound so plausible, you really want to believe them.

But eventually Barbara learned how to love her husband genuinely by refusing to pick up the pieces, to make excuses, or to rescue him from the consequences of his behavior. She let him stay in the local jail in spite of his pleadings for her to bail him out. She let him lose his job rather than intervening on his behalf. When he went on a drinking binge, she took the children and went to her mother's.

That was the last straw for Dan. He came begging and pleading for Barbara to return, but she was able to say no to his tears. She told him that she would not return until he entered a treatment program and agreed to go through marriage counseling with her. Dan came back begging the next night, and she repeated her answer. A week later, he was in a treatment program.

The Bible is clear that we are to "clothe [ourselves] with love," as Paul wrote in Colossians 3. But loving people doesn't mean letting them walk all over us; rather, it means doing what is ultimately best for them. Barbara was learning that tough love is the only love an alcoholic understands.

Father, sometimes we think that gentle, tender love is the only way to be Christlike. But I know that's not always the way you love; when I read through the Bible, I see times when you imposed consequences so that people would be motivated to change. Please help me to know when tough love is appropriate in my marriage, and help me to implement it with my spouse's best interests in mind.

HOPE FOR THE ALCOHOLIC

We know that our old sinful selves were crucified with Christ so that sin might lose its power in our lives. We are no longer slaves to sin. For when we died with Christ we were set free from the power of sin. ROMANS 6:6-7

HOW CAN YOU BE A POSITIVE AGENT for change while living with an alcoholic? Like Barbara, whom we read about yesterday, you may need to say something like this: "I love you too much to sit here and let you destroy yourself and me. The next time you come home drunk, I will take the children and move in with my parents."

This may seem like a very unchristian action. But in reality, it may be the only kind of love an alcoholic can understand. Alcoholics will be motivated to seek help only when they realize they are about to lose something important.

There is hope; deliverance is possible for the alcoholic. Romans 6 and many other places in the Bible make clear that as believers, we are no longer enslaved to sin. Christ has set us free from its power! He can transform our lives and break down any remaining areas where sin has its hold on us. Many Christians can give testimony that they were once enslaved to alcohol, but now they are free. For a few it happened instantaneously. For most it happened with the help of a Christian treatment program, the support of caring professionals, and a family that learned how to be a part of the healing process.

If you are married to an alcoholic, begin by getting help for yourself. Learn how you can be a part of the cure. Call your church and ask what local group might help you. Check out local treatment programs. Be ready with information when your spouse decides to turn for help.

Heavenly Father, thank you that there is hope for the alcoholic and for his or her family. Whether it is this issue or some other sin that is affecting our marriage, I pray for wisdom, for transformation, and for a willingness to change. Help me to trust that you can break the power of sin in our marriage.

WHEN YOU'RE ANGRY AT YOURSELF

Fools vent their anger, but the wise quietly hold it back. PROVERBS 29:11

FROM TIME TO TIME, most of us do stupid things. Then we get angry at ourselves. This anger may be mild, medium, or malicious, depending on what we have done. If I get to my car parked in the garage and realize that I left my key in the second-story bedroom, my anger toward myself may be mild. If I lock my keys in the car in the shopping center parking lot, my anger may be medium. But if I lose my keys on a hunting trip one hundred miles from the nearest civilization, my anger at myself may be malicious.

How does this affect marriage? When I am angry at myself, I may take it out on my spouse. Likely, he or she will see the unfairness of that and respond in anger, beginning an unpleasant exchange. Wouldn't it be better to say to myself: *Self, you did a stupid thing, and it's going to cost you some time. But don't make it worse by stewing or lashing out at someone who's not to blame. Now, how can the problem be solved?* Once I've done that, I can get on with the solution.

King Solomon wrote very bluntly that someone who vents his anger—particularly at someone who had nothing to do with the situation, I'll add—is foolish, but the one who can control it is wise. It's always better to move on from your frustration, which is nonproductive, and think about how you can improve the situation.

Doing a stupid thing does not make you stupid. Don't beat up on yourself, and please, don't take it out on your spouse.

> *Lord Jesus, I waste a lot of time and emotional energy being upset at myself. Too often that spills over into the way I treat my spouse, and I know that's neither fair nor kind. Please help me to move away from my frustration and instead look for a way to solve the problem I'm facing. Thank you, Lord, for having compassion on our weaknesses.*

ADDRESSING SELF-FOCUSED ANGER

His unfailing love toward those who fear him is as great as the height of the heavens above the earth. He has removed our sins as far from us as the east is from the west. PSALM 103:11-12

I WANT TO GIVE YOU four steps for responding to self-focused anger. First, admit your anger. "I am really feeling angry at myself," is the first statement of healing.

Second, examine your anger by asking yourself, *Did I do something wrong?* The answer to this question will help you determine if your anger is definitive or distorted. Definitive anger means you did something morally wrong. Distorted anger means you disappointed yourself but did no moral wrong. Forgetting to take your husband's shirts to the laundry is not sinful. Forgetting is not a sin; it is a part of our humanity.

Third, confess any wrongdoing to God and to the person you wronged.

Fourth, choose to forgive yourself. There is nothing to be gained by condemning yourself with comments like "I deserve to suffer; look what I did. I was so stupid. I did what I knew was wrong. I don't deserve forgiveness." Remember, Satan is the accuser (see Job 1:6). God is the forgiver. Why not side with God? Psalm 103 tells us that he "has removed our sins as far from us as the east is from the west." In other words, our sins are completely gone. If the Lord has forgiven you, then you can forgive yourself. And once you've done that, you will be better able to relate to your spouse openly, without blame or anger.

Father, you know how easy it is for me to get angry at myself and how hard it can be for me to get out of the self-blaming mind-set. When I do something I shouldn't, please help me to be willing to confess the wrongdoing and ask for your forgiveness. I know that's the only way to resolve my anger. And as I process this anger, please help me not to lash out at my spouse but rather to be loving.

BUILDING A FIRM FOUNDATION

[Jesus said,] "I will show you what it's like when someone comes to me, listens to my teaching, and then follows it. It is like a person building a house who digs deep and lays the foundation on solid rock. When the floodwaters rise and break against that house, it stands firm because it is well built."

LUKE 6:47-48

A STRONG FOUNDATION is the key to a strong marriage. Jesus told the story of a wise person who built a house on a foundation of solid rock. When storms and floods came, the house was not shaken. Contrast that to the foolish person, who built a house with no foundation. It collapsed at the first storm. The foundation in our relationship with God is faith, trust, and obedience. In our marriage, the foundation is oneness.

In God's plan, marriage involves two people, husband and wife, becoming one unit. They choose to share life more deeply with each other than with anyone else. This intimacy involves all aspects of life. Ideally, before we get married, we should explore the foundation for oneness. Intellectually, are we on the same wavelength? Can we talk and understand each other? Emotionally, are we able to share our feelings without fear of rejection? Socially, do we enjoy similar activities? Spiritually, are we marching to the beat of the same drummer?

After marriage, we build on this foundation. If the foundation is shaky, then it will be more difficult to build intimacy. But build we must, for that is the heart of what marriage is all about. If we choose to disengage and live separate lives, we are violating God's design for marriage. Creating intimacy may be difficult, but we have all of God's help when we commit ourselves to following his plan.

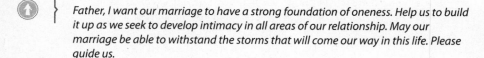

Father, I want our marriage to have a strong foundation of oneness. Help us to build it up as we seek to develop intimacy in all areas of our relationship. May our marriage be able to withstand the storms that will come our way in this life. Please guide us.

THE FOUNDATION OF SPIRITUAL INTIMACY

No one can lay any foundation other than the one we already have—Jesus Christ. 1 CORINTHIANS 3:11

SPIRITUAL INTIMACY is often the most difficult area of marriage, and yet it is the most important. Our relationship with God affects everything else we do. The apostle Paul wrote in 1 Corinthians 3 that the only foundation for believers is Jesus Christ. Trusting in him for our salvation provides the basis and direction for the rest of our lives.

Obviously, we must each maintain our own personal walk with God. We cannot do that for each other. But as married partners, we can share that walk, and in so doing, we encourage each other and build intimacy. Let me share some ideas for improving spiritual intimacy:

1. Share with each other one thing you liked about the worship service you attended. (That's far more edifying than sharing the things you did not like.)

2. Share a Scripture verse you read in your own devotional time. Don't use this to preach at your husband or wife, but to share what you found encouraging or insightful.

3. Pray together. Start with silent prayer if you like; hold hands and pray silently. Say amen aloud when you're finished, and wait for your spouse to say amen. It is not that difficult, and it will draw you closer together.

Just as our relationship with God affects other aspects of our life, so spiritual intimacy will affect all other aspects of our marriage. As we each grow closer to God, we grow closer to each other. Spiritual intimacy will enhance emotional, intellectual, and physical intimacy. All of these are part of becoming *one* in marriage.

Lord Jesus, I know that you are the foundation of my life. Nothing else can take that most important place. I pray that our relationship with you would also be central to our marriage. Help us to share the challenges and encouragements we face as we grow nearer to you. May we draw closer together as our spiritual intimacy grows.

PATTERNS OF COMMUNICATION

May the words of my mouth and the meditation of my heart be pleasing to you, O LORD, my rock and my redeemer. PSALM 19:14

ALL OF US ARE COMMUNICATORS. The question is, what kind of communicators? Simply put, communication is sharing life with another. It is the process whereby two individuals choose to reveal some of their thoughts, feelings, and experiences to each other.

On the surface level, communication seems simple enough. One may wonder why research indicates that lack of communication is one of the major problems in relationships. One reason is that our emotions often get in the way of genuine interaction. Feelings of hurt, anger, fear, disappointment, frustration, or low self-esteem often hinder our openness.

In our efforts to maintain emotional stability, we develop various patterns of communication. After a while, we are not even aware of these patterns; we are simply doing what comes naturally to us. Chances are that you, as individuals and as a couple, have developed some positive patterns and also some negative.

In the next few days, we will explore some of the negative patterns we can fall into and seek to change them. As the psalmist says above, we want the words that come from our mouths—and especially those directed to our spouse—to be helpful, loving, and pleasing to God.

Lord Jesus, I'm grateful for the things my spouse and I can share. Please help us to be willing to consider how we can improve our communication.

AVOIDING APPEASEMENT

We will speak the truth in love, growing in every way more and more like Christ, who is the head of his body, the church. EPHESIANS 4:15

MARRIAGE EXPERTS have discovered some common communication patterns that are detrimental to communication. One such pattern is what is sometimes called the Dove. In this pattern, one partner placates the other in order to avoid his or her wrath. It's the "peace at any price" syndrome. Typical statements from a Dove are "That's fine with me" or "Whatever makes you happy makes me happy."

Doves are always trying to appease the other person, often apologizing for things that may have upset the partner, no matter how insignificant. They almost never disagree with their spouse openly, no matter how they feel. Often the Dove pattern grows out of low self-esteem. The placater may think, *My ideas are not worth anything, so why express them?* He or she may also fear the spouse's response to disagreement.

It should be obvious that this pattern of communication does not build authentic marriages. Honesty honors God and reflects his image. Psalm 31:5 even refers to the Lord as "the God of truth" (NIV). We must learn to speak the truth—with grace and in love, to be sure, as the apostle Paul encourages in the verse above—but we must speak the truth.

Lord God, it's clear from Scripture that truth is of paramount importance to you. Help us as a couple to commit to speaking the truth to each other, lovingly. Let me not be afraid to say what I think or what needs to be said.

BLAMING EACH OTHER

Now there is no condemnation for those who belong to Christ Jesus. And because you belong to him, the power of the life-giving Spirit has freed you from the power of sin that leads to death. ROMANS 8:1-2

IF POSITIVE COMMUNICATION enhances a relationship, then negative communication sabotages it. Another common pattern of negative communication is the Hawk. Typical phrases from a Hawk include "It's all your fault" or "If you had listened to me, we wouldn't be in this mess." In this communication style, one spouse blames the other for everything. The Hawk is the boss, the dictator, and the one in charge who never does anything wrong. He or she might even veer into verbally abusive statements such as, "You never do anything right," "You always botch it up," "How could you be so stupid?" or, "If it weren't for you, everything would be fine." The Hawk never takes responsibility for a problem.

Usually, Hawks are suffering from low self-esteem. They cannot admit that they are wrong because that would confirm the sense of failure they already feel. The Hawk needs the healing touch of the biblical reality: All are sinners, but in Christ we are forgiven. There is no condemnation for those who are in Christ, as Romans 8 tells us; instead, if we have confessed our sins, we are free from them. If Christ does not condemn us, how can we condemn each other? Marital communication is one forgiven sinner talking to another.

If you see the Hawk pattern at work in your marriage, ask for God's forgiveness and make a fresh start.

> *Lord, I need the reminder that both of us in this relationship are sinners. We both need the humility to admit when we are wrong and the patience to deal with each other with love and respect. Please forgive us for the way we have hurt each other, and help us to start fresh.*

WHEN REASON IS TOO REASONABLE

Be happy with those who are happy, and weep with those who weep.

ROMANS 12:15

WITHOUT REALIZING IT, many of us have developed negative communication patterns that are destroying our marriages. Another such pattern is Mr. Owl or Mrs. Calm, Cool, and Collected. This is the "let's be reasonable" syndrome. These people are more like computers than humans, and they can give you logical answers to everything.

They will calmly explain anything about which you may have a question. They will make the answer sound so reasonable that you will wonder how anyone could have ever thought otherwise. These folks usually think of themselves as being reasonable and intelligent. They pride themselves on not showing emotion, and when someone else shows emotion, they calmly sit until the storm is over and then proceed with their reasoning.

The reality is that this kind of dispassionate reason doesn't always follow God's ideal for us. Romans 12:15 encourages us to rejoice with people who are rejoicing and mourn with those who are grieving. In other words, we are to enter into their situation and comfort them by experiencing some of their emotions with them.

The sad thing is that Mr. Owl and Mrs. Calm, Cool, and Collected don't realize that they have a problem. They wonder why their spouse doesn't appreciate their superior wisdom. Will someone please knock them off their roost?

Lord Jesus, it's easy for me to be overly rational. Forgive me for ignoring my spouse's feelings in my arrogance. Please give me the humility to realize that my way is not perfect. Teach me to appreciate my spouse's emotions and to enter into them with compassion.

IGNORING THE ISSUES

Understand this, my dear brothers and sisters: You must all be quick to listen, slow to speak, and slow to get angry. JAMES 1:19

THE LAST NEGATIVE COMMUNICATION PATTERN we'll discuss is the Ostrich: "Ignore it and it will go away." This pattern involves one person basically ignoring any of the other person's actions and comments that he or she finds disagreeable. The Ostrich seldom responds directly to what the other person says. Instead, she changes the subject and moves on.

Ostriches are activists. If they are talkers, they will rattle on and on about nothing related to anything. If they are doers, then they will constantly be involved in activity. If you ask a question about what they are doing, you will seldom get a direct answer.

The Ostrich sometimes develops a singsong style of talking. You can interrupt her and make your own comments, but then she will start talking again—often on a topic unrelated to what you have just said or even to what she was saying beforehand. Her conversation goes in all directions and seldom reaches any conclusions. If you open a topic of conversation she finds uncomfortable, she may immediately change the subject.

James has the best advice for this person: Be quick to listen and slow to speak. Make sure you hear and understand what the other person says before you jump in. The Bible is clear that ignoring unpleasant issues—especially being confronted with something we have done wrong and need to correct—is foolish and leads to trouble (see Proverbs 10:17).

If you or your spouse has Ostrich tendencies, you may need the help of a counselor. Without this, the ignoring will continue—and that's a flimsy base for honest, direct communication.

Father, this tendency to ignore the difficult issues in our relationship affects both of us at times. Help me to realize how destructive that is. Please show us the right way to address conflicts and struggles head-on, with grace and courage.

CHANGING THE PATTERN

Let your conversation be gracious and attractive so that you will have the right response for everyone. COLOSSIANS 4:6

IN THE PAST SEVERAL DAYS, we have looked at some unhealthy patterns of communication. We've discussed the Dove, the Hawk, the Owl, and the Ostrich. Today I want to suggest five ways to change those patterns.

First, identify the unhealthy pattern. Which one of the four is most prominent in your marriage?

Second, admit that the pattern is detrimental to your relationship. For example, say to yourself, "I am a Hawk, and it's hurting my marriage."

Third, decide that you want to see the pattern changed. Changes don't happen automatically with the passing of time. Things change only when we decide to change them.

Fourth, replace old patterns with new patterns. Get a good book on communication and find out what healthy communication looks like. Then begin working those ideas into your marriage. Yes, it takes time and effort, but it pays great dividends.

Finally, admit when you fall back into old patterns. No communication pattern will be changed overnight, and a relapse does not mean failure. It is a normal part of changing bad habits. Be persistent, and eventually you and your spouse will see change.

Let your goal be to follow the apostle Paul's advice and share "gracious and attractive" communication between the two of you.

Heavenly Father, I pray for the wisdom to see the negative communication patterns in my own life and in our relationship. Please help us to see the problems, be willing to change, and then make a change. I want my conversation to honor you.

LOVE = RIGHTEOUSNESS

Love means doing what God has commanded us, and he has commanded us to love one another, just as you heard from the beginning. 2 JOHN 1:6

SOMETIMES AN INDIVIDUAL will say to his or her spouse, "I want you to be happy. If leaving me will make you happy, then leave. It hurts, but I want you to be happy." On the surface that may sound loving and self-sacrificial, but in reality it is neither. Real love seeks the other person's good. And according to the Scriptures, breaking the marital covenant is not good. (See 1 Corinthians 7:10-11 for one example.)

A person's greatest good is found not in happiness but in righteousness. If happiness is found by doing something that is wrong, the happiness will be fleeting because the pleasures of sin are always shortlived. (See Hebrews 11:25.) So Christians must never encourage divorce in pursuit of happiness. Instead, we need to encourage each other to righteousness. As the apostle John wrote in the passage above, love means following God's commandments, or living righteously.

The real question is, what does the Bible teach us to do in our present situation? If you don't know the answer, then find a godly pastor who is acquainted with biblical principles for marital relationships. Once we know what is right, as believers we must seek it at all costs.

Father, thank you for this helpful definition of love. It's not about making my spouse happy at all costs. Rather, it's about encouraging my mate to do what is right and what is ultimately best for him or her—following your commands. Please help me to honor my marriage vows even in the midst of struggle, and not simply to look for the easiest solution.

WALKING TOWARD RECONCILIATION BY FAITH

Faith is the confidence that what we hope for will actually happen; it gives us assurance about things we cannot see. HEBREWS 11:1

WHEN THINGS GET TOUGH in your marriage, it may seem easier to give up and pursue your own happiness, especially when the feelings of love have evaporated. However, the Christian's call is not to the easy road but to the right road. I can promise you that after the pain of reconciliation, the right road leads to both happiness and love.

The choice to pursue reconciliation is a step of faith. You cannot see the warmth of emotional love returning to your relationship. You cannot see differences being resolved. You cannot see the intimacy you desire in a marriage. Therefore, you must take the first steps by faith, not by sight. But it is not blind faith; it is faith based on the counsel of God. With your hand in God's hand, you must walk with him, trusting his wisdom that honoring the marriage covenant is the right thing to do.

When you step out in faith to seek reconciliation with your mate, you join the ranks of the biblical greats. Read Hebrews 11 for many examples of people who acted in faith, without any guarantees that things would go their way. The only assurance they had that things would ultimately turn out for the best was the promise of God. You have the same. Do you need more?

Father, I am challenged to step out in faith. When our marriage hits a rough spot, help me to work toward reconciliation because it's the right thing to do. I may not have any guarantees that my spouse will be receptive, but I have your promise to be with me. Please give me the strength to make the right choice.

SERVING INSTEAD OF DEMANDING

[Jesus said,] "Whoever wants to be a leader among you must be your servant, and whoever wants to be first among you must become your slave. For even the Son of Man came not to be served but to serve others and to give his life as a ransom for many." MATTHEW 20:26-28

THE KEY THAT UNLOCKS the door to a happy marriage is learning to serve your spouse. I must confess that it took me a number of years to discover this key. When I got married, I was thinking about how happy my wife was going to make me. When she did not perform to my satisfaction, I was disappointed, hurt, angry, and hostile. Not a pretty picture.

Have you been there? You make demands on your spouse and then get angry when he or she does not do what you demand. You might respond with, "Why don't you do this? You know how important it is to me." Or, "How could you do that? You know how it makes me feel." With such statements, you try to manipulate your spouse's behavior.

Have you discovered that it doesn't work? People don't respond well to demands. Instead, try serving. Jesus told his disciples that anyone who wants to be a leader needs to first be a servant. We should follow his example and serve others.

Try doing something for your spouse that you know he or she would like you to do. Developing your serve has far more potential than continuing to make demands. Do something good for your spouse today!

Lord Jesus, thank you for your example of service. Help me not to make demands on my spouse, but instead to genuinely serve.

SERVING AS HUSBANDS AND WIVES

And further, submit to one another out of reverence for Christ. For wives, this means submit to your husbands as to the Lord. . . . For husbands, this means love your wives, just as Christ loved the church. EPHESIANS 5:21-22, 25

A MUTUAL ATTITUDE OF SERVICE on the part of both husband and wife leads to a growing marriage. But the service must be mutual. A submitting, serving wife and a tyrannical, demanding husband will never create a happy marriage. A domineering wife and a passive husband will also fail to find marital fulfillment.

The husband must learn to serve his wife as Christ served the church. The wife must serve her husband as she serves the Lord. Mutual service brings mutual joy.

Tennis players spend hours each week improving their serves. Should you give any less attention to improving the one aspect of your relationship that has the potential to make it great? Developing your serve could make the difference between success and failure in your marriage.

Are you willing to ask God to give you the attitude of Christ toward your spouse? To help you serve as he served? It's a prayer God will answer, and it will lead you to a growing marriage.

Father, I ask that you will work in my heart and give me a Christlike attitude toward my spouse. Help me to serve as you served—wholeheartedly, lovingly, and not expecting anything in return.

FREEDOM TO SERVE

You have been called to live in freedom, my brothers and sisters. But don't use your freedom to satisfy your sinful nature. Instead, use your freedom to serve one another in love. GALATIANS 5:13

IN THE PAST COUPLE OF DAYS, we've talked about developing our serve. We must learn to accept the servant attitude of Christ. When you and your spouse serve each other, you both become winners.

One thing that encourages service is the expression of appreciation. Has your spouse served you in some way this week? Think! Has he or she taken out the trash, cooked a meal, washed dishes, mowed the grass, changed the baby's diaper, or washed the dog? If so, why not express your gratitude? You might say, "You know, I didn't tell you this earlier, but I really appreciate your washing the dog. That's something that I find very difficult. I know it's messy, and I appreciate it."

Look for something your spouse has done for you and express appreciation. Then do something good for your spouse. Mutual service and mutual appreciation lead to a great marriage. They aren't required, but they can be given freely, as the above passage from Galatians points out. And it is in giving our lives away to each other that we discover the joy of service.

Father, thank you for all the ways my loved one serves me. Help me not to take those actions for granted but to express my appreciation wholeheartedly and often. Help me to serve him or her as well.

THE GIFT OF ANGER

God is my shield, saving those whose hearts are true and right. God is an honest judge. He is angry with the wicked every day. PSALM 7:10-11

ANGER IS OFTEN SEEN as an enemy to a good marriage, but I believe God intended it to be a friend. The emotion of anger is a gift from God. It reflects our concern for right and our love for people.

The passage above from Psalm 7 shows that the Lord is angry toward those who do wrong. Why? The psalm goes on to talk about these people setting traps for others and intending violence. Their capacity for harming others is large, and that disregard for others makes the Lord angry.

In the same way, if our spouse is committing a wrong, we may become angry because we know it will hurt people—including our spouse. In the example from Psalms, God's anger and resulting actions may lead the wrong-doers to repentance. Our anger, likewise, should motivate us to try to influence our spouse to stop the wrong behavior and do what is right.

In God's plan, anger serves a good end. However, as with all of God's gifts, Satan seeks to pervert God's plan. Often, he is successful. When we succumb to Satan, our anger makes the situation worse rather than better. Perhaps we respond in judgment rather than with concern, or we're self-righteous or cutting in the way we express ourselves.

The best thing we can do when we are angry is to pray. We need to ask God to show us how we can have a positive influence on our spouse. Remember, the purpose of our anger is to motivate us to cooperate with God in helping our spouse turn away from sinful behavior.

Father, when I am angry with my spouse, please help me to figure out the reasons why. When my anger is justified because my spouse is doing something wrong or harmful, give me wisdom about how to respond. I know my focus needs to be on encouraging my spouse back to the right path.

CONFRONTING IN MEEKNESS

Dear brothers and sisters, if another believer is overcome by some sin, you who are godly should gently and humbly help that person back onto the right path. And be careful not to fall into the same temptation yourself. GALATIANS 6:1

WHEN WAS THE LAST TIME you were angry with your spouse? What did you do? Did your behavior make the situation better or worse? The Scriptures say that when we encounter a brother or sister in Christ who is doing wrong, we are to seek restoration "in the spirit of meekness" (Galatians 6:1, KJV). In other words, we must be gentle and humble because we ourselves also do wrong from time to time. We are not in the position to judge, but we can gently remind our spouse of the right way.

Loving confrontation is the most positive approach when you are angry with your spouse. Perhaps you are angry because you believe your spouse has done or said something that is wrong. Or perhaps she failed to do something you think she should have done. A meek approach might be, "Honey, I may be misunderstanding this, but I'm really feeling hurt and angry and I need your help. Is this a good time to talk?"

Share your perception and then listen to your spouse. You can't make him do right, but you can influence him. You will know your anger has served its purpose when you hear, "I'm sorry. I was wrong. With God's help I will not do that again. Will you forgive me?"

Heavenly Father, help me always to be gentle and humble when I confront my spouse about something he or she is doing that is wrong. I know how prone I am to failure, and I want to extend grace to my spouse as well. Please help me to use my anger wisely—not to lash out, but to motivate me to lovingly confront when it is needed.

POSITIVE ANGER MANAGEMENT

Turn from your rage! Do not lose your temper—it only leads to harm.

PSALM 37:8

AS WE'VE SEEN, anger is an inevitable part of any relationship, including marriage. We've talked about some of the reasons behind it, but today I'd like to focus on the practical. Here are six suggestions on how to handle your anger toward your spouse.

1. Admit to yourself, "It's okay to feel anger."

2. Remind yourself, "It's not okay to lash out at my spouse or to withdraw in silence."

3. Pray that God will give you wisdom on how to handle your anger.

4. Seek an explanation before passing judgment. You might say, "Honey, something is bothering me, but I might be misunderstanding the situation. Can I ask you a question?"

5. Seek a resolution; don't seek to win the argument. If you win, your spouse loses. You don't want to be married to a loser, do you? The right question is, "How can we solve this problem?"

6. Affirm your love for your spouse. "I love you and I don't want anything to stand between us," might be an appropriate statement.

As the psalmist reminds us, losing our temper only leads to harm. By contrast, these six steps pave the way for a good resolution. Positive anger management may well save your marriage.

Father, thank you for these ideas on how to handle my anger toward my spouse. Please help me to put them into practice. May I not sin in my anger; may I be respectful and loving toward my spouse.

OUR PRIMARY NEED

Three things will last forever—faith, hope, and love—and the greatest of these is love. 1 CORINTHIANS 13:13

LOVE AND MARRIAGE—they go together like a horse and carriage. Right? Well, they should, and in a healthy marriage, they do. Most people agree that our deepest emotional need is to feel loved. The apostle Paul even identifies love as the greatest thing, and King David wrote that God's "unfailing love is better than life itself" (Psalm 63:3). There's no question that God's steady love for us can be our emotional rock. But we also need to experience human love. And if we are married, the person whose love we long for the most is our spouse. In fact, if we feel loved, everything else is workable. If we don't feel loved, our conflicts become battlefields.

Now, don't misunderstand me. I'm not suggesting that love is our only need. Psychologists have observed that we also have basic emotional needs for security, self-worth, and significance. However, love interfaces with all of these.

If I feel loved, then I can relax, knowing that my spouse will do me no ill. I feel secure in his or her presence. I can face the uncertainties in my vocation. I may have enemies in other areas of my life, but with my spouse I feel secure. In the next two days, I'll talk about how to effectively meet your spouse's need for emotional love.

> *Lord Jesus, thank you for your love that never fails. And thank you for the love I can share with my spouse. Please help me to love effectively, so that he or she will feel secure in our relationship.*

UNDERSTANDING OUR VALUE

See how very much our Father loves us, for he calls us his children, and that is what we are! 1 JOHN 3:1

OFTEN, MARITAL LOVE makes the difference between low self-esteem and healthy self-esteem. Love makes a difference in the way I perceive myself.

In reality, of course, all of us are of great value simply because we are made in the image of God. The apostle John makes clear that God calls us his children because he loves us so much. The Bible also uses the image of sheep. Psalm 100:3 says, "He made us, and we are his. We are his people, the sheep of his pasture." In short, we are loved and valued, we belong, and we are cared for. That's a wonderful message for any believer's self-worth.

But not all of us *feel* valuable. In marriage, we can be God's instrument for building our mate's self-esteem. The best way to do that is to love our spouse and communicate God's truth to him or her. Speaking our spouse's love language and keeping his or her love tank full also communicates worth. After all, if my spouse loves me, I must be worth something.

Do you know your spouse's primary love language—what really makes him or her feel loved? Then ask God to give you the ability to speak that language well, whether it's physical touch, words of affirmation, quality time, gifts, or acts of service. Watch your spouse blossom into the person God intends him or her to be. Love makes a difference.

Heavenly Father, thank you for allowing us to call you Father! You have adopted us as your children, and you care for us as tenderly as a shepherd cares for sheep. Thank you for valuing us. Please help me as I strive to communicate that value to my spouse through my expressions of love.

FINDING OUR SIGNIFICANCE

Above all, you must live as citizens of heaven, conducting yourselves in a manner worthy of the Good News about Christ. Then . . . I will know that you are standing together with one spirit and one purpose, fighting together for the faith, which is the Good News. PHILIPPIANS 1:27

THE NEED FOR SIGNIFICANCE drives much of our behavior. We want our lives to count for something. In reality, I am significant because God made me. Life does have meaning. There is a higher purpose—to share God's love with others by spreading the Good News. The apostle Paul encouraged believers to be united in this purpose, and that still holds true today. When we communicate God's love, we are doing something highly significant.

However, I may not feel significant until someone expresses love to me. When my spouse lovingly invests time, energy, and effort in me, I feel valuable. But surprisingly, when I choose to love my spouse and give my life for his or her well-being, I feel even more valuable. Why? Because it is more blessed to give than to receive.

Christ is our example. He gave up his life for the church (see Ephesians 5:25); consequently, God "highly exalted Him" (Philippians 2:9, NASB). One of your greatest contributions to the cause of Christ is to love your spouse.

Father, I am thankful for the significance you give me. I want to fulfill your purposes for me and share your love with others. Please help me to start by loving my spouse well and selflessly. Through that, may he or she feel significant too.

FORGETTING THE PAST

Forgetting the past and looking forward to what lies ahead, I press on to reach the end of the race and receive the heavenly prize for which God, through Christ Jesus, is calling us. PHILIPPIANS 3:13-14

ACCORDING TO 1 CORINTHIANS 13, love "keeps no record of wrongs." How many times in a counseling session have I listened as a husband or wife detailed each other's past failures? The hurt, pain, and disappointment are all felt as though the wrongdoing happened yesterday. I ask you, of what value is that?

All of us have sin in our past. Yes, we are guilty of dreadful failures, but the great message of Christmas is that God will forgive. And once we are forgiven, God never reminds us of past failures. In fact, in Isaiah 43:25, he tells us that he "will never think of them again." What a promise!

We need to follow God's example. If your mate confesses and asks forgiveness, you must never again bring up the past. Remember, your well-being is not determined by the past, but by what you do with the future. What is important is how you treat each other today, not how you treated each other last month or last year.

Follow the apostle Paul's example from Philippians 3 and forget the past, concentrating instead on the future and your end goal—to live a Christlike life. Forgetting the past is the key that can open the future, bringing reconciliation between you and your spouse.

Father, on this Christmas Day, I want to thank you for sending Jesus to the world to save us. His sacrifice makes it possible for you to forgive us and forget the past! Please help me to stop looking back at my spouse's past failures and rehashing the hurt. Instead, I want to look forward to the growth and reconciliation we can experience in the future. Show me how to forgive and love like you do, Lord.

LOVE DOES NOT SEEK ITS OWN

[Paul said,] "I have been a constant example of how you can help those in need by working hard. You should remember the words of the Lord Jesus: 'It is more blessed to give than to receive.'" ACTS 20:35

HAPPINESS IS A UNIQUE COMMODITY. It is never found by the person shopping for it. Lonely men and women in every age have admitted the futility of their search for happiness, most notably King Solomon in the book of Ecclesiastes. This wealthy, powerful king, with servants to cater to his every whim, found most things in life to be tedious, meaningless, and devoid of joy.

Most of us get married assuming that we are going to be happy. After the wedding, we find that our mate does not always seek to make us happy. Perhaps our spouse even demands more and more of our time, energy, and resources for his or her own happiness. We feel cheated and used, so we fight for our rights. We demand that our spouse do certain things for us, or we give up and seek happiness elsewhere.

Part of the apostle Paul's definition of love in 1 Corinthians 13 is that it is "not self-seeking." Genuine happiness is the by-product of making someone else happy. I wonder what would have happened if King Solomon had found someone to serve? Don't the Scriptures say, "It is more blessed to give than to receive" (Acts 20:35)?

Do you want to be happy? Discover someone else's needs, and seek to meet them. Why not begin with your spouse? "How may I help you?" is a good question with which to begin.

Lord Jesus, you told us that blessing comes from giving, not receiving. Please help me to turn around my expectations. I don't want to waste my time and energy grasping at happiness only to be disappointed. Instead, show me how to reach out to my spouse, giving to him or her. I want to bring happiness to my mate through the way I express my love.

BEGINNING AN IN-LAW RELATIONSHIP RIGHT

Respect everyone, and love your Christian brothers and sisters. 1 PETER 2:17

WHEN YOU BECOME a mother-in-law or father-in-law, you enter a whole new world of relationships. Don't just let it happen. Talk about it.

Before your son or daughter gets married, talk about what life will be like after the wedding. Talk with your spouse; talk with your child; and talk with your future son- or daughter-in-law.

You want to have good relationships, so talk about what would make them good. Listen to each other. Respect each other's ideas. Agree on a game plan. Answer the following questions:

- What should the new son-in-law or daughter-in-law call us?

- If we will be living in the same area, will we call each other before we show up at the door? Or will we just drop by anytime?

- What kind of contact will we have after the wedding? How often will we call each other or visit?

- Are we open to invitations for dinner? Will each couple give the other the freedom to say no if we have other plans?

- Will we help the young couple financially? If so, how can we do it without the younger couple feeling controlled?

When we treat our family members—and new family members—with love and respect, we are following the apostle Peter's advice. We are also setting the stage for strong family relationships in the years to come. Preparing for life after the wedding is fully as important as planning for the wedding.

Heavenly Father, I want to have a good relationship with my son- or daughter-in-law, whether I'm in that situation now or whether it's still far in the future. Thank you for the reminder that proactive communication, love, and respect are always beneficial. May our family relationships grow ever stronger, more supportive, and more loving.

ACTIONS OVER EMOTIONS

Let's not get tired of doing what is good. At just the right time we will reap a harvest of blessing if we don't give up. GALATIANS 6:9

MY CHALLENGE FOR YOU today is to love your spouse, even when you have negative emotions toward him or her. You may ask, "Isn't that being hypocritical?" My answer is no. Claiming to feel something that you do not feel is hypocritical, but *acting* lovingly regardless of your emotions is not. When you express kindness by a thoughtful act or a gift, you do not have to claim any warm emotional feeling. You are simply choosing to be kind.

The Bible tells us not to get tired of doing the right thing. When we treat our spouse kindly and lovingly, we are doing what pleases God. He promises that eventually, if we persevere, we will see blessing.

It is the same thing we do every morning. I don't know about you, but if I got out of bed only on the mornings that I felt like getting out of bed, I'd have bedsores. Almost every morning, I act in spite of my feelings and get up when the alarm goes off. Later I feel good about having gotten up—most days, at least.

Negative feelings are more often alleviated when they are ignored rather than pampered. When you act positively in spite of negative emotions, it tends to change the emotional climate between husband and wife. Resentment dissipates, and both spouses are more open to each other. Perhaps this is the blessing God promises! Once you're at that point, then together you can deal with the issue that initially stimulated your negative feelings.

Father, please give me the perseverance to treat my spouse kindly, even when I don't feel like it and even when I feel like giving up. I know that when I express your love, the atmosphere between me and my spouse can change. I need your will and determination to move beyond my emotions and do the right thing. Thank you for helping me, Lord.

TRANSFORMING POWER OF LOVE

The Holy Spirit produces this kind of fruit in our lives: love, joy, peace, patience, kindness, goodness, faithfulness, gentleness, and self-control. There is no law against these things! GALATIANS 5:22-23

THE STORY IS TOLD of a woman who went to a marriage counselor for advice. "I want to divorce my husband," she said, "and I want to hurt him as much as I can."

"In that case," the counselor advised, "start showering him with compliments. When you have become indispensable to him—when he thinks you love him devotedly—then start the divorce action. That's the way to hurt him most."

Some months later, the wife returned to report that she had followed the counselor's advice.

"Good," said the counselor. "Now's the time to file for divorce."

"Divorce?" said the woman. "Never! I've fallen in love with the guy."

Loving words and actions change not only the spouse; they change the one speaking and acting lovingly. Didn't Jesus say, "Love your enemies" (Matthew 5:44)? Perhaps your spouse qualifies, at least at certain moments! It may seem impossible, but Galatians 5 reassures us that it's not all up to us. The Holy Spirit, who dwells within believers, produces godly attributes in us: love, joy, peace, patience, kindness, goodness, faithfulness, gentleness, and self-control. What a list! All we need to do is allow him to work within us.

Loving your spouse in the power of the Holy Spirit will never make things worse. Who knows? Things may get better. Go against your emotions, and give love a chance.

Father, I am so grateful for the gift of the Holy Spirit, who is able to produce wonderful fruit in me. Please help me to get out of the way and allow the Spirit to work. With your help, I can love my spouse through my actions, even when I don't feel like doing it. I want to be transformed by your love, Lord.

WHAT IS YOUR LEGACY?

Follow my example, as I follow the example of Christ.

1 CORINTHIANS 11:1 (NIV)

AMONG THE THINGS you will leave behind when you die is a marital legacy. Your example will without a doubt influence the lives of your children and others who observe it. Few things are more important than building the kind of marriage that you would be happy to have your children emulate.

When I ask older parents, "What do you wish for your adult children?" their response is often, "I want them to be happily married and to rear their children to be loving, caring citizens." That's a worthy goal. What are you doing to foster that goal? I want to suggest that the model of your own marriage is the greatest factor in helping your children have happy marriages.

The question is, will you leave a positive or a negative legacy? Many young adults struggle greatly because of the influence of the negative example set by their parents' marriage. Others are blessed greatly by a positive model.

It is not too late. As long as you are alive, you have time to work on the marital legacy you will leave behind. The best thing we can do is what Paul did: follow the example of Christ. The more closely we follow Jesus and treat each other the way he calls us to, the more Christlike our legacy will be.

Lord Jesus, I know that the only way I can leave a strong legacy is by following your example. Please help me to become more and more like you in the way I treat my spouse and the way I approach our marriage. I want to leave a positive example for those around us. Thank you, Lord.

A POSITIVE MARITAL LEGACY

Be an example to all believers in what you say, in the way you live, in your love, your faith, and your purity. 1 TIMOTHY 4:12

WHAT KIND OF LEGACY will you leave your children? When you die, you will leave some material legacy: money, clothes, furniture, cars, and so forth. But the most powerful legacy you will leave your children is the legacy of your marriage.

John buried his seventy-eight-year-old father a year after his mother passed away. His father had lived in a nursing home for several years, and his money had run out. He had no financial legacy to leave. "Before he died," John recalled, "he told me he wanted me to have his wedding band. After his death, when I went to the nursing home, they gave me a bag with Dad's clothes. At the bottom was a small plastic bag containing his wedding band. Now that ring is on my dresser. I look at it every day and remind myself of Dad's faithful marriage to Mom for over fifty years. I think about all he did for me when I was young, and I pray that I will be the kind of husband and father he was."

John's words speak of a legacy far more valuable than material property. The apostle Paul wrote to Timothy, encouraging him to be an example in the way he lived, believed, and loved. That's a challenge to us as well. What will your children think someday when they look at your wedding ring?

Lord Jesus, I want to leave a positive legacy. Please help my spouse and me to love each other well, even as we weather challenges in our relationship. May those around us see our marriage and be encouraged.

TOPICAL INDEX

SCRIPTURE INDEX

ABOUT THE AUTHOR

DR. GARY CHAPMAN is the author of the perennial best seller *The Five Love Languages* (over 4 million copies sold) and numerous other marriage and family books. He also coauthored a fiction series based on *The Four Seasons of Marriage* with best-selling author Catherine Palmer. Dr. Chapman is the director of Marriage and Family Life Consultants, Inc.; an internationally known speaker; and the host of *A Love Language Minute,* a syndicated radio program heard on more than two hundred stations across North America. He and his wife, Karolyn, live in North Carolina.